看我从4到7
核心雅思语法 36招

孙良晨 闻特 编著

机械工业出版社
CHINA MACHINE PRESS

这不是单纯意义的语法书!

这是从万千语法知识中提取出来的专门针对雅思考试、考生应试时注意的夯实英语基础语言水平、提升语言逻辑能力、强化语感的如何获取雅思高分的参考用书!

从英语语言时态、虚拟语气、句式复杂程度、从句、语言格调等,精心整理出36招和雅思考试密切相关的内容,以时尚、简洁的语言将雅思考试应重点关注的语法点娓娓道来!

夯实基础固然是重中之重,但准确无误、令考官信服的流利表达才是获取高分的最佳途径,通过本书的阅读,雅思考试分数从4到7手到擒来!

衷心祝愿考生认真学习本书后,能获取雅思高分!

图书在版编目(CIP)数据

从4到7:核心雅思语法,看我36招 / 孙良晨,闻特编著.
—北京:机械工业出版社,2017.8
(智课大讲堂系列)
ISBN 978-7-111-59002-6

Ⅰ.①从… Ⅱ.①孙… ②闻… Ⅲ.①IELTS-语法 Ⅳ.①H314

中国版本图书馆 CIP 数据核字(2018)第 014452 号

机械工业出版社(北京市百万庄大街22号 邮政编码100037)
策划编辑:唐绮峰　　责任编辑:唐绮峰
版式设计:悠米兹　　责任印制:张　博
三河市宏达印刷有限公司印刷
2018年3月第1版·第1次印刷
184mm×260mm·18 印张·374 千字
标准书号:ISBN 978-7-111-59002-6
定价:49.80 元

凡购本书,如有缺页、倒页、脱页,由本社发行部调换

电话服务　　　　　　　　　网络服务
服务咨询热线:(010)88361066　　机工官网:www.cmpbook.com
读者购书热线:(010)68326294　　机工官博:weibo.com/cmp1952
　　　　　　(010)88379203　　金 书 网:www.golden-book.com
封面无防伪标均为盗版　　　　教育服务网:www.cmpedu.com

推荐序
FOREWORD

无论英语国内考试还是出国考试，几乎所有考生都说自己的英语语法是弱项，很少有例外，这大概就是中英文语言间最本质不同的体现了。语法就是各种语序和表达方式的总合，其内涵是东西方文化和思维方式的差异，而不单单只是个语言问题。

无数老师尝试过挑战语法教学这一难关，但传统的教学模式还是效果不彰，因为没有在压力下的反复运用练习，就不会有真正意义上的掌握。这本书中的36招是个很不错的点子，雅思考试就像考生背后的鞭子，而从千百种语法现象中挑选出的这36个知识点就像前面开路的锥子。其指向性与精炼的实战技巧结合，双管齐下，事半功倍显而易见。

我始终认为，任何脱离了实际应用的语言学习都是无意义地浪费时间，捧着语法书只适合做研究。在语法学习中，不停地运用所学知识才是王道。就像我们大多数人说中文的时候，并不会意识到每一个词的语法成分、每一句话的语序概念，但这并不妨碍我们说出正确的句子，因为通过从婴儿期到现在的学习，所有的语法规则已经深入骨髓，变成了我们大脑中独特的神经轴突连接方式的一部分。学习英语也是一样，虽然我们不再有十几甚至几十年的时间来建立新的语言习惯，但我们用语法示范简化了学习过程，用目的性强的练习巩固吸收，我们学习的速度也会快一些。虽然达不到英语母语水平，但在常用的一些点上，还是能胜任日常学习、工作和生活的要求的。

我很高兴地看到本书完全采用了新的讲解方法：语言丰富而有趣，避免了传统的、枯燥的说教；最新的真题做示范，最大化了目的性和针对性。而每节后面的练习不只是练习，还加入了很多容易犯错的知识点讲解，考虑基本上可以说很全面了。希望大家能够在阅读时，享受学习的过程，利用它在备考雅思的同时，也能突破语法难关，为下一步的学术学习奠基。

韦晓亮
2017.07

前 言
PREFACE

在雅思教学中，我们经常听到"烤鸭"们抱怨自己的语法基础不好、不知道该怎么说、怎么写，而实战中我们也发现，开口提笔语法必错也确实是中国考生的口语、写作成绩难超 5.5 分的最重要原因之一。

至于应对方法，时间充裕的同学会去读基础班复习一下基本语法，时间有限的同学只能抓着老师临时抱佛脚似地改改错。根据我们的经验，这些都不是最好的办法。重学一遍语法后，大家还是不会使用，因为语法基础差并不是大家初高中没听懂，而是缺乏有针对性的实践。语法就是剪刀、针、线这些工具，其实用法大家都明白，但真做起衣服来总是会扎到手。比如定语从句大家都知道，但写起文章来又有几个人脑海里会出现除了 that 以外的其他引导词的定语从句呢？老师改错相对效率高一些，因为和实战结合起来了，缺陷在于老师会被学生的思路限制，没办法示范一些有效的语法拿分点。最好的办法还是从理论到实践、用理论来指导实战。

本书就是针对这些问题，结合近年真题，由浅入深地对 36 个在雅思考试中可以有效提分的语法点进行实战用法的讲解和示范，大家消化吸收以后，就可以在考场上有目的地应用，而不是泛泛地空谈语法或者大海捞针似地改错。相应地，每一章都包含了口语和写作两个部分，用最新的真实考题来说明相应语法点的使用技巧，再配以针对常见错误的改错和实战练习巩固知识。细节上，我们还对语法点的最佳使用之处（比如应用于口语 Part 1~3、议论文或者图表作文的哪一部分）以及可供模仿的句式和变通方法（比如同义词汇的替换选项）都做了列举，以便最小化大家备考的工作量、最大化最终成绩。

因时间有限，书中的错漏之处在所难免，希望大家不吝赐教。预祝各位考试顺利，学业有成。

孙良晨　闻特

2017 年 6 月 28 日

目 录
CONTENTS

推荐序
前 言

如何明白使用别人乱用的时态
- 6 分起手式　三大基本时态滴水不漏 …………………… 2
- 7 分惊鸿一瞥　四大完成时显一即可 …………………… 11
- 7 分垫鼎之作　三大进行时稳扎稳打 …………………… 19
- 6 分老招新用　主动使用被动语态 ……………………… 28
- 8 分冲天杀阵　一招鲜的独立主格 ……………………… 37

如何变幻莫测地使用虚拟语气
- 6 分浮想联翩　if 虚拟的独特用法 ……………………… 46
- 7 分独辟蹊径　不用 if 如何虚拟 ………………………… 54

如何只记几个字就搞定关联词
- 7 分培元筑基　介词与众不同 …………………………… 62
- 7 分养神移气　连词巧妙过渡 …………………………… 71

如何使短句变复杂
- 7 分定海针　有特色的定语 ……………………………… 80
- 7 分巧修饰　精准的状语 ………………………………… 87
- 7 分共分享　独特的同位语 ……………………………… 94
- 7 分神来笔　吸睛的插入语 ……………………………… 100

如何让文章的句子种类不再单一

7分 以情动人　少见的疑问句、感叹句、祈使句 …………… 110
6分 似有还无　常被遗忘的 there be …………………………… 119
7分 如何说不　怪异的否定结构 ………………………………… 125
6分 孰优孰劣　多变的比较结构 ………………………………… 134
6分 兄弟情深　出彩的并列结构 ………………………………… 142

如何只用一句话提升全文的语法格调

7分 倒行逆施　常被忽略的部分倒装 …………………………… 150
8分 石破天惊　被完全遗忘的完全倒装 ………………………… 157
6分 重点突出　中文没有的强调结构 …………………………… 164

高大上地巧妙运用从句

6分 画"鸭"点睛　宾语从句、表语从句脱离套路 …………… 172
6分 虎踞"鸭"盘　定语从句烂俗写出新意 …………………… 180
7分 群"鸭"有首　主语从句出手保证不错 …………………… 187
7分 成"鸭"配套　同位语从句复杂但不臃肿 ………………… 194
6分 来"鸭"去脉　原因状语从句老调换词新弹 ……………… 200
6分 望子"屠"鸭　结果状语从句换个表达顺序 ……………… 209
6分 巧立名目　目的状语从句解决类文章必备 ………………… 216
6分 恰逢其时　时间状语从句注意少见用法 …………………… 223
7分 辨物居方　条件状语从句显得客观学术 …………………… 233
7分 见贤思齐　比较状语从句为分析提供参照 ………………… 240
7分 亢"鸭"有悔　让步状语从句突显思维缜密 ……………… 247
7分 见"鸭"在田　地点状语从句地图题必备 ………………… 254
7分 活"鸭"活现　方式状语从句给论述提供细节 …………… 259
华山论剑　终极必杀技——长难句 ………………………………… 265

减少常见错误一定要把握细节

功成收式　少了这些错误再提 1~2 分 …………………………… 274

如何明白使用
别人乱用的时态

6分起手式　三大基本时态滴水不漏

口语部分

雅思口语中的语法是最敏感的扣分点之一。甚至在雅思口语考题当中，有一类题型就叫作时态类考题，是考官专门挑出来考核考生的时态能力的考题。

我们先来看一看什么是时态类考题（Part 1）：

基本信息题：工作学习、家乡、住房

How was your first day at school?（Work and study）
What do you want to do in the future?（Work and study）
What's your plan for the future?（Work and study）
Has your hometown changed a lot in the past few years?（Hometown）
Do you want to live in the countryside in the future?（Hometown）
Do you prefer to live in a house or apartment in the future?（House and flat）

生活休闲类：周末、熬夜、假期、帮助他人、独处、着急

What did you do last weekend?（Weekends）
Did you stay up when you were little?（Staying up）（2016年9月新题）
When was the last time you helped others?（Helping others）
Do you wish to have more time alone?（Being alone）
When was the last time you did things in a hurry?（Being in a hurry）（2016年9月新题）
Do you think there should be more holidays? Why?（Holidays）

学习文化类：数学、历史、博物馆、书写、老师学生

When did you start to learn math?（Math）
When was the last time you read a history book?（History）
Do you have any interesting experiences of going to the museum?（Museum）
Do you think handwriting will be replaced in the future?（Handwriting）
Do you want to be a teacher in the future?（Teacher and students）

媒体类：手机短信、社交网络

Do you think phones will be replaced in the future? (Mobile phone and text messages)

Will you use more social networks in the future? (Social network)

自然、交通类：天空、树木，公共交通工具

Have you learned anything about stars or planets at school? (Sky)

Have you been to any forests? (Trees and forests)

Have you climbed a tree before? (Tree)

How to improve the public transport in the future? (Public transport)

购物视频爱好类：衣服、小吃、运动、照片

What's the difference between clothes in the past and clothes now? (Clothes)

Are the snacks you have today different from those in the past? (Snacks) (2015年9月新题)

Do you want to attend any sports competitions in the future? (Sports)

Have you taken any family photos before? (Photograph)

这就是一个常见时态类考题，基本上每个类别的题目都有。考官在考你这些题的时候，很想知道你的时态能不能都用对。

还有 Part 2 的经历题，或者人物、地点题、物品题里描述经历的部分，都要求你说清楚，这个事儿是什么时候发生的、什么时候认识的这个人、什么时候去这个旅游景点、什么时候买的东西等。所以，掌握时态技巧，是考 6 分的第一步，也是一个得分保障。

而回答这种题的基本技巧就是先**说清楚时间状语**（所谓讲故事说经历，就是时间、地点、人物、事件）。

来看这个题：

How was your first day at school?

On the first day, if I remember well, it was really exciting. I was taken to the campus by my parents and I spent likely 1 hour touring around the campus and honestly I also felt a little bit nervous, because the life ahead of me seemed to be more difficult. That's why I felt a little bit worried. But anyway, it was excellent to meet many new faces, including my classmates and teachers.

第一天，如果我没记错的话，特别令人兴奋。我爸妈带我去学校，我花了大概 1 小时转了一下校园。老实说，我也有点紧张，因为之后的生活好像要更难了，这就是为什么我有点小担忧。但是不管怎么说，能认识很多新面孔，包括我的同学和老师，还是一件很棒的事情。

文中动词的正确过去时你都能用对吗？如果不能，我们建议大家，在考试前一定要把时态类的考题单独拿出来练习一番。熟悉一下所有动词的过去式，强迫自己用英式思维口述日记：I got up in the morning, washed my face, brushed my teeth, cooked some breakfast for myself...

但是如果说，你的时态实在掌握不好，还有一个星期就要考试了，有什么办法能快速提高语法能力吗？作为一个神奇的老师，我要说："当然有！"

其实就算在女王的国度大不列颠，很多英国人也会说错时态，所以他们会有很多简单策略来规避掉自己对过去时的不熟悉。

送大家 6 个技巧，助大家快速上 6：

1» 当你要描述一系列动作的时候，使用总—分结构<u>只用一个简单的过去时，后面的内容全部用动名词列举出来</u>：

◇ On the first day, I **did** a lot of things actually, like touring around the campus, meeting up with new friends, introducing myself to everyone I met, something like that.

2» **多使用过去进行时来进行描述**，有很多同学经常用错过去式，而且自己没有意识，但是过去进行时 I was doing something 是很难错的，因为 was 是一个大家都很敏感的不容易错的词。怎么来用呢，先举个例子。

◇ Last weekend, I **went** to a bookstore to buy some tool books. I **saw** a beautiful girl. She **was** beautiful. I **talked** with her. But she **didn't** like me.

上周末，我去书店买工具书，我看到一个漂亮的姑娘。她很美，我和她聊了聊，但是她不喜欢我。

全都是动词过去式很容易出错对吧？我们套用策略再来一次：

◇ Last weekend, I was enjoying my time（整理几个可以用在很多表述里的万能的动词）in a bookstore. I saw a girl. **I was thinking**（内心戏带入）: "Wow, the girl next to me is so beautiful! She is great! Can I ask for her number or ask her out?"（双引号里的词可以不用顾忌时态）Then, after trying, nothing happened.

周末，我在一个书店里享受生活。我看到一个女孩，我就想："哇，旁边这位姑娘真好看！她太棒了！我能不能要个电话约她出去呢？"于是，我试了一下，但什么也没发生。

3» 类似的方式是**使用被动语态**：比如 I was told/asked，对话内容可以不考虑时态，对于被动语态的过去时是不容易出错的。

◇ Last weekend, I **was taken** to the city—Xiamen by my mother. I **was told** the city is a famous leisure city. Many beautiful houses could be seen there.

上周末，我妈带我去厦门。我听说这是个有名的休闲城，可以看到很多漂亮的房子。

4» **多使用描述性语言**：It's like，可以有效规避时态错误，It's like I can never be this happy in my life.（后面谈及感受的部分，可以不用太过在意语法）

5. 能用缩写的地方决不拆开 It's = it is；it was；it has。They'd like to。It's 可以表达多种意思。所以在讲形容词的时候，养成好的讲话习惯，千万别拆开。

It's great！It's cool！It's just wonderful！（时态是不可能错的）

It's been a long day.

It's gonna be great！

6. 多使用听不清楚的过去时。I liked to/I used to 表示过去经常做某事。

◇ I liked to play basketball in the past, but now I almost have no time to do it. I also like to go swimming. 在动作行为前面加上 like to 来表达习惯，是不是再也不担心过去时问题了？因为听起来都差不多。

说完了过去时，我们来看现在时。表达一般现在时的得分亮点主要在于：使用副词！

通常我们在回答雅思口语问题的时候会对具体情况进行分类：usually/often 表示常态，sometimes 表示偶尔，I remember there was a time 就会使用过去时，来举例具体信息。比如：

> **What do you like to do at the weekends?**
> Well, for most of the time, I often like to stay at home to do some laundry, but sometimes I also invite some friends to hang out and meet up in a karaoke bar or some other places...

> 大多数时间，我经常在家洗衣服，但有时候我也叫朋友出去玩，约K歌或者去别的地儿……

很多人在翻译中文句子的时候经常会犯一个很常见的错误，就是把中文里的"我会怎样"，翻译成 I will。这是一个非常普遍的错误。I will 表达的是将来时态。如果要说：On the weekend, I will watch TV. 这句话表达的不是常态，而是以后的打算。所以，我们在口语里经常把"会"翻译成 often，来表示一般时态里的常态，或者用 like to 来表示习惯。或者其他代替词：I'd like to/I usually/normally 等

那么将来时怎么用呢？What's your plan for the future?

I will become an engineer. 太普通了。I'm bound to（我一定会）become an engineer. 用 be bound to，表示板上钉钉一定会，听起来就更高级了吧？be bound to 是一个不定式表示将来时的用法，If everything goes smoothly（如果一切顺利），I would like to become an engineer. 可以添加状语从句来加强语气。Hopefully（希望），I can be an engineer in the future.

所以，除了 be going to 表达打算，will 表达肯定推测。

你能分得清虚拟语气和肯定推测的区别吗？下面用一个简单的例子说明一下。我对你

说：You will be successful！这句话听起来！舒服！I hope you can be successful！有没有听起来觉得我没那么确定的语气，这样说你生气吗？我希望你能成功，其实潜台词是我不确定你能不能成功。

所以，对于将来时态，我们要搞清楚，有哪些表达方式，它们的区别是什么？这样就有语感了。

一般将来时可用于预测，认为某事可能或肯定会发生，通常用助动词 will，在 I 和 we 后面也可以用 shall，它常与 if 等条件从句连用，表示随着一件事情的发生，另一件事就将发生。

一般将来时还用来表示说话者的打算，它和 be going to 的区别在于：be going to 所指的事往往是预先决定或安排好的，临时决定的话就要用 will。

◇ "The phone is ringing." "I'll answer it."

"电话响了。""我去接！"

所以问句 "Will you…?" 就常用于请求邀请，询问预先考虑好的事儿就用 "Are you going to…?" 好了。

当然，**现在进行时也可以表示将来**：They are coming for dinner. 这种进行时表达的是已经确定的未来计划，而且马上就要发生了。

I hope/wish 也可以用于一般将来时，表示对将来的期望。

当然，不定式 to do 也可以表示想做但是还没做的将来要做的事，比如：**I'm about to leave.** 我要走了。

而将来进行时是一种特殊的用法，用来表示肯定的、已经决定了的事。

◇ I'll be waiting here. 我会一直在这里等你的。

◇ Don't call me after seven because I'll be studying at the library to morrow.

七点后别打电话给我，因为我明天要在图书馆学习。

◇ I'll be working all day tomorrow. 我明天要工作一整天。

全部都是很肯定的语气，你学会了吗？

因为篇幅有限，在这里不多赘述，更多雅思口语相关学习，请各位读者搜索并添加微信公众号"晨说会道"（Liangchensun），有更多精彩内容与大家分享。

01 改错

下面的句子哪里用错了？

周末的时候我会去打篮球。

On weekends, I will play basketball.

02 大闯关

1）如果考官问你
"Have you got any interesting experiences of going to the museum?"
你能随口把下面这个意思表达出来吗？
"有一次，我去了伦敦的哈利·波特博物馆，在那里我了解了哈利·波特系列电影制作期间所使用的技术，还看到了为了电影效果而制作的机器人。"

2）如何翻译下面的句子？
我希望未来我能考进牛津大学。

参考答案

01 will 应该改成 often，usually，normally，like to 等词。

02 1）There was a time when I went to the Harry Potter Museum in London, where I did lots of things, like seeing all the technologies used in making these films and robots which were made for the film effects.

2）I wish I could be accepted by Oxford University.

写 作 部 分

雅思考试第一要点就是三大基本时态：一般现在时、一般过去时和一般将来时。

| 2011 年的我 | 2017 年的我 | 2050 年的我 |

I was a student. 　　I'm an English teacher. 　　I'll make a name for myself as a famous actor.

小鲜肉，一般过去时　　帅大叔，一般现在时　　老腊肉，一般将来时

准确使用这三种时态，是达到六分的语法关键。

1 一般现在时

写作中的时态选择，先看 TASK 2 议论文。如果你语法不好，全篇都用一般现在时，50% 的概率你用对了。为什么只有 50%？因为下面这些题目，除了举例子那一两句话，确实全篇只用到一般现在时，但只占 50%，也就是从 2014 年 1 月 9 日到 2017 年 6 月 3 日，165 套卷纸，正好出现过 79 次。以后这种趋势也不会出现大的变动。

这类题目要求分析某一种已经存在的现象。

这类题目通常会先说这个已经存在的事实，然后要求考生评价或分析发生原因，比如：

▶ 评价

> 2014 年 4 月 26 日　线上工作和学习的方式取代现实的方式好不好？

> Around the world, more adults can work from home and more children can study from home as computer technologies become cheaper and more accessible. Do you think it is a positive or negative development?

▶ 分析原因

> 2012 年 3 月 8 日　工作和生活失衡的原因和解决方法。

> Nowadays, many people aim to achieve the balance between their work and lives. But few people achieve it. What are the causes of the problem? How could people overcome it?

既然是讨论眼下的事，那肯定全篇用一般现在时都应该是对的，除非你要举过去发生过的例子来论证，就需要用一般过去时，但那只是一两句，注意时态就行了。

那么 TASK 1 呢？一般现在时在图表作文中有两处必用：

一是流程图，描述常态的情况，肯定是一般现在时。

二是地图题，有可能题目没说明这个地图是哪一年的，比如就说这是个学生宿舍的平面图，那就是一般现在时；还有就是地图下面标了"present"，也是一般现在时。

2 一般将来时

大作文中用到这种时态有两种情况。

一是要你评价某些人的提议，我们要怎么做之类的，比如：

> 2014 年 5 月 15 日　该为雇员们每年至少放 4 周假吗？

> Some people think that the employers should give staff at least four weeks' holiday a year as employees can be better at their work. To what extend do you agree or disagree with this view?

提到意见，还没实现，用一般将来时。

二是科技类，分析将来的科技发展，比如：

> 2013 年 8 月 29 日　电脑比人脑聪明是好事吗？

> Some scientists think it is very soon that computers will be more intelligent than humans. Some people think it is a positive development, while others think it is a negative development. Discuss both views and give your opinion.

题目中提到的事还没发生，全篇用一般将来时。

图表作文中，一般将来时用于任何涉及将来时间的信息，比如线性图从 1990 年画到了 2050 年，今年（2017 年）之后就用一般将来时。这里还有一点需要注意，就是题目中有没有限定图表的制作时间，比如剑桥雅思 9 A 类 Test 4 的线性图，题目说，这个图是从 2008 年的一份报告中摘出来的，那 2008 年以后就是一般将来时，因为后面的数据都是推测的。

用一般将来时的时候，要注意用词的问题：

be going to 在写作中不能用，那是表示你计划好了已经，就要去做，不做不行。

will 少用，因为基本这是说明一种比较肯定的情况，除非你很肯定，比如环保类的考题，你说"不可回收材料将会破坏环境"，这一点是肯定的，那用 will 就没问题。

但是国外在写论文的时候，建议你十分慎重地使用 will，因为有点绝对，学术么，世上很少有绝对的事，那不科学。

那用什么呢？下列这五个在你文章里换着用：

> would, could, may, might, be supposed to

3　一般过去时

一般过去时在议论文里应用非常有限，只有两种情况：

一是举例子，当用过去发生的事来证明论点时，要用一般过去时，比如：

> 2014 年 2 月 15 日　成功靠努力和决心还是金钱、外貌等其他因素？

我认为两边的意见都有道理，举例子：

> Bill Gates attributed his success to his mother's financial support, his hard work and talent.
>
> 比尔·盖茨将他的成功归功于他母亲的经济支持以及他的努力和才干。

图表作文中一般过去时是最常用的时态，因为一般的数据或其他信息都是已经发生过的，我们统计出来的。所以，在考场上要注意数据图表的时间，只要没有涉及将来的时间，那就用一般过去时。

01 改错：写作挑错

看看下面的句子，你能找出错误吗？

2014年9月20日　为提高生活质量，发展中国家该把钱用于推广新技术还是提供免费教育？

There is never a country that can succeed only by the achievement in one side of material production and spiritual life.

从没有一个国家仅仅凭借在物质生产或精神生活中一个方面的成就就取得了成功。

02 大闯关：写作闯关

你能翻译出下面的句子吗？注意一般将来时和一般现在时的混搭。

2013年7月6日　太空旅行的发展是好事吗？

太空旅行将会给随行的宇航员带来不必要的风险，因为游客不具备专业知识，可能会做出危险的举动。

参考答案

01　因为描述的情况是在过去发生的，"从没"就是"这个情况以前没有出现过"，那么实际应该使用一般过去时。我们在写作时需要注意，描述根据过去经验得出的结论时，需要考虑一般过去时。

There was never a country that could succeed only by the achievement in one side of material production and spiritual life.

02　Space travel would bring unnecessary risks to the accompanying astronauts, because the travellers are unprofessional and may take some dangerous actions.

四大完成时显一即可

口语部分

现在完成时是用来表示与现在有联系的过去，通俗一点说，就是这事"做完了""做过了"，所以很多同学在翻译自己的中文的时候，经常遇到，"见过""梦到了""去过""认识他好多年了""从6点他就在这""我这辈子都在""好几世纪了""有过四次了""自从""第二次来了""已经等了几小时了"。

所以我们观察一下以上的中文表达，不难发现，完成时态对应的除了"已经""过""了"这么明显的标记以外，还可以和一段时间、几次、几小时等具有延续性特质的词连用。

比如：

> I've known him for years. 我认识他好多年了。

而现在完成进行时通常表达强调不久前刚发生的事儿持续到了现在。

> I've been waiting outside for two hours. 我在外面等了两个小时了。

我们从口语的用法开始说起：

基本信息题，**表达所处的一般状态**：（学科、家乡、住哪）——最常考的必考题

> Do you work or are you a student?

一般人就回答 I'm a student. 这样的答案是很难有亮点的。雅思口语评分标准中词汇项里6分描述有一句话叫"能成功地进行改述"。我们在这里就可以培养一下自己的时态使用意识：
Currently, I've been studying in Beijing University in my third year.

现在完成进行时就用出来了，表达的是什么呢？就是我现在正在上学，而且还在上学。这个时态就要比一般时态能表达出更为细腻的意思来。

再看一例：

> What's your major?

你打算说 My major is... 吗?

这样说更好: The major I've been studying is called English, which is genuinely a good major.

The major I've been studying...我现在正在学的这个学科是……，定语后置和现在完成时的结合，可以让考官眼前一亮。

以此类推你会了吗?

> Where is your hometown? 改述
>
> The city I've been living is called Yinchuan, which is the capital city of Ningxia Hui Autonomous Region.
> Do you live in a house or apartment?
> Currently, I've been living in a 3-bedroom apartment.

现在完成时还可以表达经验。主要使用位置在于文化媒体类题，譬如: museum, travel, collection, reading, films 等题。

来看一例:

> Do you like traveling?
>
> Yes, absolutely. I've been to many exotic places and I genuinely think travel broadens the mind.
> 那当然，我去过很多有异域情调的地方，我真心觉得旅行可以开阔视野。

以此类推，museum, reading 都可以这样说。

> I've been to many cultural related museums. I genuinely think museums are wonderful places to enrich your knowledge.
> 我去过很多与文化有关的博物馆，我真心觉得博物馆是个长知识的好地方。

现在完成时还可以表达"从未"的心态

在 Part 2 里的地点题，我们经常需要解释一下，我为什么要去这个地方，为什么要做这件事。是因为我们从未做过!

> There was a time when my best friend Jack came to me and said: "Hey, Steven, I heard the travel plan on Lonely Planet is on sale. You haven't been there before, have you? How about going traveling to Thailand together?" I was thinking: "That sounds good. Why not have a try?"
>
> 有一次，我最好的朋友杰克来找我说："嘿，史蒂芬，我听说孤独星球的旅行团打折呢，你之前没去过吧？去过吗？要不咱一起去泰国吧！"我当时想："听起来不错啊，为什么不试试呢？"

你看，多种时态的加分点就体现出来了，这就是在 Part 2 的直接对话和内心戏引用的用法。

现在完成时还可以表达赞美

我们经常用"这是我这辈子见过最好的……"表达对某事物的一种肯定。用英文表达，就需要用到完成时了：

◇ This is the most relaxing place I've ever been to in my life. 这是我这辈子去过的最放松的地方。

◇ This is the best ever restaurant I've ever tried in my life. 这是我这辈子试过最好的饭馆。

◇ This is the most fantastic experience I've ever had in my life. 这是我这辈子最爽的体验。

这个用法经常出现在 Part 2 的结尾段，用于总结。

而过去完成时常用在谈话中提及在过去特定时间之前发生的事情，常见于雅思口语考试 Part 2，描述人物：

> I would say a person who is good at a foreign language that I had known before I went to college is called Steven who is my English teacher.

或者描述地点：

> I would say a place near the water that I had been to last year before Spring Festival is called Xiamen, which is a beautiful coastal city located in the south of China.

从这里我们不难看出，过去完成时常用在由 after, before, as soon as, when 等引导的时间状语从句中。

这种用法常出现在描写经历的题目中。

◇ He asked what had happened when he was out. 他问他不在何时发生过什么事。

- I had met him once before. 我以前见过他一次。
- I wondered who had taken the money. 我想知道是谁拿了钱。

而过去完成进行时则表达过去特定时间之前发生的事存在了一段时间或一直持续着。比如说，描述购物经历这个题目，考生会说，（买这双鞋之前）我（当时）一直想跑步来着，这句话就可以说成：I had been wanting to go jogging.

或者再看两个例子：

- I had been waiting for three hours when I finally saw her. 我看到她的时候已经等了3小时了。（常见等人经历题目中）
- I had been expecting some miraculous change. 我一直在期望有什么奇迹般的变化发生。（常见早起经历看日出的描述中，用来描述当时的心情）

01 改错：口语改错

你能看出下列答案的第一句话有什么语法错误吗？

Describe a place which is contaminated

You should say：

  Where it is

  When you went there

  Why you went there and who you were with

And explain how you felt about it.

I would say a place that was contaminated by pollution is a river near my school that I had been studying when I was young.

02 大闯关：口语闯关

1) 如果考官在 Part 2 让你描述 "Describe a famous person in your country"，你能随口把下面这个意思表达出来吗？

"我要说的是一个我两年前认识的名人，名叫彭于晏，是个特别高颜值的男演员。"

2) 翻译下列句子。

我听过好多歌，我真心觉得歌曲特别能够给人以启发。

我朋友有一天来找我，说："嘿，哥们儿，你没去过黄山吧？那地儿是看日出最好的地儿。最近飞机票打折，我准备下周去玩，要不跟我一起去吧？"我心想："听起来不错啊，去！"

参考答案

01 过去上学的学校可以用一般过去时、过去完成时,就是不能用过去完成进行时,因为这个动作已经截止了,没有持续。所以,正确说法应改为:I would say a place that was contaminated by pollution is a river near my school that I used to study in when I was young.

02 1) I would say a famous person that I got to know about 2 years ago is called Peng Yuyan, who is an extremely handsome actor.

2) My friend came to me one day and said, "Hey, mate. You haven't been to the Yellow Mountain before, have you? Which is the most suitable place to see the sunrise. I was told recently the flight ticket to there is rather cheap. I'm going there next week. Would you like to join me?" I was thinking, "That's sounds good. Yes, OK!"

写作部分

这几种时态在 TASK 1 和 TASK 2 中都用得到,而且都是拿分点,因为很少有人会用。

现在完成时是强调现在已经做完了,那么就可以在议论文中用来说明一个已经被证实了的论据。

比如:

> 2015 年 9 月 19 日　每一个人都该素食以确保健康吗?

我们回答说不是,"营养不足",人不吃肉就得瘦,这是常识。那我说两句话:

> Long-term lack of animal proteins could lead to malnutrition and many diseases.
>
> 长期缺乏动物蛋白可能导致营养不良和很多疾病。

> It has been proven that vegetarians usually are beset by night blindness and poor memory due to vitamin A and B deficiency.
>
> 现已证明:素食主义者通常会由于缺乏维生素 A 和 B 而被夜盲症和糟糕的记忆力所困扰。

后一句用的就是现在完成时,强调以前的经验对现在的影响,用来证明前一句话。特别适合于放在文章论述部分的第三句,第一句论点、第二句论据、第三句用过去的经验或事例进行解释。

这一句"It has been proven that..."的同义备选项还有：

> It has been accepted by the majority that...
> It has been supported by the facts that...

还有很多，因为涉及的语法拿分点还有主语从句，所以大家可以参考主语从句那一章。

现在完成时还用于下面这个问过去的题目，过去五年A类和G类总共300道题，类似的题目只在A类出现了一次：

> 2013年4月6日 过去一百年人类进步的领域，没进步的领域

这题的内容范围有点大，不过全篇都得用一般过去时和现在完成时才对。

现在完成进行时和过去完成进行时主要用于图表作文的地图题，表示过去一段时间一直存在的一个建筑或者河流道路这些地理现象，比如：

面对包含两个以上地图的多图题的时候，我们需要首先以现在完成进行时态（has been doing 图表时间从过去持续到现在）、过去完成进行时（had been doing 图表时间涉及过去某一时间段）来说明其中一直没有改变的建筑或自然结构的持续状态，比如下图：

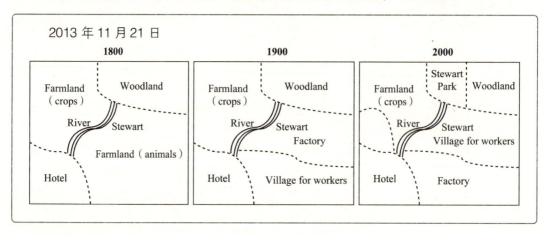

这三幅图中的河流一直未变，我们需要用过去完成进行时说明这种持续状态：

> During the two centuries, River Stewart had been running from northeast to southwest.

这就是过去完成进行时的用法，用来说明1800到2000两百年间一直存在的河流。

如果最后一幅图的时间不是2000而是"present"，那么这句话就要用现在完成进行时，从1800到现在这条河流都在。

那么这个句式就是：

During the whole period, 某一建筑 has / had been lying in 方位.

During the whole period, 某一河流 has / had been running from 某一方位 to 另一方位.
During the whole period, 某一道路 has / had been connecting 某一方位 with 另一方位.
现在完成进行时除了用于上面的地图题，还用于线性图，比如：

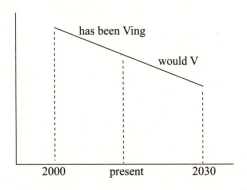

描述 2000—2030 这条线的时候，要用到两种时态，2000 到现在是过去完成进行时（has been Ving），现在到 2030 是一般将来时，可以写成：

> The number has been dropping from 2000 to the present and would keep that until 2030.

也就是说，穿越当下时间的变化，必须分割，采用两个不同的时态分别描述。当然，我们也可以用形容词＋名词的形式进行描述，这个时候就不用考虑时态变化了。比如上一句我们可以改成：There was a slow decrease lasting 3 decades after 2000.

01　改错：写作挑错

看看下面的句子，有错吗？

2014 年 7 月 26 日　个人无力解决环境问题还是必须做出行动？

Human beings have recognized the environmental hazards of white pollution for a century, but nothing has been done.

早在一个世纪前，人类已经认识到白色污染的环境危害了，但不为所动。

02　大闯关：写作闯关

看看下面这道题，你能随手翻译出下面的句子吗？注意现在完成时的应用。

2016 年 2 月 18 日　环境破坏是无药可救了还是尚有可为？

各国京都议定书（Tokyo Protocol）显示，世界大多数国家在减排（emission reduction）上已经取得了共识（reach a consensus）。

参考答案

01　recognize 是一个不可持续的动作，后面不可以连接表示一个时间段的时间状语"for a century"。

Human beings have recognized the environmental hazards of white pollution in the last century, but nothing has been done.

人类在 20 世纪已经认识到白色污染的环境危害了，但不为所动。

而其否定状态"没认识到"就是个可持续的状态，可以连接时间段：

Most people have not recognized the environmental hazards of white pollution for a century.

一个世纪了，大多数人都没认识到白色污染的环境危害。

02　It has been proven by Tokyo Protocol that most countries in the world have reached a consensus on emission reduction.

三大进行时稳扎稳打

口语部分

时态变化是口语考试的一个高级得分点,所谓高级体现在"全都能用对"和"变化"这两个技能上。那么,除了你平时熟悉的"During weekends, I always play basketball with my friends."和"I have a friend. His name is Tom. We have been best friends since high school. He is friendly and kind. We are best friends because we have similar hobbies."这样的简单时态,什么时候才能变化时态,用上我们学过的高级时态呢?

1 现在进行时

现在进行时有三个用处:
❶ 表示说话时正在进行的动作或存在的情况(口语考试很少用,大部分题是说过去);
❷ 虽然说话时并没有真正在做,但在现阶段正在从事、到现在还没有结束的事儿(常用来说明基本信息题,现在在哪住、在哪上学、在哪工作等问题);
❸ 与频度副词 always, constantly, continually, forever 连用,表示抱怨(这个很常用)
要想掌握这个时态的用法,大家只需要记住几个万能句子就可以了。
表示说话时,正在进行的动作:

> I think travelling by bus is a big trouble. What I'm saying is its disadvantages in belonging safety, uncomfortableness, and over exposure to potential diseases.
>
> I don't like science at all. I'm talking about physics, chemistry, especially chemistry which I think is just like Greek to me.

在这一用法中,现在进行时用于解释说明前面没有解释清楚的信息。
在基本信息题中,表达现阶段进行的事情就和上一章现在完成时的用法类似了,有些细微差别。例如:

> Currently, I'm studying in Xi'an International Studies University as a freshman. Right now, I'm living in a small duplex house which I share with 3 other guys.

当然，只要是描述现状的，都可以用现在进行时，比如：

> Recently, I'm struggling with the IELTS exam, so on the weekends, the only thing I do is practice my English.

在雅思口语真题中，可以使用以上表达现状的说法的题目有：

> **Work or study**
> Do you work or are you a student?
> What's your major?

> **Hometown/House or flat**
> Where's your hometown?
> Do you live in a house or flat?

> **Weekends/Leisure/Friends or social network/sleep**
> What do you like to do at weekends?
> How do you like to relax?
> How long do you spend time with your friends?
> What kinds of social networks do you use?
> How many hours do you sleep every day?

这些询问生活习惯的题是现在进行时常出现的地方，你可以用 currently... 表达现在很忙，学习很累，在做什么之类的表示现阶段进行的事情。

现在进行时还有一个用处，就是表示已确定的未来计划，或者表达强烈的愿望，比如：

> I'm craving for traveling around the world. 我十分渴望周游世界。
> I'm longing for buying a big house. 我一直想要个大房子。

2 过去进行时

这个时态在雅思口语考试中运用广泛，对雅思考试有一些了解的同学们都知道，雅思考官最喜欢问关于过去的话题，在 Part 2 中的 80% 的描述题都是要介绍我如何认识这个人（人物题）、什么时候去过这个景点（地点题）、什么时候买的这个东西（物品题）、什么时候看的电视节目（媒体题）、什么时候的经历（事件经历题）。

所以，过去进行时是所有考生必须要学会的时态用法。

怎么用呢？过去进行时的本质是用来描述口语中的场景。例如：

我上周在公交车站等公交车，看到一个美女想要电话，想描述得细致一些给你，怎么说呢？

> I was waiting for the bus at the bus station. Then I saw a good-looking girl standing by my side. I was thinking: "Wow, she looks like an angel!" So, I moved towards her and tried to start a conversation. She seemed rather offended, frowned and said, "Get out of my sight!"
>
> 我那会儿正在公交站等公交，然后我看见一个特别好看的女孩站我边上。我就想："哇，这长相沉鱼落雁啊！"所以，我就朝她挪步，想跟她聊聊天。她好像特别反感，皱了个眉头，说了句："滚开！"

过去进行时会把你拉进一个场景里去，让你和我一起回味一下发生了什么事情，还可以告诉听者在这个场景中，我的内心戏、内心感受。

如果没有过去进行时，这个小段就成这样了：

> I waited for the bus, saw a good-looking girl standing by my side and moved towards her and tried to start a conversation. She seemed rather offended, frowned and said, "Get out!"
>
> 我等公交车，看到一个漂亮女孩站我旁边，我靠近她和她聊天，她好像特别烦我，皱眉说了句，"滚！"

全部是一般过去时的表述只能表达我做过什么事，但是无法带给你更细节的体会和场景。

如何说出一个场景呢？从场景的四要素开始学起：

1. 时间 2. 地点 3. 道具/第一印象描述 4. 内心感受

> 回答一个 Do you like music? 的场景
>
> Yes, I like music very much.
> （时间）Every time when I feel tired,
> （地点）no matter where I am, on a bus or staying at home
> （道具）I like to put on my earphones and hide myself in the world of music.
> （内心感受）Before I broke up with my girlfriend, I was thinking, "Music is a cure to sadness." and later I found it's true.

> **一个认识好朋友时的场景**
>
> I'd like to talk about one of my best friends whose name is Jacie. She is a lovely girl and also my high school classmate.
> （时间）At that time, it was on the first day, in the orientation.
> （地点）We were asked to have an ice-breaking party in the classroom.
> （描述）She showed up with a long dress in white color, walking elegantly.
> （内心感受）**I was thinking**, "Wow, she is beautiful!"
> （在场景中的细节行为描述都可以用过去进行时）
> She was talking like an angel.
> She was smiling with charm.

过去进行时也可以用在其他场景中，大家可以试着描述一下吃小吃的场景，开车去旅游的场景等。

3 将来进行时

这是一个表达愿望、决心的时态，用于表示已经决定的、肯定会发生的事。

我记得上次考雅思，考官出来我马上要站起来跟他打招呼，他说他要上厕所，过一会儿回来：Just one minute, I'll be right back.

然后我回答：That's all right. I'll be right here waiting for you. 这其实是一句歌词，我酷酷地把它用这了，那次考官给了我 8 分。

不过，在整个 12 分钟口语考试中，关于将来时态的题目倒不是很多。

Part 1 出现的都是关于将来的打算，如：对未来交通的看法，以后会不会买车等问题。

> What's your plan for the future?
> Do you want to live in the countryside in the future?
> Will you use more social networks in the future?
> How to improve the public transportation in the future?
> Do you want to learn arts in the future?
> What technologies do you want to learn in the future?

在回答这些将来时的问题时，通常就只有两个态度，一个是不确定的虚拟语气表达将来时的态度：

> I think perhaps **I would have** a try some day.
> 我想我可能以后会试试。

一个是无比肯定的将来进行时的态度：

> I think I'll be looking forward to seeing the future that one day I can become an engineer as my father.
> 我想我一定会无比期待这样的未来，有一天我成为一个像我爸那样的工程师。

或

> I'll be studying in Canada next year. 我明年要去加拿大学习。
> If that comes true, I'll be thinking the world is crazy.
> 如果这个说法成真了，我一定会觉得世界疯了吧！

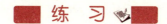

01 改错

你能看出下列句子有什么语法错误吗？

* Perhaps, next year I'll be studying in UK.

* Do you like eating snacks?
　Yes, I like eating snacks. I was thinking：
　"Snacks are the most wonderful thing in the world."

* Where do you live?
　Currently, I've lived in a dormitory at school.

02 大闯关

1）试用过去进行时描述一个吃小吃的场景。
　回答这个问题："Do you like snacks?"

2）翻译下列句子。
　我明年一定会去澳洲读书。
　我十分想周游世界。

参考答案

01　perhaps 表示可能，代表未来的打算不是很确定，就不能使用将来进行时这种表示对一定会发生的事情推测的时态。要么是"Perhaps, I would be studying in UK next year."要么是"For sure, I'll be studying in UK next year."。

　　这道题的过去进行时使用错误，前面并没有明显的表示过去的时间状语，这个时态蹦出来就莫名其妙了。过去进行时只能用来描述过去发生的场景，如果你说 When I was young，再接这个句子就对了。

现在完成时表示这件事已经做完了，那么你现在就应该不在学校住了。

现在完成时和现在完成进行时的区别就在此，后者表示动作还在持续。比如英语中会常问，你学英语学了几年了？回答：

I've been studying English for more than 10 years.（学了十几年还在学）

I've studied English for more than 10 years.（可能是 1998 年到 2009 年在学，之后就没学了）

02 1) Yeah, snack is my poison. Every time when I get out of the underground station and smell something savory or pot. I am frozen in my steps. When I was young, my mother also said, "Don't eat that. It's dirty." I was always thinking, "There is a person who just lives in my heart and always says go eat it, eat it!" So I easily gave up and started to lick my fingers.

2) I'll be studying in Australia next year.

I'm craving for touring around the world.

写作部分

1 现在进行时

在议论文写作中，常用一般现在时讨论当下的情况，其实现在进行时有时会有更好的效果。因为它强调的是现在正在做的事、当下正持续的现状或我们正在作出的努力。语气比一般现在时要强很多。

有一种特殊的用法，大家可以了解一下，就是用现在进行时用在否定结构中可以表示决心：

I am not waiting any longer. I must sell my kidney and buy an iPhone 7.

我决心不再等了。我必须卖肾买个 iPhone 7。

再如：

> 2015 年 9 月 26 日   为什么一些国家废物回收量不足？如何鼓励回收？
>
> 鉴于在污染上治理上的庞大开支，很多政府正停止等待、开始鼓励使用可回收材料，比如在英国的废弃物填埋税。
>
> In view of the heavy expenditures on pollution control, many governments are not waiting any longer and start to encourage the use of recyclable materials, such as the landfill tax in UK.

这里又涉及一个论述材料的问题，建议大家写作文的时候多用现实生活的和西方的材料：比如新闻时事、历史典故，而不是用一些华丽的大词堆砌，前者能够让论述更有说服力并容易引起共鸣。比如上面例子里的 landfill tax，是英、美、澳等国最先出现的环保税的一种，埋不可回收的废物时就得多付钱，从而抬高不可回收材料的使用成本、逼着大家使用可回收材料。记住这个例子的语法和内容，环保类题目可以借用。

那么句式的骨架就可以总结为：

In view of 某种情况，相关人士/政府 are not waiting any longer and start to 采取某种措施，such as 举例.

再举个例子：

> 2016 年 4 月 2 日　多元文化给国家带来的好处多于坏处吗？

> In view of the severe shortage of technical laborers, many industrial nations are not waiting any longer and are starting to apply more positive multicultural policies to encourage population inflow, such as a lower immigration threshold in America.
>
> 鉴于严重的技术人才短缺，很多工业化国家正停止等待、开始实施更加积极的多元文化政策去吸引人口流入，比如美国降低的移民门槛。

我们还可以以列表的方式提供更多选项：

鉴于	某种情况	相关人士/政府	正停止等待、开始	采取某种措施	包括了/例如	例子
Based on In consideration of In the light of In view of	名词短语	名词短语	are not waiting any longer and start to	动词短语	containing including involving such as	名词短语.

在图表作文中（特别是线形图），现在进行时有一种特殊的用法：对于 go, comes, fly, move, stay, return 这些词，现在进行时与其一起使用可以表示将来，比如：

> 数据将于 2020 年回归 180 吨。
> The number is returning to 180 tonnes in 2020.

2　过去进行时

过去进行时比较少见，是描述过去某一时刻正在发生的事情的。

比如在 George Orwell 的动物庄园（Animal Farm）的第一段就有：

> Mr. Jones kicked off his boots ... and made his way up to bed, where Mrs. Jones was already snoring.

在一般的议论文题目中使用起来很困难，但是在小作文的线性图中却可以用来描述两条线交叉，比如下图：

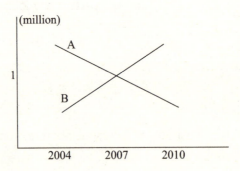

我们模仿上面动物庄园里的那句话：

> A started to decline in 2004 and crossed with B at 1 million in 2007 where the latter was climbing.

这句话我们在写交叉点的时候可以拿来用，它的骨架就可以简化为：

A 线 started to 某种变化 in 时间 and crossed with B 线 at 交叉点数据 in 交叉点时间 where the latter was Ving 某种变化.

对照这个骨架和上一句的示例，记住它，并在考场上使用。

01 改错：写作挑错

看看下面的句子，挑挑毛病吧。

1) 2016 年 4 月 16 日　新城镇建公园和体育设施比建购物中心重要吗？

City planners are recognizing that leisure facilities have the same important ance as material supply and must be built proportionally.

城镇规划者们正逐渐认识到，休闲设施和物资供给对保证生活质量同等重要，必须按比例修建。

2) 2016 年 3 月 19 日　医疗保健应该免费还是人们该自己付医疗保健费用？

When people will be faced with huge medical bills, they could recognize the importance of free public healthcare.

什么时候人们将要面对巨额医疗账单了，他们才能认识到免费公立医疗的重要性。

02 大闯关：写作闯关

试着针对下面的题目翻译句子。

2016年3月31日　为什么孩子们花更多时间在电脑游戏上、更少时间在运动上？它是积极的还是消极的？

鉴于长时间静坐对健康的坏处，很多家长现在不再等待教育部门的指导性建议，开始限制他们的孩子花在屏幕前的时间。

参考答案

01　1）表示情感、认知、愿望的动词不能用现在进行时，这些词例如：hate、know、mind、recognize、think、want、wish、understand 等，应该用一般现在时表示。
City planners recognize that leisure facilities are as important material supply and must be built proportionally.

2）不能算错，读起来有点别扭。在时间、条件状语从句中，有时习惯用进行时代替一般现在时。
When (people are 可省略) facing with huge medical bills, they could recognize the importance of free public healthcare.

02　In view of the negative effects of sedentariness on health, many parents are not waiting for the guidance from education sectors and start to limit the time their children spent in front of screens.

主动使用被动语态

口语部分

在雅思口语中被动语态是个特别容易被人忽视的加分点。来看这些句子，不同的说法感觉就不一样。

> A 同学：I'd like to talk about a place Xiamen. It's located in the south part of China. I went there with my best friend during the last summer holiday.
>
> B 同学：I would say a place near the water that I had been to 2 years ago in summer holiday with my friend is called Xiamen, which is located in the southern part of China.

同样的信息，但是 B 同学给人的感觉就不一样。在一个句子中套用了多种语法结构。对于被动语态这个知识点，最容易被忽略的就是 is called（被叫作）结构。通常大家都会直接说 is...，很少有人会刻意强调名称。这算是一个清晰传递信息的技巧。

再看一句：

> A 同学：Before I went to this place, my friend searched for some information about this place on the Internet. He said Xiamen is a leisure city. In 2007, it ranked in the top 10 tourist cities in China.
>
> B 同学：Before I went to this place, I was told that Xiamen, the leisure city in 2007, was on the list of top 10 tourist cities in China. Thanks to my friend's searching work on the Internet.

做引入信息的时候，可以用到 I was told that...

比如，说到水果，可以说 I was told that an apple a day keeps the doctor away. 或者，说到污染，可以说 I was told that in Beijing the haze and PM2.5 have already influenced the death rate of lung cancers in a bad way. 提到历史，你可以说 I was told that in traditional Chinese culture, there's an old saying. Take history as mirror, you'll know rise and fall.（我听过传统中国文化里有句古话，以史为鉴可以知兴替。）

如果是在 **Part 2** 题里，想要描述一个名人，一个老人，一个好朋友的事迹，也可以用这一句，I was told that he has been to 14 different countries in only 2 years. That fascinated me. 题目要求描述一个常坐飞机的人，可以说：

I was told he was a professional cameraman.

除此之外，被动语态还可以被用在表达惊讶的情绪中。这一组句子的备选项有：

我很震惊	震惊的内容
I was surprised that	句子
I was amazed by	名词短语
I was shocked that	句子
I was impressed that	句子

描述一个未来想住的房子，也可以使用被动语态：

> The first time I saw this house in a movie, I was amazed by its style and imagination of using plastic bottles to build a house.

描述一个你敬仰的老人，可以使用被动语态：

> I was shocked that Doctor Tu Youyou used her own body as human experimental subject and finally found how to tackle the malaria problem.

我们还可以把被动语态用于转折的句子中，譬如：

> Do you prefer to eat in the restaurant or eat at home?

> Well, nowadays, a lot of newspapers often report recycled oil being used in restaurants, that being said（话虽这么说）, you can't ignore the advantages restaurants bring to us, for example, save my time on dish washing and cooking and provide me with various choices.

用被动语态表达干的不错的或者干得不好

好的	不好的
well-educated 受到良好教育的	ill-educated 素质差的
well-decorated 装修的不错的	ill-decorated 装修很烂的
well-performed 表现不错的	ill-performed 表现不好的
well-said 说得真好	ill-said 说的真烂
well-written 写的不错的	ill-written 写的差劲的

- His body is very well-built. 他身材非常好。
- He is medium built. 他中等身材。

在口语中表达活儿干完了：

> She is very strict. Every day she has to check if the flower is watered, homework is done, socks are washed and then she allows us to go to bed.

还可以表达一些众所周知的事情、媒体报道、大众观点：

It is often reported that… 媒体经常报道……；It's supposed to be a controversial issue. 这应该是个具有争议性的问题。It is commonly known that…众所周知……；It is said that…据说……

还有几个常用的被动语态表达：

- My timetable is always packed and fully occupied.
  我的时间表总是很满。
- This phenomenon is often described from a negative aspect.
  这个现象总是从负面被描述出来的。
- In school, we were not allowed to wear whatever we wanted.
  在学校不是想穿什么就能穿什么。
- Her face is always filled with smile.
  她总是面带微笑。
- I like the feeling of being needed.
  我喜欢被需要的感觉。
- Instead of being warmed up by the clothes she gave me, my heart was melted by her.
  与其说她给我的衣服让我感到温暖，不如说我的心已经被她融化了。

被动语态出现的位置通常都比较固定，所以学会这一章，在口语表达中可以自如运用被动语态。

01 改错：口语挑错

看看下面的句子，挑挑毛病吧。

1) I was so surprised. I didn't expect that she would gave me pajamas. I was thinking,

"How considerate she is." Can you imagine that? If you saw my facial expression, you would know it's mixed with happiness, satisfaction and being moved.

我特别惊喜，我没想到她会送我一件睡衣。我就想："她好体贴啊！"你能想象吗？如果你看到我的表情，你就知道我脸上混杂着开心、满意和感动。

2）At about 4 o'clock, I was woken up by my friend. He just slapped my face and said, "Hey, rise and shine! It's about that time." I was thinking, "Who the hell is that? Leave me alone. I'm so sleepy." Honestly, if I had a knife in my hand, I would definitely kill him. My head was so heavy. I felt like my head was hit by a rod or something.

大约4点钟，我的朋友把我叫醒了。他拍拍我的脸蛋说："嘿，快起床！时间到了。"我当时想："到底是谁在叫我？让我自己待会儿，我太困了。"说实话，如果当时我有一把刀，我一定会杀了他。我的头好沉，好像被一个杆子或别的东西撞了似的。

02 大闯关：口语闯关

试试针对下面的题目翻译一句。

Do you like eating fruits?

我超爱吃水果，夏天的时候几乎天天吃。以前我总听人说，"一天吃个苹果就不用看医生了"。苹果富含维生素，对身体很有好处。

参考答案

01 1）并列结构 happiness，satisfaction 都是名词，后面的 moved 是个形容词，与前者不匹配了，所以要慎用"感动"这个词，应该为 being moved 被感动，就变成名词的形式了。

2）有时候要小心一个词的过去分词和原型形式一样。hit 的过去分词就是 hit，类似的词还有 put，let，hurt，read，shut，spread，cut，set，千万不要写错，或者读错了。

02 Fruit is my poison. In the summer I eat fruits almost every day. I was told before that an apple a day keeps the doctor away. Apples are rich in vitamins, so they've very healthy.

写作部分

在写作中，我们可以使用下面两种被动语态的特殊用法来给文章增色：

1 和主语补足语合并使用

比如：

> 2016 年 4 月 21 日　如何解决不断增加的消费品生产对环境的危害？

> Popularizing biodegradable materials are thought to be the main way to minimize the pollution caused by household waste.
>
> 推广可降解材料被认为是最小化生活垃圾所造成的污染的主要途径。

这一句的主干就是：

相关事项 is/are thought to 某一意义（主语补足语）。

相关事项被认为是……。

句子很短，但是包含了两个语法拿分点：一个是被动语态"被认为"，另一个是句尾不定式作主语补足语。逻辑上这一句可以用来提出论点。

再如：

> 2016 年 3 月 31 日　为什么孩子们花更多时间在电脑游戏上、更少时间在运动上？它是积极的还是消极的？

> Playing video games, including violent shooting games, is believed to boost a range of cognitive skills, such as a sense of direction, reasoning, memory and perception.
>
> 有人相信，玩电游，包括暴力射击游戏，可以加强一系列的认知技能，比如：方向感、推理、记忆力和觉察力。

那么，这一句的备选项可以总结为：

相关事项	被认为	某一意义
名词/动名词短语	is/are adviced to is/are believed to is/are presumed to is/are predicted to be is/are proposed to is/are proved to is/are recommended to is/are suggested to is/are thought to	动词短语

2 和主语从句同时使用

> 2016 年 3 月 12 日　现代社会不需要动物性食品和产品了吗?

> It has been noted that the taste, nutrition or quality of artificial alternatives cannot compare with animal products.
>
> 人们已经注意到，人工替代品的口味、营养或者质量不能和动物产品相比。

这一句的主干是：
It has been noted that ...
人们已经注意到……。

拿分点是 it 作形式主语，that 引导后置的主语从句，具体细节大家可以参照第二十四招：主语从句的讲解，同时又包含了被动语态。这一句可以用于论据分析部分，用来讲道理。

再如：

> 2016 年 3 月 5 日　不该相信记者吗？记者最重要的素质是什么？

> It is believed that curiosity, namely being interested in how things work, should be the number one quality a great reporter must have.
>
> 人们相信，好奇心，即对事物如何发展感兴趣，应该是一个出色的记者必须拥有的第一素质。

注意这个例句中出现了两处被动语态：一处是"is believed"，另一处是"being interested in"。

那么，这一句的备选项可以总结为：

人们相信	意见部分
It has been widely accepted that	
It has been proved that	
It is advised that	
It is believed that	句子
It is recommended that	
It is suggested that	
It should be noted that	

需要注意的是，其实上面表格里的时态是多种可选的：既可以用现在完成时表示既成事实 has been noted，也可以用将来时表示建议 should be noted，还可以用一般现在时表示

现存状态 is noted。

图表题中，被动语态主要用于流程图和地图中对于变化的描述。

先看流程图，大部分加工流程图中施动者（比如工人）是不出现的，那么我们不得不依赖被动语态来说明加工过程。一般流程图包含大约 6 个加工步骤，我就列出 6 个不同的句式来供大家参考，都涉及被动语态。

- 选项一：

原料 is 加工过程（动词被动语态）by a 设备（so that 加工结果（句子））．

原料将由某种设备进行某种处理（以便得到某种结果）。

- 选项二：

原料 is placed in a 设备 to be 加工过程（动词被动语态）（for 加工结果（名词／动名词词组））．

原材料被放置于设备内进行某种加工（以便实现某种加工结果）。

- 选项三：

原料 is transferred to a 设备 so as to be 加工过程（动词被动语态）and 加工结果（动词词组）．

原材料被运送到某一设备并进行某种加工（并达到了某一结果）。

- 选项四：

原料 is passed to a 设备 for 加工过程（动名词词组）（and turns to 加工结果（动词词组））．

原料被送到某种设备处进行某种处理（并变成了某一结果）。

- 选项五：

In order to further process 原料（to 加工结果（动词词组）），流程（名词／动名词词组）is done with the help of a 设备．

为了对原料进行进一步的加工（以得到某种结果），某一流程在某一设备的帮助下被完成。

- 选项六：

As a close, 原料 is packed up / delivered to 用户．

作为收尾，原料被打包／运给用户。

这些句式，除了选项六之外，其余在实战中的顺序都是可调的，在句首加上下面这词表示顺序就更好了：

> At the beginning, Next, Then, After that, Afterwards, Following that, At the 序数词 stage, At stage 数字, Finally 等

在闯关部分，我们会看到针对这些句式的流程图练习。

在地图题中，建筑和自然景貌的变化也一样要用被动语态，因为建设者在图中不会出现，这一点相对简单，但是涉及的动词相对多变，下面是一些描述特殊地点变化的词，注意所有的动词都是以被动形式出现的：

> **Trees, forests**: cleared, cut-down, chopped-down, removed, planted
> **Roads, bridges and railways lines**: constructed, built, extended, expanded, removed
> **Leisure facilities**: opened, set up, developed

01 改错：写作挑错

看看下面的句子读起来顺口吗？问题在哪里呢？

2014年5月10日 男性应该帮女性做家务吗？

It would be cruel and unreasonable to push men to do housework, because more rest is needed by them to replenish energy.

强迫男性做家务是残忍和不通情理的，因为更多的休息被他们需要来补充体力。

02 大闯关：写作闯关

试试用本章提供的流程图句式描述出下面图表的关键加工过程。

2014年1月11日

The flow chart below describes the processes of making bottles by recycling glass products.

The process of glass recycling

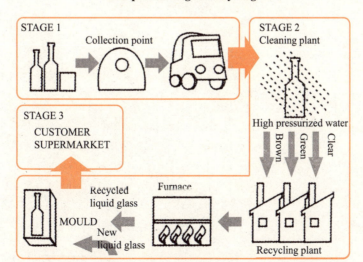

参考答案

01 实际生活中,被动语态常用于施动者没出现的情况,比如:那个苹果被吃了。这句里被谁吃的没提,那被动语态就是对的。否则,在施动者出现的情况下,一般用正常语序比较顺口,这是一个表述习惯的问题,中英文在这一点上是一致的。

所以上面的翻译读起来很怪异,应该改为:

It would be cruel and unreasonable to push men to do housework, because they do need more rest to replenish energy.

强迫男性做家务是残忍和不通情理的,因为他们确实需要更多的休息来补充体力。

02 There is a flow chart showing the process of the recycle usage of glass.

The process contains six steps according to the time sequence.

First, **used glass products** are **collected** in **collection points**, so that they could be **transferred to a cleaning plant by trucks**.

After that, **these used glass products** are placed **under high pressurized water** to be **cleaned**.

Then, **the cleaned ones** are **classified by colors**, **including brown**, **green and clear** and are **transferred to a recycling plant**.

Following that, **the glass products** are passed to a **furnace** for **heating** and turns to **recycled liquid glass**.

In order to further process **recycled and new liquid glass** to **produce new bottles**, **the final production** is done with the help of a **mould**.

After that, **the new bottles** are **delivered to customers and supermarkets.**

一招鲜的独立主格

口语部分

首先解释一下什么叫"格"。英语是一个特别讲究结构的语言，任何一个句子都应该有主谓结构，简单讲，就是只要是句子就应该有"动词"，但是独立主格中就没有动词，于是它就形成了一个格。

独立主格结构不是短语，它里面其实有动词的概念，但是没有动词的形式，因为**动词全部都是以非谓语动词的形式体现的（多数情况是 ing 的形式）**。

这一个语法现象之所以显得高级，是因为它看起来毫无章法，只是把一件事的逻辑堆在一起，没有从句的先行词和连接词，但是却节省了表达时间，看起来简单、易懂。

独立主格在句子结构中相当于状语从句，表时间和表伴随的用法比较常见。来看一例：(Part 2 常用开头)

> 许多雅思考生在谈论一个话题的时候习惯说：
> When it comes to this topic, I'd like to share with you one of my experience.

这是一个 when 引导的时间状语从句，可以用独立主格结构改写：

> For the topic being mentioned, I would start by sharing a story of mine.

注意，在这个句子中，前半句话没有任何引导词，作了后半句话的从句，两句话的主语还都不一样，第一句主语是 topic，第二句主语是 I。但是你很容易就听懂了，这就是独立主格的特点，前半句只给 -ing 形式的动词，后半句按照主句的形式表达。

学习独立主格结构，我们主要培养自己在这一领域的语感。

再看一例：(看天的经历)

> Because the night is dark and frosty, we brought some hot chocolate and a torch.
> The night being dark and frosty, we then brought some hot chocolate and a torch.

下面，让我们来连番轰炸语感：

（表时间）中国人喜欢游泳
With the summer coming with hot temperature, you will see swimming pools filled with crowds of people, like a hot pot full of dumplings, from my way of seeing it.

（表条件）如果有机会我一定要去一次西班牙
Chances are there, I will definitely go to Spain for once.

（表原因）因为运动使人健康，所以我很喜欢运动
Sports give me a healthy lifestyle, I like sports. I like them very much.

（表伴随）所有水果都富含维生素，猕猴桃含量最高
All the fruits are rich in vitamins, with kiwis being the best of all.

（表补充说明）一个向你道歉的人
I can't say anything to him at that moment, he is treating me so well.

其实，所谓独立主格结构，就是把这几种状语从句，去掉连接词，然后把动词变成 being，动词 ing 或者 done，然后句子原有意思靠意会来体现逻辑。

当然能表示非谓语动词的可不只有 ing，要是会用 done 结构的独立主格，那才更酷炫。

With the homework done, she finally went back home. （由 when 从句改装过后的句子）
With the journey finished, I started to feel tired. （由 when 从句改装过后的句子）
With more time given, I will tour around the city. （由 if 从句改装后的句子）
With more chances given, I won't fail it again. （由 if 从句改装后的句子）
Later, after the article was published, people started to realize how important health is. （由 after 从句改装后的句子）

独立主格+不定式的结构也有，不定式的用法通常用在将来时和否定句中：

If this exam I do not fail, I'm sure I'll be going to Britain next year.
With nobody to write anything by hand, I think computer might really be the major way to record words.

还有几种比较怪的方式，独立主格＋介词短语/形容词、副词

> He is thinking, eyes on the floor. （重要的对话）
>
> In the photo, I sat in the first row, mouth half open. （自己的照片）
>
> She looked confused about what I said, then I took out my mobile phone, screen on, finger on the app, key words typed in the search engine, and information about her destination popped upon the screen. （帮助别人的经历-指路/第一次使用外语的经历）

特殊句型：独立主格＋there being 和 it being

> If I have enough time, say on holidays or weekends, what I like to do is to go for a movie or sing in the karaoke bar. There being no time for leisure, the only thing I do is to relax by taking showers. （你喜欢怎么放松自己？）
>
> It being a problem of lacking public awareness, littering is a problem we never solve. （环境法）

再看一些句子来刷语感：（常坐飞机的人）

> I would say a person who often travels by plane that I had met about 2 years ago when I traveled from Beijing to Shanghai is called Steven, who is a professional photographer.
>
> At that time, I was sitting by the aisle on a plane, this man sitting by the window, face in a magazine, both feet on my chair, looking extremely tired. I was thinking："What a person！"
>
> "Excuse me, sir！" said the Air hostess, turning to me and said sorry, her facial expression looking embarrassed, hands rubbed with each other briskly.

独立主格结构尤其适合描述场景，具有很强的描述性，可以把连续的动作放在一起在最短的时间内讲完，听的人也比较容易理解。

01 改错：口语改错

下列句子改成独立主格结构的句子，你觉得改对了吗？

He looked at me in the eyes, his hands were crossed in front of his legs.

答：He looking at me in the eyes, with his hands crossed in front of his legs.

02 大闯关：口语闯关

试着用本章提供的句式描述出下面"帮助他人"的经历：

Describe an experience when you had to help a stranger.
You should say
When it happened
Who you helped
How he benefited from you help
And explain how you felt about it

我正在地铁站买票，忽然有人拍我肩膀，我一回头，看见一个老太太带着孩子，手缩在袖子里，衣服别在裤子里，看起来像有事儿要说。

参考答案

01 这两个句子，句子主干是 he looked at me in the eyes, 那后半句是什么？应该是 his hands crossed in front of his legs 是独立主格结构作伴随状语，其中，his hands 是 crossed in front of his legs. 的逻辑主语，两者为被动关系，所以动词是过去分词。答句中，He looking at me in the eyes, his hands were crossed in front of his legs. 前半句是独立主格结构作伴随状语，he 是 looking at me 的逻辑主语，两者之间是主动关系，所以用现在分词.

但是 his hands were crossed under his head。成了句子的主干，从语法规则上看好像是正确的，但是说话者要凸显的内容错位了。说话者显然想凸显他看着我这个动作，而不是交叉手。因为"主体"比"手"重要，所以改错的时候也要判断语境。

02 At that time, I was in a subway station, buying a ticket. Somebody patted my shoulder, I turned around and saw an old lady. She was accompanied by a child, hands hidden in his sleeves, with the lower hem of his clothes stuffed in the trousers, and seemed to have something to say.

写作部分

独立主格就是和主句有关系的从句（两句的主语不一样），从句中的非谓语动词为现在分词形式（主动）或者过去分词形式（被动）。从句作主句的时间、条件、原因或者伴随状语。

> Because Angelababy is a beautiful and smart lady, she drew Mr. Huang's attention.
> 因为Angelababy是位聪明漂亮的女士，所以她引起了黄先生的注意。

这句话包含一个原因状语从句，这个原因状语还可以以状语的形式出现：

> Being a beautiful and smart lady, Angelababy drew Mr. Huang's attention.
> 作为一位聪明漂亮的女士，Angelababy引起了黄先生的注意。

这句是非谓语动词作状语，其逻辑主语和主句一致。如果不一致呢，比如下面这句：

> Because Angelababy is a beautiful and smart lady, Mr. Huang married her.
> 因为Angelababy是位聪明漂亮的女士，所以黄先生娶了她。

还是一个原因状语从句，但是从句里的主语和主句不一致，其实也可以换种表达方式：

> Angelababy being a beautiful and smart lady, Mr. Huang married her.
> Angelababy是位聪明漂亮的女士，所以黄先生娶了她。

上面这句就包含独立主格结构，非谓语动词作状语，逻辑主语和主句不一致，必须另带主语。

这里讲解的用法是表示因果关系的，在议论文中这一逻辑关系最常见。另外独立主格还可以用于时间、条件或者伴随关系。

例如：

> **2015年6月27日　为什么公众缺乏安全感？如何解决？**
>
> 如果论点是"estranged interpersonal relationship"：
> Coolness growing between social members, the feeling of being disconnected and helpless makes people feel emotionally unsafe.
> 由于在社会成员间之间冷漠的滋生，隔离和无助的感觉让人们情绪上觉得不安全。

这一例句里我们用独立主格做主句的原因状语来进行深入解释。

这一句式我们把用法公式化，就是：

> 主语 + 非谓语动词（being / Ving / Ved）表语 / 宾语，主语 be / v + 表语 / 宾语。
> 从句（原因，也就是深入解释），主句（结果，也就是论据）

因为某一深层原因，产生了某种情况。

再如：

> 2015 年 6 月 18 日　青少年犯罪的原因分析和解决措施

> 如果论点是"home issues"。
> The children from broken families lacking parental supervision will have more common delinquent behaviors and character among these juveniles.
> 由于来自破裂家庭的孩子缺乏父母的监管，违法行为和性格缺陷在他们中更加常见。

上面适用于议论文写作，表达因果联系，在图表作文中也可以使用独立主格结构，不过表示时间关联的情况更加常见，比如对下图的描述：

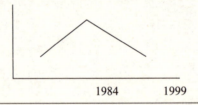

> When the growth was over in 1984, the number started to drop and kept that tendency until 1999.
> 当增长在 1984 年结束后，数字开始下降、并保持了这一趋势直到 1999 年。

这一句可以用独立主格结构表达：

> The growth being over in 1984, the number started to drop and kept that tendency until 1999. 这一表达方式可以说明两种变化的衔接。

01 改错：写作挑错

看看下面的句子有错吗？

2016 年 2 月 27 日　产假的好处大于坏处吗？

如果劳动力供给情况变好，实行更长的产假也就成为可能。

Having better conditions in labor supply, applying for longer maternity leave will become possible.

02　大闯关：写作闯关

试着用独立主格结构的句子翻译下面的句子。

2013 年 2 月 23 日　没有足够学习科学课程的学生的原因及影响

由于学术研究任务和晦涩的教科书将学生们搞得筋疲力尽，当下的招生问题就成了必然的结果。

参考答案

01　此句使用了 Ving 作状语，但是不对。这一句的完整表述是：

If the conditions in labor supply are better, applying for longer maternity leave will become possible.

这里是虚拟语气，从句和主句之间是条件关系。题目中翻译的错误在于，从句和主句的主语不一致，不能省略从句的主语、用 Ving 作状语。

这里适用独立主格：

The conditions in labor supply (being) better, applying for longer maternity leave will become possible.

这里的 being 可以省略，变成逻辑主语 + *adj.* 这种不带系动词的"主 + 系 + 表"结构，也是独立主格的一种特殊的形式。

02　Both academic research missions and complex textbooks make students completely exhausted, so current recruitment problems become a necessary consequence.

如何变幻莫测地使用虚拟语气

if 虚拟的独特用法

口语部分

以前 Barenaked Ladies 写过一首歌，歌名叫 If I had a million dollars，歌词是这样的：If I had a million dollar, I would by you a big house. If I had a million dollars, I'd buy you a K-car. If I had a million dollars, I'd buy fur clothes. 翻译成中文其实特别通俗易懂，就是：如果我有一百万，我就给你买个房。如果我有一百万，我就给你买个车，如果我有一百万，我就给你买件貂皮衣服。

这首歌就用到了虚拟语气。所谓虚拟语气，就是表达和现实生活相反的，或者不确定的条件下，我的行为会怎样。虚拟语气的句子通常是用来表决心的，表达的是感受，其实不一定会这么做。

举个例子，雅思考官问你，你喜欢学英语吗？你说如果猪会飞的话，那我就喜欢学英语。考官问你，你喜欢学历史吗？你说，太阳要打西边出来，我就喜欢历史。这两句话用英文表达就是

> If pigs could fly, I would love studying English.
> If the sun were to rise from the west, I would like my history class.

这种答题方式是不是比 Definitely not. 更加精彩？所以，认真观察一下，含虚拟语气的句子和普通 if 从句有什么不同，核心点就在下面这几个词上：

If I could help you,	I would help you.
If I had a million dollar,	I would travel around the world.
If I were you,	I wouldn't accept this.

> 如果我能帮你，我一定帮你。（我到底帮没帮你？）
> 如果我有足够的钱，我就去环游世界。（我有没有足够的钱？）
> 如果我是你，我就不会接受这个。（我可能是你吗？）

所以，什么叫虚拟语气，就是你也不知道，不确定，觉得不可能，你觉得太夸张，这时候就可以把动词都换成 could，had，were 的形式，来表达你的假设和感受。比如，我早上特

别困，我室友还把我叫起来让我开门。我的心情就是：

> At that time, I feel if he **had not been** my friend, I **would have** beaten him.

总的来说，英语中能被称作语气的一共就只有三种：分别为陈述语气、祈使语气和虚拟语气。

在 if 从句虚拟语气中，主要需要区分的就是这个语气所假设的内容，是与现在事实相反，还是与过去事实相反，还是与将来事实相反。

与现在事实相反的公式是：

> 从句：if + 主语 + 过去时（be 动词用 were）
> 主句：主语 + should/would/might/could + do

什么是与现在事实相反？比如，如果我是你，如果我知道他的号码（假设我知道，其实我不知道），如果我有足够的时间，如果我有足够多的钱，现在时就要变成过去时。

> If I knew his number, I would tell you.

这种用法许多考生会经常弄错，因为很多情况不需要假设。比如：

> 如果你见过她，你一定会喜欢她。（假设你见过她，你是有可能见过她的）
> If you see her, you will like her for sure.

> 如果我有机会，我一定会再来的。（我是有可能有机会的，不与事实相反）
> If I have a chance, I will come again for sure.

与现在事实相反的假设大多数是：如果猪会飞，如果太阳打西边出来，如果我是你，如果我知道等这种根本不可能的事儿。

与过去事实相反的公式是：

> 从句：if + 主语 + had done
> 主句：主语 + should/would/might/could + have done

与过去事实相反的用法通常是在表达后悔、埋怨等，有种早知如此何必当初的感觉。

> 如果我有机会再选一个专业，我就不会这么耽误自己。
> If I had got a chance to choose my major again, I wouldn't have wronged myself.

再比如：

> 如果我当时记得他跟我说的这件事儿，我不会这么后悔。
> If I had remembered what he told me, I shouldn't have been this regretful.

但是，有时候从句和主句的动词也许不是在同一时刻发生的，我们把这种情况叫错综条件句。主句的时态，要进行相应地调整：

> 如果我生在富裕家庭，我现在可能也是成功人士了。
> If I had been born in a rich family, I would be successful, too.

我们要做的是分清楚主句到底是当时的感受，还是在现在才产生效果的。比如在等人经历这道题中：

> If you have told me that you were going to be late, I wouldn't have waited this impatiently.
> 如果你早告诉我你要迟到，我就不会这么没耐心地等了。

虚拟语气还有一种用法是对将来极其微小的可能的推测：雅思口语里经常出现将来时态的题目，比如聊聊未来交通、未来教育、未来环境、未来手机、未来打字还是写字、未来换工作、外星人等。我们来一起试试：

> If aliens should come to earth one day, I would be scared about it.
> 如果外星人来地球了，我会很害怕。

> If there were no participation of teachers in future education, children would be staying at home all day in front of computer, day dreaming all the time and become extremely fat.
> 如果未来教育老师们都消失了，孩子们就会整天坐在电脑旁走神，并且变得很胖。

> If handwriting should vanish in the future, the older generation would be joining a parade on the street to promote traditional culture.
> 如果手写在未来消失了，老一辈的人就会上街游行呼吁发扬传统文化了。

> If mobile phones were to stop working for even one day, youngsters would be committing suicide directly because of that.
> 手机哪怕仅有一天不能使用了，年轻人也会为此都得直接去自杀了。

> If every company were to give me a great job with high salary, of course I would choose the one with the highest satisfaction.
> 如果每个公司都给我一份高收入的工作，我肯定选工作满意度最高的那个。

高级的虚拟语气需要我们好好多念几遍，在题目中套用几次。在考试的时候用上，会为你增分不少！

虚拟语气表示强烈愿望的还有一个词组叫作 if only，表达"要是我能……该多好呀！"。比如当我第一次见到我的偶像时：

> At that time, I was thinking: "If only I could know him."

或者你的室友打鼾，你也可以发出感慨：

> If only he didn't snore！真希望他别打鼾了！
> If only he wouldn't eat so noisily. 真希望他吃东西别发出噪声。

同样的句型只要注意虚拟语气中时态的使用就可以了：

> If only I were rich. 要是我有钱就好了。
> If only I could swim. 要是我会游泳就好了。
> If only I had remembered to buy some fruit. 我要是记得买水果就好了。
> If only I had more money, I could buy new clothes. 要是我有更多的钱就好了，我就可以买新衣服了。

你能试着自己多造几个句子吗？

01 改错：口语挑错

在 Part 2，描述一个早起的经历。第四问 and explain how you felt about it。一个学生说：I felt really sleepy and exhausted. I was thinking, "Don't touch me. Leave me alone." My head was really dizzy. It's like my head was hit by a stick. If I could sleep for one more hour, I would say thank you for one thousand times.

你认为以上这个例子中的虚拟语气用对了吗？

02 大闯关：口语闯关

试着用 if 引导的虚拟语气形式翻译下面的句子：

1）如果有一天人类被人工智能统治了，大概我们人类就会插着呼吸管躺在一个容器里，想象自己是个大力士，坐拥无数美女，过着逍遥的生活。

2）如果我能重来一次，我一定从小学就开始好好学习，天天什么也不干，只看书。

参考答案

01 上面的句子使用了虚拟语气的形式，If I could…I would，但是这句表达的意思是一个条状状语从句，是一个真实的条件，如果让我再睡会，我就谢谢你。完全是真实会发生的事情，并不是假设。虚拟语气往往用于表达情绪或者与现实相反的情况，比如 If the Pacific Ocean were to dry up，如果太平洋的水会干（根本不可能发生），I would…。所以在这里如果使用虚拟语气表达情绪，需要一个很有反差感的条件，比如我们经常用到的一个套路：If I could beat him, I would definitely beat him to death.

02 1) If artificial intelligence should conquer all human beings, probably we human beings would be lying in a container with a respirator, thinking of ourselves as muscle men, sitting with lots of beautiful girls in our arms, living a luxurious life.

2) If I could start all over again, I would have studied hard, and done nothing except for reading.

写作部分

if 引导的虚拟语气可以说学过英语的人都会，因为从语义上和中文意思上没有任何区别，都是"如果……，会……"的意思。在使用时，需要注意的要点是从句和主句的时态问题，简而言之，if 引导的从句的时态落后于主语一步即可：

常见情况	从句时态	主句时态
对现在情况的假设	一般过去时	would, could, should, might + 动词原形
对过去情况的假设	过去完成时	would, could, should, might + 现在完成时
对将来情况的假设	一般过去时 should/were to + 动词原形	would, could, should, might + 动词原形

（1）对现在的假设

If God gave me a second chance right now, I would say three words to the girl: I love you.

如果上天现在再给我一次机会，我会对那个女孩说三个字：我爱你。

（2）对过去的假设

If God had given me a second chance yesterday, I would have said three words to the girl: I love you.

如果上天昨天再给我一次机会，我就已经对那个女孩说了三个字：我爱你。

(3) 对将来的假设

If God should give me a second chance tomorrow, I would say three words to the girl: I love you.

如果上天明天会再给我一次机会,我将会对那个女孩说三个字:我爱你。

在议论文中,最常用的是对将来的假设,特别是在要求针对问题提出解决方法的文章中,解决措施都是在未来才能实施,所以 if 引导的虚拟语气十分合适。

> 2012 年 7 月 21 日　车流量大会导致的问题和解决方法

> The issue will be less of a problem if the municipal authorities could divert traffic by way of strengthening public transportation capabilities.
>
> 如果市政当局能够通过加强公共交通运载能力来分流交通,问题将会缓解。

这一句的语法拿分点为:虚拟语气,以及介词短语作补语。逻辑内容说明了措施和效果两点。句子的骨架可以简化为:

> The issue would be less of a problem if sb.(相关人士)could 实施某一解决方案(动词词组)by way of 具体措施(名词/动名词词组).
>
> 如果相关人士能通过某些具体措施来实施某一解决方案,形势就一定会好转。

这一用法还可以参考以下例句:

> 2012 年 9 月 12 日　年轻人物质条件变好却不开心的原因和解决方法

> Besides, an upturn would show if the community could provide much help in reducing competitive pressure by offering more free training opportunities.
>
> 另外,如果社区可以通过提供更多免费的培训机会来减轻竞争压力,情况一定会有所好转。

这一句的表意可以总结为下表:

形势一定会好转	如果相关人士能	采取某种解决方案	通过	某些具体措施
An upturn would show An improvement will be seen The issue will be less of a problem The problem will be solved, at least partly, The situation will improve	if sb. could	动词短语	by by means of by way of through via	名词/ 动名词短语

图表作文中,虚拟语气的适用范围极小,因为图表是对事实的描述,不存在虚拟的必要性。不过,在一类特殊的流程图(工作流程图)中可以使用虚拟语气。

工作流程图主要描述人员工作的流程,比如考驾照、面试等,是从 2014 年开始出现的新题型,它比常见的加工流程图难度更大,因为其中一些步骤有成功和失败两个分支,需要分别交代。

工作流程图每一步的描述要点是:参与人员、处理过程(涉及地点的需要带入交代)和处理目的。比如:申请工作,

第一步:参与人员:申请人

处理过程:填写申请表(地点:网上)

处理目的:审核学历和工作资历

工作流程图(例如下图):

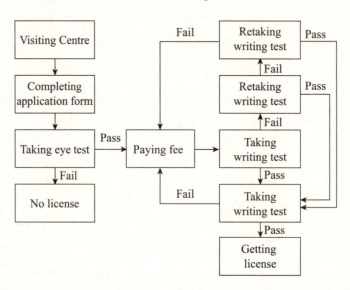

在描述分支的时候,我们可以说,如果成功了会怎样,而失败了又会怎样,这样就需要使用虚拟语气。我们来看下面的句式:

> The next step would be 流程(名词/动名词词组) if the result of the last one was pass, so that 目的(句子). But the failures have to 失败者的流程(动词词组) / quit.
>
> 如果上一步通过了,下一步将会是某一流程,以便达到某一目的。但失败者则必须进行某一步骤/退出。

比如针对 driving test 那一步:

> The next step would be a driving test if the result of the writing test was pass, so that the applicants' driving skills could be examined. But the applicants who fail will have to retake the test at most twice before they are asked to pay the fee again.

01 改错：写作挑错

看看下面的句子有错吗？

2012 年 8 月 11 日　青年毕业即失业的影响和解决方法

如果高等教育机构能够在上次教改中加强了学术学习和职业培训之间的联系，失业率绝不会这样高。

The unemployment rate would not be so high if higher education institutions could strengthen the bond between academic study and occupational training in the last education reform.

02 大闯关：写作闯关

试着用 if 引导的虚拟语气翻译下面的句子。

2016 年 6 月 16 日　人们孤立生活不认识邻居的原因及解决方法

如果人们能够通过摆脱电子依赖的生活方式来在真实的生活中参与更多的社交活动，问题至少会得到部分解决。

参考答案

01 这是一个混合了不同时间的虚拟语气，从句是针对过去发生的事，主句是针对现在的情况，表示：如果过去……，那么现在会……。这种情况下，从句需要用过去完成时，主语需要用 would, could, should, might + 动词原形，就是混合了两种不同情况下虚拟语气中主从句的时态。那么这句的正确翻译应该是：

The unemployment rate would not be so high if higher education institutions had strengthened the bond between academic study and occupational training in the last education reform.

02 The problem will be solved, at least partly, if individuals could participate in more social events in real life via casting off their cyberholic lifestyle.

不用 if 如何虚拟

口语部分

其实很多时候，虚拟语气说的就是时态问题。比如：

> Everybody thinks it's about time the school **improved** its meal service.

我们在使用 It is (about/high) time (that) 这个词组时，后面接过去时的从句，表达建议或忠告，也是虚拟语气的重要用法。意思是"早该做这件事了"，既然想表达"早该"，用过去时就是虚拟语气的一种体现，其实还没做，但是早该做了。

> It's time we stopped. 早该停了。
> It's about time you had your hair cut. 你该找时间理理发了。

在口语表达中，提到建议的时候可以用到虚拟语气的这一用法。比如：

> 1. Nowadays, many people complain about the air pollution. Do you have any good suggestions?
> 2. Do you think the museum should be free?

> 1. 我们早该这样治理雾霾了。It's high time we dealt with haze and smog.
> 2. 我们早该让博物馆免费了。It's about time that museum provided free entrance.

第二个特别常见的虚拟语气是 I wish I could 句型，表达"我希望我能够"，但是事实往往和希望的不太一样。比如：

> I wish I could live here forever. 我希望我能在这儿住一辈子。（只是说说，没法实现）
> I wish I could walk with you hand-in-hand till the end of the time. （分手时候才说，表示遗憾）

口语考试中可以用虚拟语气来表达强烈渴望，别忘了在考官问你 Do you have any plans for the future? 时，轻描淡写地要个分儿，让考官知道你的心意，暗送秋波。

> I wish I could get a 7 on this exam.（未来打算）

或者在所有 Part 2 描述未来住的房子，未来的法律，以及表达对某事的怀念时，说：

> I wish I could afford this house before 40 years old.（未来想住的房子）
> I wish I could experience this all over again.（开心的事儿）

当然也可以表达抱怨和羡慕：

> I wish I lived near New York. 我希望我住的离纽约近一点儿
> I wish he could have come and seen this. 要是他那时能来看到这个就好了。（死去的爷爷）

再比如，描述朋友弄坏了我的东西，我被朋友弄醒，或者别人说了伤害我的话：

> I wish I had never lent him anything. 我真希望我没借给他。（生气经历）
> She wishes she hadn't said that. 她希望他没有说过那样的话。（道歉经历）

但是，注意，纯粹希望将来将如何的时候就不能虚拟语气了！不能用 wish，要用 hope，如：I hope you like this house.

虚拟语气条件句，有一些是不需要用 if 来引导的，可作条件状语成分的词有：without, but for, under…condition, otherwise, but。这些句子与 if 引导的虚拟条件句有一定的转化关系。比如：

> if 引导：If I had had enough money, I would have bought the car.
> 不由 if 引导：I would have bought the car, but I didn't have enough money.

> if 引导：if something went against my conscience, I would never do it.
> 不由 if 引导：I would never do anything that went against my conscience.

> if 引导：One would believe that only if one were a fool.
> 不由 if 引导：Who but a fool would believe that?

其实，语法都是形式，只有对时态的感觉才是对语言的真正掌控。我们要把虚拟语气化成一种感觉，在表示假设，愿望，羡慕，渴望等强烈情绪时，对于假设是否与现实相反保持敏感，才能将虚拟语气运用自如。

> I could do nothing without you.（事实上我已经成功了，do nothing 是与现实相反的假设）
>
> We could have done better under more favorable conditions.（事实上已经做不了更好的了）

英语中有个很常见的插入语大家应该很熟悉，in fact, as a matter of fact, indeed, in reality。这些短语如何在虚拟语气中使用呢？先看它的另一个用法：

> They agreed to buy the house as it is. 看样子他们同意买那套房子。

但如果我想表达"在某种程度上说"，"可以说"，但是表达的内容不是真实的，是夸大的。我就可以用 as it were 这个插入语。比如描述你最喜欢的朋友：

> He's my best friend, my brother as it were. 他是我最好的朋友，就好像是我的兄弟。

01 改错：口语挑错

看看下面的句子有错吗？

What's your plan for the future?
Well, hopefully, if everything goes smoothly, I wish I could become an engineer.

02 大闯关：口语闯关

试着用没有 if 的虚拟语气翻译下面的句子。

1）如果不是雅思没考到 6.5，我早就已经出国了。
2）要不是看在我们都是朋友的份上我想给她留面子，我早就爆发了。
3）我要说的常伴的家人是我老爸，可以说他是我的灵魂伴侣。

参考答案

01 题目中问 plan，表示的是清晰的计划，虚拟语气通常用来表达不太可能发生的事，遥不可及的奢望。那么回答部分倒不能算错，就是表达的意思会有歧义，考官会觉得，你到底想不想做 engineer？正确的说法应该用表示更肯定意思的 hope：I hope to become an engineer. 或者 I'll be doing engineering work.（将来进行时）

02　1）I would have been abroad, but I didn't get a 6.5 on the IELTS test.

　　2）I would have exploded in anger, but for the sake that we were friends, I had to save her face.

　　3）The person that I spend the most time with is my father, who is a soul mate to me, as it were.

写作部分

虚拟语气表示的是假定的含义，如同中文一样，表示假定，我们不一定总是使用"如果"，还有很多情况也能表达一样的含义：

1 表达"像……"的含义时

> I always eat as much as I can in the buffet as though my stomach was bottomless.
> 在自助餐上我总是尽可能多吃，就像我的胃是无底洞一样。

这句话中，as though 引导的从句里（胃是无底洞）是和现实不符的、虚拟的。这种用法实际是用比喻的方式进行说明，可以在议论文中用于逻辑展开。

表达"像……一样"的含义时，我们使用的是 as though 或者 as if，后面接的从句的时态是：

	像……一样	从句时态
现在	as if as though	一般过去时
过去		过去完成时
将来		would, could, should, might + 动词原形 were to + 动词原形

举个实战的例子：

> 2015 年 5 月 30 日　对国际旅游的负面看法的由来和解决方法

> Some foreign tourists behave randomly regardless of local religious requirements and cultural backgrounds as if they were In their own country.
> 很多外国游客行为随意、无视当地的宗教要求和文化背景，就如同他们还在他们自己的国家一样。

2 和条件状语从句结合

> There is no chance for me to marry Angelina Jolie, unless she is crazy.
> 我是没机会娶 Angelina Jolie 的,除非她疯了。

这句话包含由 unless 引导的条件状语从句,从句中的情况是不存在的,所以是虚拟的。当从句是"主 + 系 + 表"结构时,系动词可以用 be,表达虚拟的含义。这一句可以用于强调成立的前提条件。

> 2016 年 2 月 20 日　针对小孩的广告需要被禁止吗?

> The sales in related industries, such as toy production, definitely will drop after imposing bans on advertising, unless alternative marketing channels are available.
> 在实施对广告的禁令后,相关行业(比如玩具制造业)的销售绝对会下降,除非能得到其他市场推广渠道。

3 和让步状语从句结合

> Whether it be in medical practice or English teaching, I can garner a reputation.
> 无论在医疗上还是在英语教学上,我都能赢得声誉。

这句话包含了由 whether 引导的让步状语从句,其中虚拟语气的用法和上面条件状语从句一样,当从句是"主 + 系 + 表"结构时,系动词可以用 be,表达虚拟的含义。同样的还包括了由 even though 引导的从句。这一句可以用于强调作用范围。

> 2016 年 2 月 18 日　环境破坏是无药可救了还是尚有可为?

> Vegetation planting changed the environment conditions in the worst zones like Chernobyl even though the process was very slow.
> 植被种植改变了像切尔诺贝利这样最糟糕的区域的环境条件,尽管进程很缓慢。

练习

01 改错：写作挑错

看看下面的句子有错吗？

2016年1月23日　新闻媒体对人们的影响增大是负面变化吗？

在海湾战争期间，要不是像CNN、BBC和NBC这样的大众传媒的持续报道，全世界的观众绝对没机会随时了解伊拉克正在发生的事。

During the Gulf War, audiences all over the world would never get a chance to keep updated of what was going on in Iraq if it wasn't for the continuous reports from the mass media like CNN, BBC and NBC.

02 大闯关：写作闯关

试着用这一节的技巧翻译下面的句子。

2016年2月13日　同意应该鼓励建筑地方化、多样化吗？

无论外形独特还是大众，控制建筑成本并最大化市场价格都是选择相应设计时考量的唯一标准。

> **参考答案**
>
> 01　but for 或者 without 引导的条件状语表达的也是一种虚拟的状态，对过去情况进行假设时（比如上面句子里的"世界的观众绝对没机会……"），主句需要用 would, could, should, might + 现在完成时，那么上面的句子应该是：
> During the Gulf War, audiences all over the world would never have gotten a chance to keep abreast of what was going on in Iraq if it wasn't for the continuous reports from the mass media like CNN, BBC and NBC.
>
> 02　Whether the appearance is unique or common, to control the cost and maximize market price are the only criterion for choosing the corresponding designs.

如何只记几个字
就搞定关联词

介词与众不同

口语部分

　　介词是许多英语学习者最头疼的问题,"我希望在这次考试中取得好的成绩"是用 in the exam 还是 on the exam?我在街上看到了一个明星是用 on the street 还是 in the street?对我来说是 for me 还是 to me?

　　中国人为什么害怕介词,主要是因为汉语表达中介词的使用频率非常小,而英语则不同,介词丰富而且使用频率特别高,对于习惯于逐字逐句汉译英的同学,可能就很容易犯错误了。

　　给几个汉译英的句子大家感受一下:

> 她穿着一件蓝衬衣。
> 他反对这个方案。
> 他很喜欢电影。

这些句子你会怎么翻译,你会不会先想到的是:

> She is wearing a blue shirt.
> He opposes this plan.
> She likes films very much.

但是这里要注意了,中国人在汉语表达中有过度使用动词的习惯,英语是一个极简模式,不喜欢重复,能用功能词就不用动作词,所以要想讲的地道一些就要有这样的感觉:

> She is in a blue shirt.
> He is against this plan.
> She is fond of films.

但是许多同学没有使用介词的意识,就会经常犯错误,错误率最高的是遗漏介词或画蛇添足:

> We didn't listen to him.（正确说法是：listen to him）
> He did not notice a dinosaur was approaching him.（approach 本来有接近某人的意思，to 多余）
> She married with a second rich man.（with 多余）
> Jacie knocked the door.（正确说法是：knocked at the door）
> I agree her.（正确说法是：agree with her）

许多人喜欢用汉语来逐字翻译，她和一个富二代结婚了，就非要把"和"翻译出来，结果就错了，殊不知 marry 本身就是及物动词，同一时间一个人只能和一个人结婚，没有必要带 with。

我们怎么才能学好介词？第一是要常背固定搭配；第二是要专门买一本 Collocation Dictionary（词语搭配词典），每天看 10 个，很有必要；第三要搞清理解易混介词的区别。

我们先来看和时间、地点相关的 in, on, that 的用法：

> in 是范围性介词，修饰的对象必须清晰说清楚时间范围（某一清晰时间段、平面空间、立体空间）；
> on 是概念性介词，修饰的对象不在清晰范围内（可能冒出来、不好定义或者在附近）；
> at 点状介词，修饰的对象是一个清晰的时刻，小地点门口，标志性行为（睡觉时间、周末）。

比较抽象的概念我们用例子来理解：
I've got to get up _____ eight tomorrow.（时间点用 at）
She went home right _____ the end of the holiday.（right 表示一个时刻，用 at）
_____ what time do you usually start work?（时间点用 at，注意首字母大写）
She woke up at three _____ the morning?（早上是从日出到晌午，是时间段，用 in）

> 表示确切某一时刻，通常用 at；
> 表示一天里的各个部分，通常用 in；
> 可是说"在夜里"，要用 at night，如：
> Nurses often have to work at night.
> in 清晰时间段/on 概念性时段/at 点状时段

那为什么 night 不是一个时间段呢？因为 day 和 night 会随着四季变化有长短变化。我们说 at night，指快要睡觉了的那个时间点，所以用 at，说白天也不能说 in the day，要说 in the day time。

She left _____ the night of Friday, June 13th.

I first met him _____ a cold afternoon in January.
He was back home _____ July 1st.
I'm seeing her _____ Sunday morning.
What are you going to do _____ Christmas day?

这一组就有点眩晕了吧，填介词时到底是参考 night，还是后边的日期呢？只要是涉及日期，都不是时间段，而是时间概念，所以用 on！用中文体会一下，"今天上午我看到一起车祸"，其中提到的上午，是一个清晰的时间段，不是下午，也不是晚上，是早上日出到晌午的时间。"她周五早上到"，这句强调的是她周五早上来，不是周四早上，所以这里已经不深究是具体几点到几点了，只是强调概念。

另外，有修饰语的某一天，也不是时间段而是时间概念，比如 cold afternoon，强调的已经不是那个下午的某个时间段，而是那样的一个下午，描述的是整体。所以用 on！

最后，在提到节假日：圣诞节、复活节、新年时用 at，提到假日中的某一天用 on。

搞清楚时间段的逻辑概念：in February last year；in his early fifties；in her day（She was a famous beauty in her day.）。

> 表示地点的时候
> 位置是某一点：at the door, at the traffic light, at the bank, at a concert；
> 立体空间里或圈起来的平面范围：in the kitchen, in Beijing；
> 某个表面：on the floor；on the table；
> 在河流、道路、边界等线状东西之上或附近：on the street, on my way；
> 某一条线上的位置：in my way, in the street；
> 书中某一页上 on Page 25, on the cover；书里 in the first chapter。
>
>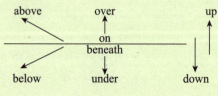

还有几个介词短语需要辨析一下："在海上"是 on the sea 还是 in the sea？当然是 on，in 表示清晰范围，潜水艇没入水中可以用 in。那如果说"在街上"用 on the street 还是 in the street 呢？通常会用 on，因为也说不清在街上哪里，"我在街上碰到一个明星"，只表达了附近的概念，没有特别清晰。这和 I'm on my way 是一个道理。在路上，但说不清是在哪里。如果有清晰位置，可以用 in。如：路中央发生了车祸：In the street, there's a car accident.

My mother is _____ the kitchen.（立体空间用 in，带屋顶的）
I lost my ball _____ the long grass.（没入草中，用 in）
There are dirty marks _____ the ceiling.（表面上，用 on）
Charles is _____ the road to London.（路上，用 on，说不清楚位置）

We live _____ a small river.（附近用 on）
Who's that girl _____ the front row?（一条线，用 in）
There's a misspelling _____ the third line.（一条线，用 in）
He kissed her _____ both cheeks.（表面，用 on）
He is blind _____ one eye.（眼睛能不能看见不是表面，用 in）
He was wounded _____ the shoulder.（身体某部位受伤，用 in）
I've got a pain _____ my back.（身体某部位疼痛，用 in）

一般涉及身体的表面时多用 on，但说到眼睛、鼻子、嘴巴等时则用 in。但是介词使用有时会有修辞意义，比如说"打某人的脸"用 in：hit him in the face，就感觉打得特别狠，脸都凹进去了。另一个特别明显的修辞就是坐在沙发上，用 in the sofa，会感觉沙发很舒服，坐的人都陷进去了。但是亲吻脸颊，就不能用 in 了。但有的时候为了修辞就会夸张，比如在街上撞到某人，表达为 run into sb.。如果说到某人脸上的表情时就得用 on 了：a sad expression on her face，谈及伤痛时一般用 in，但提及抓住人身体的某个部位时，用 by：take him by hand；grasp her by the hair。

再来看几个常见的易混介词：

> besides 和 except for

> besides 的意思是"除……之外"但包括它在内，如：
> Is anyone coming besides John? John 来了，除了他，别人还来吗？
> except 有"排除，不包括……在内"的意思，如：
> I like all drinks except whiskey. 我啥都爱喝，但我真不喜欢威士忌。

> 在不定代词后或否定词、疑问词后，except 多被 but 代替。
> Everyone was there but him.
> Who but a fool would do such a thing?
> No one but Bill knew the way.

> between 和 among 是两个人之间和三个人之间的区别。

> by，with 和 in 都可以用来表示某人做某事

> with 表示用什么工具，如：I beat him with my shoe.
> in 表示语言、声音、笔墨，如：I'll tell you the truth in a few words.
> by 表示交通工具和通信工具，如：I'll contact you by phone.

for, during, since 和 from

for 用于说明动作持续了多长时间，如：I'll be here for 2 weeks.
注意，在 stay, wait, last 等词后可以省略 for：
I stayed here 2 weeks.
during 表示在一段时间中。
since 用来表示一个持续到现在（或过去某一时刻）的动作或情况开始于什么时候，它通常与完成时连用：It's a long time since breakfast.

like 和 as

like 用来进行比较，通常涉及的不是同一个人或物，如：
He plays tennis like a professional.
as 用来表示职业、身份、作用，涉及的是同一个人物，如：
He has been playing tennis as a professional for two years.

over, across 和 through 都表示跨越、穿越

over 和 across 都可以表示位于一个狭长的东西之上，比如河沟、街道、边界：
They live just over the street/across the street.
但表示越过水中，只能用 across，如：swim across the river。
翻越障碍物要用 over，如：jump over the bench。
through 表示穿越立体空间，如：丛林、房屋、门窗、人群等。

until, till, up to, by

by 表示不迟于哪个时间，如：by the time, by tomorrow.
up to 和 till 都是到什么时间位置，如：I'll be here up to 2 o'clock.
till 不能放在句首，放在句首的只能是 until。

练 习

01 改错：口语挑错

看看下面的句子有错吗？

The place near the water I'd like to talk about is Xiamen, which is located in the southern part of China. I went to there with my best friend John. We had a lovely time there together.

The first time I met him was in the Orientation Day. In that time, he was wearing a white T-shirt and blue jeans, talking very quickly.

02 大闯关：口语闯关

翻译下列句子。

1）去年春节，我正坐在沙发上看电视，我隐约听到有人在门口。
2）我只要有空闲时间，我就爱听音乐、游泳、散步或者跑步。

参考答案

01 错误的地方在 went to there，here 和 there 是一组副词，表示方向的，和 upstairs, downstairs, westward, outside 用法类似，所以你可以联想 come here 这个用法中，here 前面就没有 to，说明 here 不是一个名词。同理，go there 中间也不能有 to。

第二题错在 in that time，这个是许多雅思考生常错的介词误用，"在那时"描述的是一个时间点，所以应该用 at that time。

02 1) Last year in Spring Festival, I was sitting on the sofa, watching TV. I vaguely heard there was someone at the door.

2) As long as I have free time, I like to listen to music, go swimming, go for a walk or go jogging.

写作部分

英语的介词太多了，还有词组里的固定搭配，数不胜数，记忆量太大，短时间搞不定，怎么办？没关系，备考雅思写作部分，你记住这一节的内容就够了。

在议论文中，常见的问题是介词使用极其单调，全篇只用"of"的比比皆是。而且还都用错了。这还是中英文的语言差异导致的，中文的学术写作推崇长句子，于是修饰词十分常见，比如"自动化生产时代发展中国家对劳动力素质的要求"。主词"人民"前面有4个修饰词，这些修饰词都是形容词，实际上以"的"结尾：自动化生产时代（的）、发展中国家（的）、对劳动力大军（的）、素质（的）"，而英文中对应"……的"就是"of"，所以，许多考生连续用多个 of 翻译这个短语。而实际上，英文中这些修饰词可不是用 of 连接的。

对比下面的错误和正确表达，注意介词的使用。

错误表达：

the requirements of qualities of labor of developing countries of the automatic production era

正确表达：

the requirements for labor qualities in developing countries in the automatic production era

介词的搭配使用是经验性的，议论文写作中大家只要掌握两点即可：

1 如何从概率上减少介词使用的错误？

答案很简单，掌握下面以论文中最常用的两个介词的用法以及一些固定的搭配即可。

（1） 议论文中 of 的常见用法

a. 表示所属关系

Bill Clinton is a friend of mine.

b. 表示关于

The law of green tax is the first step towards sustainable development.

c. 表示时空关系

in the time of cyber era

d. 某些动词后

deprive criminals of freedom

e. 对人的行为发表看法

It was kind of you to help me prepare for the interview.

（2） in 的常见用法

a. 表示领域

the application of technology in daily life

b. 表示方法

People are used to talking in common languages, such as English, in international conferences.

c. 表示数量、比例

Nine in ten children are attracted by the audio-visual effects of computer games.

下面还有一些常见的涉及介词的搭配：

> 关注 pay attention to, focus on
> 基于 base on
> 花费/投资 spend on, invest in, use in
> 鉴于 in view of, in light of, on the consideration of

2 如何用事先准备好的最少量的介词装扮出考生的水平？

实际上，单纯的十几个带有介词的词组就可以连接起一篇文章的逻辑和语法框架，比如：

> As 相关情况的变化，相关人士 have to confront with 讨论的问题. In view of 下文的原因，I think 回答问题.
> Firstly, 论点1. 论据解释, owning to 深层原因. In real life, it results in 举例子.
> Secondly, 论点2. Based on 深层原因, 论据解释. Actually, only by 相关事项 could sb. 举例子.
> But, some people hold different views. They lay stress on 反面论点1 decided by 论据解释. Also, coming with 论据解释，反面论点2.
> Personally, on account of 有利于作者立场的情况，it is more reasonable to 采纳作者立场. According to the opposite views, 采取措施弥补对立观点.

因为只有一些最简单的连接词，所以不能算是写作模版，但是从语法和逻辑的角度来看，基本可以满足6分的要求了。上面的只是个例子，按照这样的原理，我们可以利用本书中的各项语法点准备好文章的骨架，再配合上面第一点介绍的议论文最常用的介词，考场上犯错的可能性就可以降到最低。

图表题里介词的使用比较多变、但也有规律可循，首先是数据变化的介词。表示达到最高点或最低点、持平时，后面需要介绍数值时需用 at，比如：Chinese population leveled off at 1.6 billion in 2010.

表示变化的数值时，from 接起点数值，to 接终点数值，by 接变化差值，比如下表：

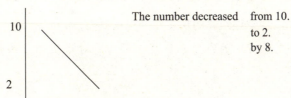

The number decreased from 10.
to 2.
by 8.

另外，使用介词比较复杂的是地图题中对方位的表达：

> on the north side of 在北面（外部）
> in the north part of 在北部（内部）
> at the northeast corner of 在东北角
> 毗邻 adjacent to, close to, next to
> 通向 access to, lead to
> 位于 lay in, site in, locate at
> 沿着 along

> 外部 outside，surround
> 位于某处的远端 / 近端 at the far / near side from somewhere

然后就是流程图，流程图主要是动词词组中的介词搭配：

> change into 变成，transfer to/deliver to 运到，be connected to 连接，consist of 由……组成，be made of 由……制成，send to 发送到，pass to 送到，transfer to 运到，flow through 流过，deliver to 运送，distribute to 分发，dispatch to 发送，transport to 运送

01 改错：写作挑错

看看下面的句子有错吗？

2016 年 4 月 30 日 购物习惯更多地取决于年龄而非其他因素吗？

What the elder can not stand is that window shopping takes energy and spare time.

令老年人无法忍受的是，逛街会占用精力和业余时间。

02 大闯关：写作闯关

试着翻译下面的句子，注意其中的介词。

2013 年 3 月 14 日 同意建筑物的功能比外观重要吗？

改善建筑物的外观对当地的商业有好处，因为它对街区房产的吸引力和销售有明显影响。

参考答案

01　of 用于 take 之后，接其所涉及的人或物。正确的应该是：What the elder cannot stand is that window shopping takes of energy and spare time.

02　Improving the appearance of a building can support local businesses, because it has a significant impact on the attractiveness and marketability of the properties in neighborhood.

连词巧妙过渡

口语部分

连接词是口语考试的一大评分要点,在流利度的这一评分项里,7分要求就有"具有一定灵活性地使用一系列连接词和语篇标记",而6分也写出了"能使用一系列连接词"的表述。那么,什么才是一系列连接词呢?

> 回答一个问题:Do you like sports?
> 多数人的回答是这样的:Yes, I like sports.
> Sports can make me healthy.
> And it's a good way to relax.
> I like to do a lot of sports, such as...

And, because, but, such as 是很多考生唯一会用的连接词。
那我们希望给大家的训练是,能够给出下面这样的回答:

> Well, I'd like to say, honestly, I'm kind of reluctant about doing sports, considering a current lifestyle of mine is a bit of working up to my neck, but I do like the feeling of playing sports, which are uplifting and refreshing. In addition, sports trigger my passion in competition, especially when I play in games in university.

所以,要想脱口而出各种连接词,要先理解口语表达的基本结构

表示原因:simply because, given that, considering, as, for, seeing that
表示转折:but the thing is, however, whereas
并列逻辑:for the first of all, in addition, what's more, more importantly
时间逻辑:usually, sometimes, especially when...
总分逻辑:off top of my head, what I enjoy the most is...
对比逻辑:Honestly, I merely have no interest about..., but if I must say...
场景:When I have free time, for example in holidays or at weekends... Whenever I

have free time... As long as I'm not busy...

强调：It's worth mentioning that...

假设和虚拟语气：say if, even if

总结：anyway, admittedly（诚然）

我们来套用一个雅思的题目吧！

> **Do you like history?**
>
> Yeah, I like history, **simply because** I am always attracted by those fantastic stories in it.
>
> **For example**, during the three kingdom periods, and the wars between seven kingdoms in chunqiu. **But the thing is**, China has a long history of over 5,000 years. **Seeing that** there're so many things to remember in history exams. It also scares me. **Usually**, I don't like stories I'm not interested in, not everything. **Sometimes** when it comes to the details of which dynasty is in which year. **Off top of my head**, what I can think about is "Geez! Go to hell!" **So**, it really depends on my mood. **Whenever I** have free time, or away from pressure. I'd like to sit somewhere and read history. **Say if** it's not boring, **admittedly**, history is **not only** absorbing, **but also** useful. **In addition**, it also educates people.
>
> **Given that** there's a saying which goes: history is like a mirror which tells you rise and fall.

所以，想要学好连接词，重要的是熟悉连接词常出现的位置，并且了解连接词的功能和作用。我们要怎么理解连接词使用的位置呢？英语思维模式里有一个词叫 GTS，全称是 From General to Specific，从一般到具体。也就是说当话题从一般谈到具体时，每一个阶段的连接词使用应该是有规律的。起句分为三种情况：

1. 用于一般性话题回答：basically/generally speaking/usually/normally
2. 用于稍微复杂一些的问题拖延时间：Let me think/How should I put it?
3. 据我所知：to my experience/in my opinion/from my point of view/to my knowledge

In my dictionary/in my case

第一个分话题点：

1. 场景：sometimes, especially when
2. 说明情况：you know
3. 举证：Nowadays, more and more people...

4. 原因：because, given that, seeing that, considering, due to the fact that/as/the reason why

第二个分话题点：

1. 观点：to be fair/actually/in fact/as a matter of fact/to be honest/frankly speaking
2. 并列：in addition, what's more, more importantly
3. 举例：for example, in that situation
4. 经历：When I was young/recently/currently/initially…

描述一个画面

1. 想象：just picture this/imagine that
2. 回忆：I remember once/I remember there was a time/On that day, if I remember well…
3. 分析：Now that/although/just in order to…
4. 解释：What I'm saying is/My point is/specifically/theoretically…
5. 比喻：It's like/It's more likely that…
6. 互动：If you must know/If I must say/I don't know if you know about this/I'm telling you this
7. 猜测：probably/perhaps/personally
8. 总结：In other words/In a word/All in all/After all/indeed/I have to say…

当然，使用连接词还要注意保持语法的平衡：比如并列连词前后的时态要一致，结构也要保持一致。如：

> They **sat** down and **talked** about something.
> I saw two men **sitting** behind and **whispering** something.

注意几个特殊的并列结构的用法

> not only…but also… 不但……而且……
> both…and… 两者都……
> neither…nor… 既不……也不……

01 改错：口语挑错

你能把下面的句子用你知道的连接词丰富一下吗？

Do you like chocolate?

Well, chocolate is my poison. The flavors vary from milk to nuts. They provide me with a fantastic tasteful enjoyment. Most chocolates are creamy and sweet. It's best to take it out when you feel exhausted at work or study. It cannot only help you gain more strength but also improve your mood.

02 大闯关：口语闯关

试着翻译下面的句子。

Do you like history?

事实上，我超喜欢历史，我觉得历史对每个人都至关重要，让人记住他们从哪里来，他们文化的意义和起源，以及他们特有的并且准备传承的精神。历史是从不缺精彩故事的书，尤其是对于像中国这样的有5000多年历史的国家。有太多精彩时期，比如唐朝、清朝，还有三国时期，都是我们获取精神财富的地方。

参考答案

01　Do you like chocolate?

Well, (in fact), chocolate is (kind of) my poison, (as) the flavors vary from milk to nuts, (which) always provide me with a fantastic tasteful enjoyment. (Usually), most chocolates are creamy and sweet, (so) it's best to take it out when you feel exhausted at work or study. It not only help you gain more strength but also improve your mood (as well) (indeed).

02　Well, as a matter of fact, I'm a big fan of history, which I think is vitally important for everyone to remember where they come from and the meaning and origin of their culture and the spirit they carry on and are going to pass on. History is a book which never lacks fantastic stories, especially for a country like China with over 5,000 years history. There're so many wonderful periods such as the Tang Dynasty, Qing Dynasty and the three-kingdom period where we can learn our spiritual treasure.

写作部分

连词有很多，按逻辑分类就有两大类、十几小类。我把最常用的几个挑出来，大家记记就好。由于议论文部分的连词和本书从句部分有重合，本书只简单示范一下用法，具体细节可以参照后面的章节。先看议论文，常用的有三种：

(1) 表示因果关系的连词

主要是用于论据分析部分，分析问题时要努力写出层层深入、抽丝剥茧的感觉来。

> 因为：for（接名词/现在分词词组）
> 　　　because、since、as、now that（接从句）
> 结果/目的：so（接独立句子）
> 　　　　　so that（接从句）

这一部分大家可以参照后面的章节：原因状语从句、结果状语从句、目的状语从句部分。这里举个例子方便大家理解：

2016 年 5 月 19 日　只有男性适合在军队工作吗？

　　Females perform better in the positions asking for attention, research and analysis, such as site inspection and unmanned aerial vehicle driving, because they are more careful and pay more attention to details.
　　女性在像现场勘查、无人机驾驶这类需要专注、研究和分析的岗位上表现得更好，因为她们更加细心和关注细节。

(2) 表示让步关系的连词

> 尽管：although，though，while
> 即使：even if，even though
> 不管：whether，no matter

这一部分大家可以参照后面的章节：让步状语从句，这里还是只举个简单的例子。

2013 年 12 月 7 日　成为负责任的游客是不可能的吗？

　　No matter how perfect environmental protection efforts are, travelling hot spots may nevertheless meet heavy pressure brought by too much domestic refuse.
　　在这种情况下，无论环保措施有多出色，旅游热点地区仍会遭遇过量的生活垃圾所带来的巨大压力。

(3) 表示时间的连词

> 当……时：as，when，while　　时间前后：before，after
> 自从：since　　　　　　　　　一旦：once
> 直到：until

这一部分请参考后面的时间状语从句部分，这里举个例子：

> **2013 年 8 月 29 日　电脑比人脑聪明是好事吗？**
>
> When it comes to artificial intelligence, the matter of prime importance is the conflict between the anticipation for tremendous convenience and the worries about side-effects.
>
> 当提到人工智能时，最重要的问题是对惊人的便利的期待和对副作用的担忧之间的矛盾。

图表作文多用以下几种连词：

（1）引导比较的连词

包括：than、as、as...as 等，最常用于倍数表达法。倍数表达常用于柱状图的数据之间的比较，下面的必须掌握：

> 常用的倍数有：twice、triple times、数字 + times
> 表示 "……是……的几倍"：... be 数字 times as many as ...
> 表示 "……比……大几倍"：... be 数字 times more than ...
> 表示 "……是……几倍的数量"：... be 数字 times the 比较的性质（length / width / height / weight / amount）of ...

跟倍数表达紧密相关的是分数表达，数据图建议这两种用法至少各用一次，拿到相应的逻辑比较和语法的分数。

分数表达除了数据对比之外，还可以用来替代直接的抄写数据（百分比可以化成近似的分数），特别是常和表示估计的形容词一起用。

> 常用的分数如下：a fold（10%）、one fifth（20%）、a quarter（25%）、a third（33%）、a half（50%）
> 分数表达法：数字（分子）序数词（分母）
> 分子 >1 时，分母用复数，比如：two fifths（2/5）
> 倍数和分数举例：A 30　　B 10
> 　　　　　　　　A is triple times as many as B.
> 　　　　　　　　A is two times more than B.
> 　　　　　　　　B is one third of A.

（2）表示转折的连词

> but、yet、while、whereas

这一类连词除了用在议论文中，还可以在数据图表中用来描述极点、也就是最大值和最小值（包括静态点和不同时间点之间变化差值的对比）。比如：

> The one showed the largest number was 最大者的名称 with 最大的数值, whereas 最小者的名称 had the smallest one, 最小的数值. The others were distributed between the two extremes.
>
> 显示最大数字的是拥有某一数值的某一单项，相反地，另一单项有最小的数字，某一数值。其余的数值散布其间。

练 习

01 改错：写作挑错

看看下面的句子有错吗？

2015 年 12 月 5 日　广告的积极作用大于消极作用吗？

False advertisements lead to prejudice for the role of advertising and poor credibility of advertising industry builds up a vicious cycle between advertising market shrinkage and endorsing more defective goods.

虚假广告会导致对广告作用的偏见，广告宣传行业糟糕的信誉会造成一个在市场萎缩和不得不更多地为劣质产品代言之间的恶性循环。

02 大闯关：写作闯关

试着翻译下面的句子，注意其中的连词。

2014 年 10 月 18 日　同意去其他地方学习另外的文化不必要吗？

生活于异种文化之中并对其深入了解不仅是一种良好的学习经历，而且是一种在适应不同文化环境上有价值的个人经历。

参考答案

01　and 属于并列连词，但不能连接两个独立的句子结构。如果两句的主语一致，需要合并主语，变成用 and 连接的并列谓语；如果主语不一致，需要用句号断句。

False advertisements lead to prejudice for the role of advertising. A poor credibility of the advertising industry builds up a vicious cycle between advertising market shrinkage and endorsing more defective goods.

02 Living in a foreign culture and understanding it is not only a great learning experience, but also a valuable personal experience in accommodation to a different culture environment.

如何使短句变复杂

有特色的定语

口语部分

熟悉英语句子成分是组句的必备功课，刚开始学英文的同学，需要对句子成分有敬畏之心。因为句子成分是我们造句子的时候最麻烦也最容易出错的部分。我们都会比较容易学会和中文语序一样的语言，比如我爱你，因为你很美。I love you, because you are beautiful. 几乎完全一样，一一对应关系。但是千万不要误以为，所有的英文都可以按照中文的语序，一个字一个字地翻译，比如英文当中的定语就是一个时常与中文语序相反的结构。

> 我喜欢的女孩是玛丽。（中文的定语只要在修饰语后加上的就可以了）
> 英文是：The girl I like is Mary.（在造句的时候要想着主语是什么）

再比如说到地点：

> 中文的语序是　中国北京市海淀区清华大学
> 英文的语序是　Tsinghua University, Haidian District, Beijing, China

你会发现英文的表达习惯是先讲清楚那个最核心的目的词，也就是作主语的词汇。我们把这个结构叫作主谓结构，而中文有时候更习惯于先描述背景知识、环境，而核心的目的传递是在字里行间中猜测出来的。所以，我们把中文这种表达形式叫作"意和"，也叫话题中心式，而英文表达叫作"形和"，更强调一件事情的直接逻辑。

再看一个例子：

> 那个村东头的老张家的小女儿找了一个男朋友，考上清华了。

这个句子要是让老外听，肯定搞不懂！首先是谁考上清华了？小女儿还是男朋友？

如果要把这个句子逐字翻译一下就会特别滑稽：The village east Old Zhang family's little daughter finds a boyfriend, goes to Tsinghua University. 完全没法理解。

通过这个例子，我相信大家能够感觉到，中文表意多靠想象，英文表意多靠逻辑。英文的表述如果语法乱了就完全听不懂，所以作为英语学习者，我们要做的是拎清楚这件事儿的逻辑。

如何使短句变复杂

正确的表达应该是：

> The youngest daughter of Old Zhang who lives in the east end of the village finds a boyfriend who's going to study in Tsinghua University.

这个句子中有好几处的语序与中文是反着的：

老张家的小女儿：The youngest daughter of Old Zhang

村东头的老张家：Old Zhang who lives in the east end of the village

其实这个句子的基本逻辑就是"小姑娘找了一个考上清华的男朋友"。如果你能理解句子的本意，那英文的主谓宾就应该是"女儿找到男朋友"，至于女儿是谁家的女儿，老张是哪个老张，男朋友是什么样的男朋友，都是这个句子的定语，需要放在主语和宾语后面补充说明。那么，什么是定语？

> 定语是用来修饰、限定、说明名词或代词的品质与特征的。主要有形容词，此外还有名词、代词、数词、介词短语、动词不定式（短语）、分词、定语从句或相当于形容词的词、短语或句子都可以作定语。汉语中常用'……的'表示。
>
> 定语的位置一般有两种：用在所修饰词之前的叫前置定语，用在所修饰词之后的叫后置定语。

在英语中，一般定语前置时的次序为：**限定词、形容词、分词、动名词和名词性定语**。但当几个形容词同时出现在名词短语之前时，我们要注意其次序。

其形容词遵循的词序为：**限观形龄色国材**，指：限定词（一般指数量）；外观（美丽等）；形状（大小，高矮，肥瘦）；年龄；颜色；国籍；材料；用途。比如：three beautiful fat 2-year-old white English boys。如果想表达"三个漂亮的胖乎乎的2岁白人英国男孩"，形容词的使用顺序就要遵循这个规律。

除此之外，大家最需要掌握的是与中文语序不同的7种定语后置。

> 1）短语作后置定语（放在名词后）
> 2）不定代词＋形容词（强制定语后置）
> 3）表示方位的副词作定语
> 4）表示能够（-ible, -able）的词作后置定语
> 5）过去分词作定语
> 6）不定式作定语
> 7）介词短语作定语

在雅思口语中，定语后置是怎样应用的呢？例如：

My hometown is a place **full of historical atmosphere**. (room, city)

English is a language **easy to learn**, but **hard to master**.

My flat is a small two-bedroom flat with a living room, a bedroom and a bathroom.

There's nothing newsworthy in today's newspaper. (some, no, any, every)

If I have something more creative, I will tell you.

The people upstairs are a pair of new couple. (here/there)

He is a person that is dependable.

This is the only transportation means available.

This is the only food edible.

Everyone involved should start to realize.

The reason mentioned is just one.

The dream to achieve needs to come true.

The boy in yellow looked at me.

这些定语后置的特殊语序需要大家反复体会，当然定语也可以放在名词前面，比如形容词 yellow pen，还有名词 paper book。不过，多体会不同才是学习语法的真谛！

01 改错：口语挑错

What's your favourite room at home?

The room I like very much is my bedroom, which has a little privacy for me.

02 大闯关：口语闯关：

翻译下列句子。

1）我想去的国家是西班牙，那是一个风景如画（picturesque）的地方。

2）未来想住的地方，在我想象中，应该是一个坐落在海边，有温暖阳光，有美丽的海鸥（sea gulls）的地方。

3）关于游泳，没有什么值得说的，因为我就不会游泳。

4）那儿的人都很友好。

参考答案

01 这是定语后置的一个考点，英语表达"最喜欢"有两种说法。The room I like, my favourite。在这个结构中，I like 作 room 的后置定语，翻译成"我喜欢的"，如果后面加了 it，那这个定语修饰的名词到底是 the room 还是 it 呢，就有重复了。

02 1) The country I want to visit is Spain, a place full of picturesque views.

2) The place I want to live in the future, in my imagination, is located near the sea, with warm sunshine and beautiful seagulls over head.

3）As for swimming, there is nothing worth to say, because I can't swim.

4）People there are very friendly.

写作部分

  定语就是修饰限定名词或者代词的词或短语，可以是名词、代词、数词、介词短语、动词不定式、分词，而定语从句我们在后面的章节再说，这里只关注于词或短语作的定语。

  定语放在所修饰的词的前后均可，比如：a beautiful girl from Xinjiang。这里 girl 有两个定语，一个是前面的形容词 beautiful，一个是后面的介词短语 from Xinjiang。

  关于定语，我建议大家掌握下面几点：

1. 形容词作定语是有一定顺序的：数观形龄色国材用，即：数量、外观、形状、年龄、情感、颜色、国籍、材料、用途。

  比如：a handsome strong young Australian boy

     一个帅气、强壮的年青澳洲小伙

  但在考试中，不建议大家使用一长串的定语。

2. 后置定语可以是短语、形容词、分词的形式，议论文中比较常用的是形容词短语、介词短语、分词短语作后置定语，这一部分是这一节的重点，下面用例子来分别说明。

  形容词短语作后置定语，例如：

> 2014 年 6 月 7 日   警察携枪会加重社会暴力吗？
>
> Upgrading police equipment is a vicious cycle easy to start but hard to keep.
>
> 升级警用装备是一个开始容易停止难的恶性循环。

  这里 easy to start but hard to keep 就是形容词短语作 a vicious cycle 的后置定语。

  介词短语作后置定语，例如：

> 2014 年 10 月 18 日   同意去其他地方学习另外的文化不必要吗？
>
> The complexity of authentic language contexts decides pure foreign language environment is the best way to understand grammars, grasp vocabulary and copy pronunciation in daily life.
>
> 真实语境的复杂性决定了外国语言环境是在日常生活中理解语法、掌握词汇和模仿发音的最佳途径。

其中 of authentic language contexts 就是介词短语作 complexity 的后置定语。

现在分词和过去分词短语都可以作后置定语，具体用哪一种取决于这一动作是前面修饰的名词主动发出的还是被动接受的。

过去分词做后置定语，例如：

> **2012 年 3 月 8 日　工作和生活失衡的原因和解决方法**
>
> The imbalance between work and life should be ascribed to the extreme working pressure brought by intense social competition.
> 工作和生活失衡确实应该归咎于激烈的社会竞争所带来的巨大的工作压力。

这里 brought by intense social competition 就是过去分词短语作后置定语，限定前面的 the extreme working pressure 的来源，注意压力是由竞争带来的，是被动关系。

现在分词作后置定语，例如：

> **2014 年 11 月 8 日　犯罪是因为后天原因还是先天原因？**
>
> The origin of some offences has been imputed to propensity for violence and anti-social personality coming from genetic defects.
> 一些违法行为的起源已经被归咎于源于基因缺陷的暴力倾向和反社会人格。

这里 coming from genetic defects 就是现在分词短语作后置定语，限定前面 propensity for violence and anti-social personality 的来源，注意暴力倾向和反社会人格来自于基因缺陷，是主动关系。

后置定语在考场上的应用：

先看议论文，根据上面的两个例子，我们可以总结出一个句式来：

主要论题（名词词组）should be ascribed to 某一原因（名词词组）brought by/coming from 深层原因（名词词组）。

主要论题应该被归咎于源于某一深层起源的某一原因。

这一句的表意可以有很多并列选项：

主要论题	应归因于	某种影响	来自于	某一原因
名词／动名词词组	应归因于 should be ascribed to should be chalked up to should be put down to should be attributed to	名词／动名词词组	过去分词短语作后置定语 associated with brought by caused by	名词／动名词词组

（续）

主要论题	应归因于	某种影响	来自于	某一原因
名词/动名词词组	应归咎于 should be blamed on has been imputed to	名词/动名词词组	现在分词短语作后置定语 accompanying with coming from originating from resulting from stemming from 介词短语作后置定语 by due to through	名词/动名词词组

再看图表作文，后置定语在图表作文里也可以应用，比如起始段介绍图表内容时我们可以用：

There is (are) 图表类别 showing 图表内容.
这是个（些）展示了某些内容的某种类别的图表。

比如：

> There is a line chart showing the consumption of fish, beef, lamb and chicken in a European country from 1979 to 2004.
> 这是个展示了 1979 至 2004 年间一个欧洲国家鱼肉、牛肉、羊肉和鸡肉消耗量的线性图。

这一句的语法拿分点包括：there be 句式和现在分词作后置定语。

01 改错：写作挑错

看看下面的句子，你能给出更好的写法吗？

2014 年 4 月 5 日 人们常换住址和工作好吗？

Frequent change of addresses and jobs builds up a vicious cycle, which starts at an unfixed lifestyle always on the run and processes to perennial adjustment and a disappointed life.

频繁换住址和工作建立了一个恶性循环，从不规律的疲于奔命的生活方式开始，进展到永无休止的调整和灰暗的生活。

02 大闯关：写作闯关

试着翻译下面的句子，一定要注意长定语的顺序。

2014 年 11 月 1 日　失业比有工作但不喜欢强吗？

大多数失业者确实遭受着伴随长期不稳定的收入而来的不断恶化的财务状况的折磨。

参考答案

01　这一句原则上并没有错误，只是我们可以用后置定语替代 which 引导的非限定性定语从句，因为后者在考场上过于常见，不能让考官惊艳。可以改成这样：

Frequent change of addresses and jobs builds up a vicious cycle starting at an unfixed lifestyle always on the run and processing to perennial adjustment and a disappointed life.

这一句实际上是双现在分词作后置定语，公式化就是：

主要论题（名词/动名词词组）builds up a virtuous / vicious cycle starting at 某一小的影响（名词/动名词词组）and processing to 某一大的影响（名词/动名词词组）.

主要论题建立起了一个良性/恶性循环，以某一小的影响开始，进而进展到某一大的影响。

还有很多并列选项：

主要论题	导致了一个连续的变化	始于	某一小的影响，	终于	某一大的影响
名词/动名词词组	builds up a virtuous / vicious cycle leads to a continuing process results in a domino effect	beginning with starting at from	名词/动名词词组	progressing to ending in to	名词/动名词词组

02　The most unemployed do suffer from deteriorating financial conditions accompanying with unsecured income.

精准的状语

口语部分

状语是英文中一个既简单又复杂的结构，说简单是因为它在英文中的语序和中文几乎一样。常见的状语从句如 because，but，if，when 引导的句子，都可以直接逐字翻译。说它复杂是因为种类繁多。

状语没有掌握好的人，往往在翻译这些字眼的时候非常困难：

1）要想 to
2）趁着、一边……一边…… while
3）刚…… as soon as
4）哪里有……哪里就有…… where
5）要是能 unless
6）……才 as
7）既然 now that
8）正如 as
9）相比较来说 comparatively
10）在其中 in which
11）就能 so that
12）有点 to some extent

当然，我们这里说的不是状语从句，就是状语。能作状语的语法成分有哪些？这一章我们来谈一谈。

句子的基本成分是主谓宾，比如：

> The man（主语）killed（谓语）my neighbor（宾语）.

上一章讲过，定语的位置是名词前后，我们先把句子变复杂一点：

> The black man who I talked with last week killed my old neighbor who is the grandfather of my classmate.

状语的位置是动词前后（副词）和句子前后。我们把状语加上：

> To tell you the truth, last night, for some reason, before 12 o'clock, the black man who I talked with last week killed my old neighbor who is the grandfather of my classmate, when he was walking back home to have dinner.

所以，你看一个好句子的丰富程度，是不是跟状语脱不了干系？状语是一个特别容易让人轻视的语法结构，表达一件事情的过程时，没有状语，只知道什么是主谓宾是很难通顺流利地组句的。换句话说，掌握了状语才真正意义上掌握了丰富表达的钥匙。

掌握状语，首先要掌握的是状语的位置。状语通常会出现在句首或者句尾，所以起句的时候就要有用状语的意识。

我们需要了解两个知识：
- 第一，是从功能上划分，状语可分为时间、地点、原因、结果、目的、比较、让步、条件、伴随。
- 第二，是从结构上划分，状语的构成可由副词、介词短语、不定式、动名词、过去分词、状语从句、表示时间的名词（some day）来充当。

1 不定式作状语

不定式作状语常出现在 Part 3 解决办法类问题中，比如：如何解决环境污染问题，交通堵塞问题，孩子不爱学习问题。

Nowadays, some people don't like to study. Do you have any methods to encourage them to study well...

> To solve the problem, punishment will be a good idea.
> 要想解决问题，惩罚是个好主意。
>
> To encourage young people to study, the best method is …
> 要想鼓励年轻人学习，最好的方法是……

2 while/as 表示"一边……一边……"

通常出现在场景描述中，比如：Do you prefer to eat out or eat at home?

> I prefer to eat at home, and enjoy the meal while the family is around.
> 我更喜欢在家吃饭，趁着家人都在身边，享受美食。

3 as soon as 刚……

通常出现在表达愿望的题目中，比如：What's your plan for the future?

> As soon as I get a 6.5 on the test, I will go abroad to UK and further my study.
> 一旦我考试考到6.5分，就会出国去英国深造。

或者谈论未来你对交通的看法，也可以说：

> In the future, as soon as flying means of transportation can be applied, traffic jam won't be a problem.
> 未来，一旦飞行交通方式得以应用，交通堵塞不会是个问题。

4 Where there is... There is... 哪有……哪就有……

通常用于表达感受，比如问你住在哪里：Where do you live?

> Where there is her, there is home. 哪里有她哪里就有家。

5 unless 除非

用于对未来的否定推断，Will handwriting be replaced in the future?

> I don't think so, unless human beings are completely ruled by artificial intelligence.
> 我认为不会，除非人类完全被人工智能取代。

6 It's long time before... 很长时间才……

用于描述长时间的等待，比如早起的经历题：

> It's long time before I fall asleep. 我过了很长时间才睡着。

01 改错：口语挑错

一到周末我就去打篮球。
When it's the weekends, I go to play basketball.

02 大闯关：口语闯关

翻译下列句子。

1）要想出人头地，就得多工作少休息。

2）趁热打铁。

3）他一边站起来一边笑着。

4）刚到家就闻到饭香了。

5）无风不起浪。

6）你要是能明天还我，我就借给你钱。

7）我们总是边走边唱。

8）我过了很长时间才睡着。

9）我慢点跑你就能追上我了。

10）既然你有钱你给她买个车呀！

11）在某种程度上这个是对的。

12）我们离不开空气，正如鱼儿离不开水啊！

参考答案

01 这是雅思考试中常见错误，when 是状语从句连接词，后面需要写完整的句子，when I was during the weekends，或者不要 when，只用介词短语表达同样的意思。on the weekends，或者 at the weekends 都对。

02 1）To get ahead, you'll have to walk long hours and take short vacations.

2）Strike while the iron is hot.

3）He smiled as he stood up.

4）I smelled the flavor of dinner as soon as I got home.

5）Where there is smoke, there is fire.

6）I could lend you some money if you return it tomorrow.

7）We always sing as we talk.

8）It's a long time before I fell asleep.

9）Let me run slower so that you could catch up with me.

10）Now that you are rich, you can buy her a car.

11）This to some extent is right.

12）We can't live without air, as water to fish.

写作部分

在议论文中，由于表示原因和目的的状语可以展示出逻辑推理的过程，所以应用得更为广泛，这里我们重点说明表示原因和目的的状语的实战用法。

1 表示原因的状语

比如：

> 2014年8月9日　危险运动应该被禁止还是人们有权去选择它们？

> Because of the pursuit for mental stimulation and self-accomplishment, many people choose to ignore the side-effects.
> 因为对心理刺激和自我完善的追求，很多人选择忽略那些副作用。

句首 because of 引导的是表示原因的状语，类似的还有：

> 2013年12月14日　年轻人离开乡村去城市的原因和评价

> Owing to the attractions of higher living standards and more opportunities, more and more young people are packed into over-crowded towns and cities.
> 由于高生活标准和更多机会的吸引，越来越多的年轻人涌入拥挤不堪的城镇。

这一句的基本结构和上一句一样，都是句首是一个表示原因的状语，只不过这里的状语是 owing to 引导的。

下面这些都可以引导表示原因的状语，而且这个状语既可以放于主句之前、也可以放在主句之后：

> because of, for, on account of, owing to, due to

2 表示目的的状语

> 2014年8月17日　把工商业从大城市移到其他地区好吗？

> In order to guarantee the rationality of industrial distribution, the authorities have to intensively analyze whether industries and businesses should be moved from urban areas to other regions.
> 为了确保产业布局的合理性，当局必须深入分析工商业是否应从城市迁移到其他地区。

这里句首的 in order to 引导的就是表示目的的状语，和表示时间的状语一样，可以放于主句之前，也可以放于主句之后。这一句可以放在议论文的起始段，用来说明讨论这一论题的意义，其主干可以表示为：

In order to guarantee 讨论意义（名词词组），相关负责人群（名词）have to intensively analyze 主要论题（名词/动名词词组或 whether，why 等引导的从句）.

为了确保相关领域的健康发展，相关人等必须深入分析主要论题这一问题。还可以参考：

> **2013 年 6 月 22 日　应该把国际新闻列为中学课程吗？**
>
> In order to guarantee the appropriate arrangement of school curriculum, educationalists have to evaluate the necessity of teaching world affairs in high school.
>
> 为了确保学校教育的课程设置的合理安排，教育学家必须评估在高中教授世界时事的必要性。

表达这一语义的并列选项可以总结为下表：

为了	确保	讨论意义，	相关人等	必须得评估	主要论题这一问题
后接动词词组 Aiming to In order to 后接动词现在分词词组 Aiming at For With the aim of	ensure guarantee insure maintain promise	名词词组，	名词词组	have to access have to analyze have to estimate have to evaluate must analyze	whether，why 等引导的从句

表达目的的状语在流程图里也有应用：

> 原料 is placed in a 设备 to be 加工过程（动词被动语态）with the aim of 加工结果（名词/动名词词组）.
>
> 原材料被放置于设备内进行某种加工，以便实现某种加工结果。

> In order to further process 原料 to 加工结果（动词词组），流程（名词/动名词词组）is done with the help of a 设备.
>
> 为了对原料进行进一步的加工以得到某种结果，某一流程在某一设备的帮助下被完成。

比如：

> The clay is placed on a metal grid to be refined with the aim of mixing with water and sand.
> 黏土被放置于金属网格上进行筛选，以便和水和沙混合。

> Then, in order to further process the mixture to form the shape of bricks, moulding is done with the help of a wire cutter.
> 然后，为了对混合物进行进一步的加工以形成砖头的形状，塑形在一个金属丝切割器的帮助下完成。

练 习

01 改错：写作挑错

看看下面的句子有错误吗？

2013年10月12日 其他因素同经济发展在衡量国家成就上一样重要吗？

To measuring national comprehensive strength accurately, sociologists have to estimate whether economic progress is the single key indicator for national success.

为了准确评估国家的综合实力，社会学家必须分析经济发展是否是一个国家成功的唯一的关键标准。

02 大闯关：写作闯关

试着翻译下面的句子，注意第一句包含的表示目的的状语、第二句包含的表示原因的状语。

2013年11月9日 青少年犯罪该接受和成人一样的惩罚吗？

为了维护司法公正和青少年权益，犯罪控制部门必须得分析青少年违法者是否应该受到和成年人一样的惩罚。因为在侵害青年人权益和威胁社会安全方面的副作用，我反对施以同样的惩罚。

参考答案

01 动词不定式 to V 可以作目的状语，放于句首时表示重点强调这一目的，这里 to measuring 是错的。

To measure national comprehensive strength accurately, sociologists have to estimate whether economic progress is the single key indicator for measuring national success.

02 Aiming at upholding judicial justice and juvenile's rights, crime control departments have to analyze whether youth offenders should receive the same punishment as adult ones. For the side-effects in violating juvenile's rights and threatening communities safety, I object to applying the same penalties.

独特的同位语

口语部分

同位语是表示前边说的和后边说的是一回事儿，后面的是前面的补充说明。最简单的同位语比如，Mr. Smith, our new teacher is such a nice person. 在这个句子中，史密斯和我们新来的老师说的就是一回事儿，但是后面在做阐释和补充。

同位语最常见的用法就是解释名字，最常出现的位置是介绍一个地方、一个人、一样东西，使用要点就是后面解释的内容要让听者更感兴趣一些。

> I'd like to talk about a place, Xiamen, a leisure city located in the south part of China.
> Speaking about family members, my brother, John is the one who I spent most time with.

第二种同位语的用法叫作部分意义同位语。比如：

> We Chinese people are not weak.
> I like all kinds of fruits, especially kiwi, the fruit rich in vitamin.

另外，要分清同位语和补语的区别，同样是补充说明，但是同位语始终是名词性质的，而补语可以由形容词、副词、名词、代词、不定式、动名词或分词短语来充当。我们要从逻辑上来区分，比如：

> The important thing is **to make money**.（主语补足语）
> All he did was (to) ruin everything.
> He remained sitting **alone** in the room.（主语补足语）

补语是来表示对结果、程度、趋向、可能、状态、数量的说明

从逻辑上讲，补语和状语的区别是这样的：

状语是在说：怎么样干？
补语是在说：干怎么样？

看下面这个补语从句，你能理解吗？

> What's troubling me is (that) I don't have much experience.
> 让我困扰的是我并没有太多经验。
> That was how they got the impression. 他们就是这样留下这些印象的。

主语补语与主语之间通常由系动词连接，系动词分为三类：
- 一类表示现状，以 be 为代表，包括 appear, feel, look, prove, seem, smell, sound, taste 等。比如：
The tea tastes more like pee. 这茶喝起来跟尿似的。
- 一类表示持续的，以 remain 为代表，包括 hold, keep, rest, stay 等。比如：
I can't stay awake another minute. 我快撑不住要睡着了。
- 还有一类是表示结果的，以 become 为代表，包括 come, fall, get, go, grow, make, turn, turn out 等。比如：
She went pale in the face and ran out of the patient room. 她脸色发白，跑出了病房。

在"作为一个……"这个结构里，主语补语和同位语有时让人分不清：

> As a father of six children, he had to do 5 part-time jobs. （主语补语）
> He, a father of six children, had to do 5 part-time jobs. （同位语）

这部分放在宾语上就是宾语补足语了，比如：

> He made her (as) his wife. （宾语补足语）
> They named their beloved son (as) Steven. （宾语补足语）
> This is their baby son Steven. （同位语）
> He thinks himself a genius. （宾语补足语）

宾语补足语常用在动词 call, name, believe, consider, feel, find 后面。
其他宾语补足语：

> Jacie's silence made Steven uneasy. （形容词作宾语补足语）
> We don't allow people to take phone calls in here （不定式作宾语补足语）
> I heard someone knocking at the door. （分词短语作宾语补足语）

练 习

01 改错：口语挑错

看看下面的句子有错吗？

The room I love the most, a room with lots of facilities like a laptop, a bed, and a guitar is my bedroom.

02 大闯关：口语闯关

试着用 if 引导的虚拟语气来翻译下面的句子。

1）我的家乡变化太大，所有东西都在变：路、交通、经济，越来越多的高楼。绿化也越来越好，给这个城市增添了一种独有的味道，一种我深深爱恋的氛围。

2）一到周末，我唯一要做的事情就是做饭。

参考答案

01 题目结构从语法上讲没有太大问题，但是交际上容易造成听者的困惑。所以这个句子看起来有一种头重脚轻的感觉。通常同位语在雅思口语中语习惯出现的位置是靠后的，相当于定语从句的位置，作解释说明。所以正确的说法是：The room I love the most is my bedroom, a room with lots of facilities like a laptop, a bed, and a guitar.

02 1）The change in my hometown is earth-shattering. Everything has changed, the road, the transportation and the economy. More and more high-rise buildings sprouted out. The greening has become better and better, which adds some spice to the atmosphere, an atmosphere I'm deeply attached to.

2）As soon as it's weekend, the only thing I need to do is cooking/all I need to do is cooking.

写 作 部 分

同位语一般是名词词组，位于修饰的名词或代词之后，补充说明后者，比如：

> I, an unfamous IELTS writing tutor, have to work hard to survive.
> 我，一个非著名雅思写作老师，不得不努力工作以维持生计。

这里 an unfamous IELTS writing tutor 就是前面 I 的同位语，对我的身份进行说明。

原则上，同位语是对前面名词或代词的说明，可以出现在名词或代词的句子成分之后。在考场上，比较容易掌握和运用的是主语和宾语的同位语。上面的例句是主语的同位语，下面我们来看两个真题示范。

1 主语的同位语

> 2015 年 7 月 11 日 广告使大众丧失了个性吗？

> Popular dress patterns, visual signs of brand identity, are helpful for customers to build self-confidence.
> 流行的服饰模式，社会定位的视觉表象，有助于帮顾客建立自信。

这里 typical visual signs of social identity 是前面主语 popular dress patterns 的同位语。这里的用法是对论述对象（广告和流行）进行逻辑解释（社会定位的典型视觉表象），所以能有助于帮顾客建立自信，那么这一句实际上包含了两层逻辑关系：

广告和流行
↓
社会定位的典型视觉表象
↓
有助于帮顾客建立自信

主语的同位语在图表作文的流程图中也可以应用：

> The raw material, 原料, has to be 第一步的加工过程（动词被动语态）in a 设备 / at 地点, so that they could change to 加工结果（名词词组）.
> 原料，即某些东西，需要相关人员用某一设备 / 在某个地点进行某种加工，以便变成某种状态。

比如：

> The raw materials, and fresh fish, have to be heavily salted and dried in the factory, so that they could change to dried fish.
> 原材料即鲜鱼，必须得在工厂里用盐腌制并烘干以便变成鱼干。

2 宾语的同位语

> 2016 年 6 月 4 日 训练年轻人竞争而不是合作的好处大于坏处吗？

> Being aggressive and competitive would lead to better preparation and stronger actions, driving forces to exceed normal limits.
> 锐意进取、勇于竞争会带来更好的准备和更有力的行动，突破极限的原动力。

这一句中，driving forces to push people to exceed their normal limits 是宾语 better preparation and stronger actions 的同位语，用来解释后者的深层意义，逻辑层次如下：

锐意进取、勇于竞争
↓
更好的准备和更有力的行动
↓
突破极限的原动力

可见，无论放在何处，同位语都可以作为逻辑上的深入解释部分用于文章对论点进行分析的主体段部分。我们再看个例子：

> 2015年4月30日　年轻人和父母同住的好处大于坏处吗？

> Boomerang children could get more family support in daily expenses, a powerful assistance in lowering living costs.
> 啃老族能在日常花销上得到家庭的支持，这是一个在降低生活成本方面非常有力的助力。

练 习

01 改错：写作挑错

看看下面的句子有错误吗？

2016年5月28日　同意所有父母都要参加照顾孩子的课程吗？

In order to reduce final medical care expenses, many public hospitals supply free childcare training on how to prevent some diseases and accidents.

为了降低最终的医疗费用，很多公立医院提供免费的育婴培训，教授年轻的父母如何避免一些疾病和意外。

02 大闯关：写作闯关

试着翻译下面的句子，注意同位语的使用：

2013年5月18日　孩子们学习历史重要还是学更实用的科目重要？

历史和艺术，我们当下生活方式的共同点，对于理解文化和提高国家认同感上是非常重要的。

参考答案

01 同位语和其前面说明的先行词的格必须一致,句法功能也相同,也就是说,前面的先行词是名词(短语),后面的同位语必须是名词或动名词(短语)的形式。上面的句子中,how to prevent some diseases and accidents 是宾语 free childcare training 的同位语,两者的词性不一致就是不合适的。

In order to reduce final medical care expenses, many public hospitals supply free childcare training, a valuable chance to teach young parents how to prevent some diseases and accidents.

02 History and art, the common ground of our current lifestyles, are vital in understanding our culture and providing a sense of national identify.

吸睛的插入语

口语部分

插入语是位置比较灵活,但不影响句子结构和成分。

> She, I think, has no interest in you. (在这个句子中,I think 去掉也不影响句子意义,故为插入语)

形容词(短语)作插入语

能用作插入语的形容词(短语)常见的有:true, wonderful, excellent, strange to say, most important of all, sure enough 等。如:

> True, it would be too bad. 真的,太糟了。
> Wonderful, we have won again. 太好了,我们又赢了。
> Strange to say, he hasn't got my letter up to now. 说来也奇怪,他到现在还没有收到我的信。
> Most important of all, we must pay the debt. 最重要的是,我们必须还账。

副词(短语)作插入语

能用作插入语的副词(短语)有:indeed, surely, still, otherwise, certainly, however, generally, personally, honestly, (un)fortunately (badly), luckily (happily) for sb., though, besides, exactly, perhaps, maybe, probably, frankly, or rather 等。如:

> When he got there, he found, however, that the weather was just lousy. 可是到了那儿之后他发现,那儿的天气太坏了。
> Otherwise, he would still be at home. (不然的话,他还会在家的。)

介词短语作插入语

能用作插入语的介词短语有：in fact, in one's opinion, in general, in a word, in other words, in a few words, of course, by the way, as a result, for example, on the contrary, on the other hand, to one's surprise, in short, as a matter of fact, in conclusion, in brief 等。如：

> You can't wait anymore-in other words, you should start at once. 你不能再等了——换言之，你得立即出发。
>
> On the contrary, we should strengthen our collaboration with them. 相反，我们应该加强和他们的合作。

V-ing（短语）作插入语

能用作插入语的 V-ing（短语）常见的有：generally speaking, strictly speaking, judging from by, talking of, considering 等。如：

> Generally speaking, the weather there is neither too cold in winter nor too hot in summer. 一般来说，那儿的气候冬天不太冷，夏天不太热。
>
> Judging by his clothes, he may be a foreign backpacker. 从衣着来判断，他可能是个外国背包客。

不定式短语作插入语

能用作插入语的不定式短语有：to be frank/honest/sure/exact, to tell you the truth, to make matters/things worse, to sum up, to start with, to begin with 等。如：

> To be frank, I don't quite agree with this opinion. 坦率地说，我不太同意这个说法。
>
> To tell you the truth, I'm not so interested in sports. 跟你说实话，我对体育的兴趣不大。
>
> To sum up, success results from persistence. 总而言之，成功是艰苦努力的结果。

句子（陈述句和一般疑问句）作插入语

能用作插入语的句子有：I am sure, I believe, I think, I know, I suppose, I hope, I'm afraid, you see, what's more, that is to say, as we know, as I see, believe it or not 等。如：

> Some old people can't get used to this fast-paced society, that is to say, they are not satisfied with their lives. 有些老人适应不了这个快节奏的社会，就是说，他们对生活其实并不满意。
>
> I believe, I will catch up with those elites sooner or later. 我相信我迟早会赶上这些精英的。
>
> He can't go abroad, because he doesn't study hard. What's more, he isn't so clever. 他不能出国，因为他学习不认真，更何况他又不太聪明。
>
> Technology, as a general rule, is the friend of scientists, as it is, I think, the friend of all the people. 一般而言，高科技是科学家的朋友。实际上，我认为高科技是全人类的朋友。

插入语的使用重在掌握语境，通常情况下出现都是为了加强语气，比如：

加强个人观点：

> Do you prefer listening to live music or recorded music?
> Recorded music, I think, is more likely to be my preference.
> (同样表达个人观点的有：I think, I believe, I suppose, I assume, I believe 等)

表达不情愿或个人信息：

> Will you live in your hometown forever?
> Living in my hometown, honestly, is not a good idea.
> (同样表达这个意思的有：to be frank, to tell you the truth 等)

强调否定意义：

> Do old people and young people like a same kind of music?
> Well, as a matter of fact, old people will, by no means, like listening to pop music, instead, they probably are more interested in opera.
> (同样表达这个意思的有：in no case, in no way 等)

强调程度：

> What benefits are there if you read novels?
> Firstly, reading, to some extent, helps you get some inspirations, especially reading autobiography, in which the experience that was told are very precious lessons.
> (同样表达这个意思的有：kind of, sort of 等)

练 习

01 改错：口语挑错

看看下面的句子有错吗？

1）Nowadays, fewer and fewer people like to go to the cinema, that being said, they are not satisfied with the effects.

2）In my eyes, playing games, to be honest, is not a waste of time, instead, is a mainstream form of leisure.

02 大闯关：口语闯关

翻译下列句子。

严格意义上说，旅游不但能够开阔视野，更能给我们一个好机会来领略各地美食。

参考答案

01 1）that being said 表达转折关系，意思是"话虽这么说"。千万不要和 that is to say 混淆，that is to say 表达的是"这就是说"，才是这个句子中正确的连接词。

2）插入语的使用要注意语气，句子的本意是说，在我眼中，玩游戏不是浪费时间，相反，是一种主流休闲方式。在这个句意里用 to be honest（诚实地说）就显得不伦不类。在表达观点时，无所谓诚实不诚实，只有表达不情愿（Honestly, I don't like it.），不希望其他人听到的建议（Honestly, is not a good choice.），才用 honestly。如果想强调一下 no 这个概念，可以用 In my eyes, playing games is by no means a waste of time, instead, is a mainstream from of leisure.

02 Strictly speaking, travel not only broadens the mind, plus it gives us a great opportunity to try every snack in different places.

写作部分

插入语灵活多变，与句子其他成分无语法关系，多用逗号与句子隔开，写文章时常用插入语来加强语气和起到连接作用，一般位于句首，可以总结为以下几种。

1 副词

表示承接：indeed 的确，naturally 自然地，obviously 显然，surely 无疑地

表示并列：besides 另外

表示转折：fortunately 幸好地，however 然而

表示个人观点：frankly 坦率地，honestly 坦诚地，personally 就个人来说

表示总结：briefly 简单地说

比如，在雅思议论文中，Discuss both views and give your own opinion 是一种特殊的提问方式，一般在评论完双方的观点后，会陈述个人的看法，这一类题目中双方的观点一般比较极端，考生采取折中的看法会比较客观，这时就可以用上面表示个人观点的副词。

	我认为应该把上文的两个观点综合起来
Frankly, Honestly, Personally,	a compromise between the above two extremes sounds more reasonable. a synthesis is more viable. I incline to give a composite suggestion. I prefer to combine the above two views together. there should be a perfect mix of the above views.

2 形容词和形容词短语

表示承接：needless to say 不用说，most important of all 最为重要的是，sure enough 十分肯定，worse still 更糟的是。比如：

> 2015 年 11 月 19 日 B 卷　国家应该经济支持体育运动队和运动员还是应该依靠非政府资源？

The financial return is uncertain and most resident could not get benefit from these programs. Worse still, excessive social support would reduce enthusiasm for production because competition and commercialisation is the only way to boom any industry including sports.

财务回报是不确定的，而且大多数人从这些项目中得不到任何好处。更糟的是，过度的社会支持会降低生产积极性，因为竞争和商业化才是使包括体育运动在内的任何行业繁荣的唯一途径。

3 分词短语

表示条件：generally speaking 一般地说，judging from ... 根据……判断，strictly speaking 严格地说。比如：

> **2015 年 2 月 7 日**　文化场所对本地人吸引力不如对游客大的原因和解决方法

> Judging from the situation that the content of exhibition usually keeps invariable for decades, local cultural hot spots cannot supply novelty value and attraction for second visit.
>
> 鉴于展出的内容通常几十年不变这一情况，地方文化热点不能为二次参观提供新鲜感和吸引力。

4　不定式短语

表示承接：to be sure 无疑地

表示总结：to conclude 总结来讲，to sum up 概括来讲，so to speak 可以说

表示个人观点：to be frank 坦率地说，to tell the truth 老实说

比如：

> **2015 年 6 月 6 日**　该给社区还是国家或国际组织提供援助？

> To be frank, without an effective supervising mechanism, I do not trust any kind of charity organizations.
>
> 坦率地说，没有一套有效的监督机制，我不相信任何一种慈善组织。

5　介词短语

表示补充：of course 当然，on the other hand 另一方面

表示总结：in conclusion 总结来说，in short 简而言之

表示举例：as a matter of fact 事实上

表示个人观点：in my opinion 就我来说

比如：

> **2014 年 3 月 1 日**　在大城市生活对健康不利吗？

> As a matter of fact, a quarter of Beijing residents are suffering from breathing problems caused by severe haze.
>
> 事实上，四分之一的北京居民正在遭受由严重的雾霾引起的呼吸系统问题的折磨。

6 代词短语

表示转折：all the same 尽管如此

表示总结：all in all 总的来说

比如：

> 2015年7月25日　同意商业应该承担起社会责任吗？

> Unlike natural persons, business is not subject to normal moral constraints. All the same, its profit-driven nature must give place to social responsibilities because it takes the largest share of new social wealth.
>
> 不像自然人，商业不受普通的道德约束。尽管如此，其逐利本性仍然必须让位于社会责任，因为它占据了新创造的社会财富的大头。

7 还有一类是短句的形式，一般放于句中或句末，起到加强语气的作用

表示承接：it seems 看来是，that is 也就是说，what is important（serious）重要（严重）的是

表示个人观点：as I see it 照我看来，I am sure 我可以肯定，I believe 我相信

表示转折：I am afraid 恐怕，I wonder 我不确定

比如下面这道近年比较抽象的一道题目：

> 2011年5月14日　该倡导传统价值观以应对贪婪和自私的泛滥吗？

> Without any real benefit induction, it is difficult for traditional values to provide necessary motivation to follow, I am afraid.
>
> 没有任何的实际利益介入，我恐怕传统价值观难以提供遵从的动力。

练 习

01 改错：写作挑错

看看下面的句子，你能找出错误吗？

Comparing with the others, China shows significant advantages and has a population of 1.3 billion. On the other extreme, less than 70 million people live in France, which is the least figure.

同其他的相比，中国显示了明显的优势并拥有 13 亿人口。另外一个极端是，少于 7000 万人住在法国，这是最小的数字。

02 大闯关：写作闯关

翻译下面的句子。

2015 年 1 月 10 日　应该让年轻人做领导者吗？

严格地说，更老的年龄不能完全等同于更丰富的经验，因为后者，照我看来，更多地取决于人生经历和性格而不是时间。

参考答案

01　这一句句首的插入语应该是过去分词短语，而不是现在分词短语，因为其隐藏的逻辑主语是 China，只能和其他国家比较，所以应该是：

Compared with the others, China shows significant advantages and has a 1.3 billion population. On the other extreme, less than 70 million people live in France, which is the least figure.

02　Strictly speaking, elder age does not equate to better capacity for work, because the latter, as I see it, more depends on life experience and personalities rather than time.

如何让文章的
句子种类不再单一

少见的疑问句、感叹句、祈使句

口语部分

我们在这里要讲的疑问句分为基础三种和进阶三种：

1 一般疑问句（yes/no 疑问句）

Will Jacie be here tomorrow? Yes, she will.
Are you staying here? No, I'm not.
Do you like music? Yes, I do.
Did you have a good time? Yes, I did.
Have you got any interesting experience in the museum? No, I haven't.
Should I tell her what happened just now? No, you shouldn't.

2 选择疑问句（A or B）

Do you prefer fashionable shoes or comfortable ones? Comfortable one.

在这里回答问题 I prefer 可以有很多替换的说法

I prefer = I'd fancy A over B
= I'm partial to…
= A is more likely to be my preference.
= B takes a better chance to win my preference.

有一种选择疑问句是与 or not 或者 or something 连用的：

Are you coming with me or not?
Did he get hurt or something?

这样的句子形式上是选择疑问句的省略式,但语气上更有煽动性和猜测性。特别适合用在邀请、判断猜测某件事情的语境里。比如看日出、邀请一起旅游、忘记事情、道歉、第一次用外语等感性的并且具有对话性质的话题中,再给大家几个例子:

> Do you mean you want to get some change or something? 你的意思是说要换点零钱吗?(第一次用外语)
> Have you seen it or not? 你看到没看到啊?(看流星)
> Did you forget or not? 你不是忘了吧?(忘事儿经历)
> Are you going to apologize or not? 你道不道歉?(道歉经历)

3 特殊疑问句

在口语考试的情境中,并不存在询问对方问题的情节。多数情况我们只回答问题,特殊疑问句只用作四个方式:

A) 自问自答:Why we need this law? Because… 为什么我们需要这个法律,因为……

B) 表达不满:I said, "What the hell you are doing?" 我说:"你干什么!"

C) 表达询问:I asked him, "What is the most significant reason for you to like traveling by plane." He said:"Because I was a pilot." 我问他:"到底是什么重要原因让你那么喜欢坐飞机?"他说:"因为我曾经是个飞行员。"

D) 朋友仗义:Every time when I say, "Who can help me?" He is always the first one who jumps out and says, "No worries, buddy. I'm on your back." He is just that kind of friend for me. 每次我说:"谁能帮帮我?"他总是第一个跳出来跟我讲:"没事儿,兄弟,有我呢!"他就是那种朋友。

考试的时候也可以用夸张的语气来表示情绪。

> Do you prefer to read newspapers or watch TV programs?

可以说:"Come on! Who still read newspapers today?" 而不是 I prefer to watch TV programs.

再如:

> Last year, in October, my girlfriend gave me a phone call. She said, "Hey, Darling. I've got something for you. Would you like to come and pick it up?" When I arrived, I saw a beautiful box wrapped with colored paper, in which there is my favorite basketball jersey of the Los Angels Lakers. I was so moved. I almost burst into tears. I was thinking, "How considerate she is!" Can you imagine that?

在英语中，声情并茂地转述他人的话是一个特别常见的场景，所以讲话的人要特别注意语调的夸张，因为语调可以传递情绪。

疑问句应用还可以分为三个目的：**表达感受、表达强烈怀疑、描述场景**。

在感受表达中最常见的疑问句就是：

> Can you imagine how exciting/disappointed I was?

可以用在刚讲完一个很令人激动或者令人失望的事情，用反问这个句子可以引起对方的共鸣。

> Who but a fool would say yes to this question? 除了傻子，谁会同意这个观点呢？
> Are you kidding me? 你不是逗我呢吧？

这个例子想表达的就是强烈的不同意，通常用在问答题中，表达出强烈的情绪。

My friend came to me and said, "Hello, sweetheart! I found the recent flight tickets to Thailand is quite reasonable and alluring. Would you like to come with me for a trip together?" 这个场景复原了对话的内容，想表达请求，常见于经历题。

下面来说特殊的三种疑问句：**否定疑问句、答语疑问句和附加疑问句**。

1. 否定疑问句通常含有特殊意义，这类疑问句常用来表示：
   A) 说话者认为那是一个事实
   B) 提出请求、邀请或建议
   C) 表示关切，感到意外或惊讶
   D) 表示对某件事没有做而感到意外或惊讶

   比如：

   > Isn't it a wonderful moment? Just you and me, sitting here, watching the moon and stars. Romantic, right?
   > 这个瞬间是不是很棒？只有你和我，坐在这儿看星星月亮，很浪漫，对吧？

2. 答语疑问句：用一个简短的问句来回应一个陈述句，表达兴趣、关心、惊奇等感受。

   > You've forgot something. Oh, have I?
   > I'd seen Tom Cruise yesterday. Oh, had you?
   > It wasn't a good film. Wasn't it? That's a pity.

3. 附加疑问句和答语疑问句的用法几乎相同，只不过是同一个人说出来的。

> You will stay in touch, won't you? Yes, I will.
> Tom didn't tell you, did he?
> We are late, aren't we?

在祈使句后面使用附加问句就要复杂一点了。来看这个句子：

> Come for dinner with us, won't you? 来和我们一起吃饭吧，来吗？

这个例子的陈述句里并没有出现助动词，那么我们该怎么选择助动词呢？助动词一共只有三个，分情景来用 won't you/will you，can you/could you，shall we。在 let us 句型后面只能用 shall we。

> Let's forget it, shall we?

但是如果这个要求不包括说话的人，就用 will you：

> Let us know your new number, will you?

其他的语境就看意思：

> Get me some tissue, can/could you?

* 特殊的特殊疑问句：我们有的时候需要区分 what 和 which 的区别。比如，What color is her hair? 这个时候就不用 which 原因是没有选择范围。

除此之外，大家还需要熟悉一些特殊的疑问句问法：

> What did you do that for? 你为什么做那件事情？
> What is this button for? 这个按钮是干什么的？
> "I'm going to Shanghai." 我要去上海。"What for？"去干吗？
> Yes, I wrote it. What of it? 那又怎么样 = So what?
> What do you say（= how about）we have a rest? 要不休息会儿？
> How come（= why）you don't know it? 你怎么会不知道呢？

我们下面再来说感叹句，感叹句的构成是用 how 和 what 引导。
公式是：

> How + 形容词 + 主语 + 谓语

比如：How beautiful the girl is!

> How + 副词 + 主语 + 谓语

比如：How nice of you（it is）to help

> How + 主语 + 谓语

用 what 引导就要和名词连用，比如：

> What a terrible mess we are involved in!
> What lousy weather we're having!
> What a lovely view it is!

除了疑问句，感叹句也是表达感受的有力武器！

> 比如见朋友的第一印象可以说：What a beautiful girl she is!
> 收到礼物的第一反应：How considerate you are!
> 遇到不满的一句抱怨：What a people!
> 去旅游景点的第一句感慨：What a paradise this place is!
> 看到日出的激动心情：What a spectacular moment!

关于祈使句在雅思口语中出现，通常只为三个目的：

> 第一个是解释：Let me explain.
> 第二个是拖时间：Let me think
> 第三个是引述：My mother always said："Don't eat that! It's dirty"

常见的祈使句，用 let 引导或 don't 引导的多一些，应用主要引述，提到别人的教诲：

> My mother always told me that：Always bear this in mind! Never trust strangers!
> Do that again and you'll be in trouble.

01 改错：口语挑错

看看下面的句子有错吗？

At that time, my friend came to see me and said, "Hey, Steven. You haven't seen the sunrise from the beach before, have you? Let's go there, together?"

那时候，我朋友来看我并且说：“嘿，史蒂芬，你没见过海边的日出吧，看过吗？要不咱一起去？"

02 大闯关：口语闯关

翻译下列句子。

1) 当我看到礼物的那一瞬间，你能想象我有多开心吗？

2) 太阳逐渐升起，把天空染成红色，海天一色，真美啊！

参考答案

01 反义疑问句的用法，是助动词和代词——对应关系。句子类型有两种，一种是反义的，一种是非反义的。简单来说，就是前肯后否，或前否后肯。所以，正确的说法是：You haven't seen the sunrise from the beach before, have you?

02 1) The moment when I saw the gift, can you imagine how happy I was?

2) The sun popped up, painted the sky into a red color, and linked the sky with the sea. What a beautiful view it is!

写作部分

由于雅思写作属于正式文体，那么语气上疑问和感叹句可以用，但不能多用，一般在议论文中最多一句比较合适，以避免过于强烈的感情色彩。祈使句多用于面对面的交流，在写作部分应该尽可能避免。图表作文中这三种句式都不可以使用。

雅思写作要求语言偏正式（formal）或半正式（semi-formal），要求符合书面语体例，避免过于口语化（informal）。

正式和非正式文体语言风格的区别主要表现在三个方面：书写方式、用词和语境。具体可以参见下表：

	Formal	Informal
书写方式	1. 不可以用缩写 比如：The government will make the decision. 2. 不可以省略从句中的代词 比如：The people who care about the issue should show their attitude. 3. 不可以省略任何句子成分 比如：The final choice depends on the situations.	1. 可以用缩写 比如：The government'll make the decision. 2. 可以省略从句中的代词 比如：The people care about the issue should show their attitude. 3. 可以省略某些句子成分 比如：Depends on the situations.

（续）

	Formal	Informal
用词	长或源于 Latin、Greek（书面化）commence、terminate、endeavor、children、improve personal financial conditions	短或源于 Anglo-Saxon（口语化）start、end、try、kids、earn more money
语境	以第三人称为主（it、they、people、there be、the situation …）；尽量减少第一人称（I、we）；杜绝第二人称（you）或直接交谈的语气（let's …）。	以第一、第二人称为主。

下面来看一下疑问句和感叹句在议论文写作中的运用：

1 疑问句

疑问句可以用于引起下文，以自问自答的方式自然过渡。比如：

> 2012 年 2 月 4 日　年轻人该遵循传统还是特立独行？
>
> It is well known that creativity is the driving power for future development, but how to balance the relationship between it and traditional rules? There are two key points.
>
> 众所周知，创造力是未来发展的驱动力，但如何去平衡它和传统规则之间的关系呢？主要有两个要点。

自问自答的部分就是对下文内容的总起。还可以用反问的形式来反驳对立的观点，比如：

> 2014 年 2 月 15 日　成功靠努力和决心还是金钱、外貌等其他因素？
>
> If good looks and family backgrounds could decide everything, how to explain the success of Abraham Lincoln?
>
> 如果美貌和家庭背景能够决定一切的话，那该如何解释亚伯拉罕·林肯的成功呢？

这一句就是运用举反证的论证方法，用反问来有力地驳斥对立的观点。
反义疑问句还可以用来表示对语意的强调，比如：

> **2014 年 7 月 26 日   个人无力解决环境问题还是必须做出行动？**
>
> Since individual activities made the current environment crisis, the solution must count on everyone's further choices and actions, needn't it?
>
> 既然个体活动造成了环境危局，那其解决必然依赖于每一个体的下一步的选择和行动，不是吗？

需要注意的是，反义疑问句使用时多出现在面对面的谈话中，为了冲淡这种非正式的语境，写作中多用于和环保、犯罪这些问题严重、语气可以更绝对一些、压根不需要回答的问题。

2 感叹句

感叹句一般用于一段说理的结束部分，简短而有力，用来加强结论的冲击力。常见的感叹句可以总结为以下两个公式，请注意二者的不同：

（1） What + 形容词 + 名词（主语）+ 动词！

比如：

> **2012 年 2 月 9 日   跨国公司和全球化的增长对每个人都有利吗？**
>
> What high unemployment rates there would be if local players have to face the cut-throat competition with their powerful international peers without any protection!
>
> 如果地方企业不得不在没有任何保护的情况下面对强大的跨国企业的激烈竞争，那将会有多高的失业率啊！

在实战中使用感叹句时，可以参考上面例句的思路，以假设的方式提出展望。

（2） How + 形容词/副词 + 主语 + 系动词/动词！

上面这句话，还可以这么说：

> How high unemployment rates would be if local players have to face the cut-throat competition with their powerful international peers without any protection!
>
> 如果地方企业不得不在没有任何保护的情况下面对强大的跨国企业的激烈竞争，那失业率将会有多高啊！

你注意到两者的区别了么？注意对比一下句子的构成吧！

练 习

01 改错：写作挑错

看看下面的句子，你能找出错误吗？

2015年6月27日　为什么人们缺乏安全感？如何解决？

None of us are safe if one of us is threatened by corruption or injustice, are we?

如果我们中有人处于腐败或执法不公的威胁下，那我们就没人是安全的，不是吗？

02 大闯关：写作闯关

翻译下面的句子。

2014年3月13日　纸质书会被电子版替代还是会维持其重要性？

没有了线上电子资源的即时更新功能，我们得花多长时间等待最新信息啊！

参考答案

01　陈述部分的主语是 anybody, anyone, everybody, everyone, somebody, someone, nobody, no one, none, neither 时，其反义疑问句的主语需用复数代词 they，所以应该是：

None of us are safe if one of us is threatened by corruption or injustice, are they?

02　What long time we have to wait for the newest information without the instant updating function of online electric resources!

6分 似有还无 常被遗忘的 there be

口语部分

很多人不习惯使用 there be 句型，所以就会经常出现 My hometown have 这样的错误用法。在英语中表达"有"的概念一共有三种：

1) have：表示物理拥有，所属，拥有，所有
2) There be：表示空间拥有，在某个时间空间存在某人某物
3) with 补语，补充说明

像"门上有个把手"就可以说 The door has a handle. 因为这是物理连接的。但是就不能说 The classroom has 4 people. 因为一旦人离开教室，这屋子里就没有人了。所以许多同学喜欢讲 My hometown has many friendly people. 这个用法就不怎么准确了。

There be 是我们接触过的第一个倒装句。

句子的主语其实是 be 后面的词，因为和中文语序不同，刚开始接触的同学会有不适感。就像翻译"树上有只鸟"，起句没有说树，逐字逐句翻译就错了，得倒着来 There is a bird in the tree.

have 什么时候可以和 there be 换用呢？有三种情况：

1. 表示某物体在结构上装备有某东西（物理连接）：

   A door has a beautiful handle.

2. 当 have 表示"包括"时，可以和 there be 换用：

   A week has seven days.

3. 当 have 表示"存在"时：

   This country has few resources.

在使用 There be 句型时，be 动词的使用遵循"就近原则"。试比较一下以下这两句话：

> There are five banks cards, two name cards and an ID card in my wallet.
> There is an ID card, two name cards and five bank cards in my wallet.

如果 There be 后面描述的是钱，不管数额多少，都算单数：

> There is 25 Australian dollars to pay.

当然，系动词也可以换成其他动词，譬如：lie, stand, used to be, seem to be, appear to be 等。

> There appears to have been a horrible terrorist's attack. 似乎发生了一起可怕的恐怖袭击。
> There is likely to be a terrible storm. 可能有一场大暴雨。

当然，也要熟悉一下其他的关于 There be 的句型和常见用法，比如：

> There is no going back. = It's impossible to go back.（表示不可能）
> How many percentages are there?（疑问句）
> There must be some good ideas in your mind.（和情态动词连用）
> There came a scent of perfume.（和动词连用）
> There being a subway station near my house is a great advantage.（There being 名词性结构）
> I expect there to be no fighting about this.（there to be 作宾语）
> There being nothing more to do, we went back to the dormitory.（there being 作状语）

了解了常见句型和用法后，我们要总结 There be 句型常出现的位置，通过使用目的来记住用法。

第一个作用就是列举作用，列举家乡的景点，小区的周边，具体的爱好。如：

> There're lots of restaurants, shops, gyms near where I live.
> There're lots of stuff that I've been interested about, for example.

第二个作用就是表决心，比如在题目为什么选这个专业中，就可以说：

> Once I made my decision, there's no regret.

第三个是感慨时光一去不复返，在所有童年类题目中，都可以说：

> Gone are the days when I was carefree all the time, there is no going back.

第四个是在所有方案解决办法题中，表示一定有更好的办法：

> Although some say it's expensive for the maintenance of antiques, I still think increasing the entrance fee is a stupid idea. There must be a better solution.

第五个是在场景描述中表达空中飘来什么气味：

> There came a scent of street snacks.

第六个是在做比较时表明优势，比如别墅好还是公寓好？

> There being less housework to do is a great advantage to live in an apartment.

第七个是表达期望某个决定判断没有悬念或质疑，比如：

> She is the best ever person I've ever seen in my life. I expect there to be no doubt about it.

练 习

01 改错：口语挑错

看看下面的句子有错吗？

Currently, my life is quite busy. There is no time to do some leisure activities.

现如今，我的生活很忙。没时间休闲。

02 大闯关：口语闯关

翻译下面的句子。

我猜在一周内我最喜欢的是周五，这是一周的最后一天，也是个绝佳的社交时间，每个人都能有个阳光灿烂的心情，因为第二天一早也不用担心早起或者工作。

参考答案

01 There be 句型中很少使用 There have 这个结构，中文讲话习惯会影响英文组句，是大家学习英文语法需要注意的地方。正确的说法是：Currently, I'm very busy in life. There is no time for leisure. 另外这个题中有些小词搭配也需要注意，busy 通常是形容人的，休闲呢也不用 do some leisure，这个搭配不地道。故改成这个说法。

02 Well, I assume the day I adore the most in a week is Friday, which is the end of the week and also a perfect social time when everyone has a sunny day in the mood, considering there're no worries about getting up late and work in the next morning.

写作部分

there be 表示"有"的意思，中文的"有"常见两种含义，一是"拥有"，表示所属关系；另一个是"存在"，表示某地有某物。There be 句型的"有"是后者。这就是一个常见的中式英文错误的出处，混淆了这两个"有"，比如：

> The tree has some apples and a snake.
> 那棵树上有苹果和一条蛇。

这就是中式直译的错误，因为表示的是"某地有某物"，应该是用 there be 句型。

> There are some apples and a snake on the tree.

我把这两种"有"的含义在一句中展示一下：

2011 年 4 月 30 日　同意对外国旅游者收取高于本地人的费用吗？

> There should be a reasonable gap between tax-payers and foreign visitors, because after paying tax and contributing to local construction, citizens have the right to enjoy lower charges.
> 在纳税人和外国游客之间应该有合理的差异，因为在纳税和给地方建设做了贡献之后，公民有权享受更低的收费。

在议论文中，我们可以稍稍加大句子的复杂度，比如：

2015 年 5 月 16 日　应该让学生评价老师吗？

> There is a tight connection between feedbacks and purposefully adjustments in teaching contents and methods.
> 在反馈和目的明确地调整教学内容和方法之间存在着紧密的联系。

这一句的句子主干可以表示为：

> There is a tight connection between 主要论题（名词/动名词词组）and 某一分论点/某一原因（名词/动名词词组）.
> 在讨论主题和某一分论点/原因之间存在着紧密的关联。

逻辑上，这一句可以用来说明分论点，备用选项可以罗列为下表：

有着	紧密的关联	在讨论主题和某一分论点／原因之间
There is	affiliation a causal relationship a close link a strong correlation a tight connection	between 主要论题（名词／动名词词组）and 某一分论点／某一原因（名词／动名词词组）.

在图表作文中，there be 用于对数据、流程或建筑的描述，相对简单，比如在线性图的描述中，我们可以把它和时间状语一起使用：

as for 单线名称, ahead of a 第二种变化（形容词＋名词）over the period between 时间起点 and 时间终点, there was a 第一种变化（形容词＋名词）from 起点数值 in 起点时间.

至于说某一条单线，在从某一时间开始到某一时间结束的第二种变化之前，有从起点时间和数值开始的第一种变化。

这一句式一句话说明了同一条线的前后两种变化，先用时间状语交代第二种变化，再用 there be 句型说明第一种变化。

应用举例：

> As for the consumption of beef, ahead of a dramatic recovery over the period between 1981 and 1983, there was a nosedive from 220 grams in 1979.
> 至于说牛肉的消耗量，在从 1981 开始到 1983 的剧烈反弹之前，有一段从 1979 年 220 克开始的直线下降。

在使用 there be 句型时，需要注意有关单复数的两个特殊点：

1. 就近原则

there be 后面是几个并列的名词或名词词组时，be 的单复数形式要和紧接着出现的第一个名词或名词词组的单复数一致，比如本节所举的第一个例子：

> There are some apples and a snake on the tree.
> There is a snake and some apples on the tree.

最常见的错误就是我们会自作聪明地做加法判断单复数：

> There is a pie chart and a table supplying some information about land degradation.

很明显，这句的错误在于应该用 is，哪怕后面接的总共是两个图表。

2. 如果 there be 后面接的名词是复数，但属于一个整体，be 用单数

比如：

> Although the decline of lamb was much slightly higher than beef after 1988, there was still 50 grams less at the end point.
> 虽然 1988 年以后羊肉的下降远远较牛肉舒缓，在终点还是有 50 克的差距。

01 改错：写作挑错

看看下面的句子，你能找出错误吗？

2014 年 12 月 6 日　高楼型密集城建还是低层型松散城建好？

People usually do not prefer there is a long distance between living and working areas.
人们通常不愿意在生活区和工作区之间存在太远的距离。

02 大闯关：写作闯关

你能翻译出下面的句子吗？注意值得记忆的词组。

2015 年 6 月 13 日　把工商业从大城市迁移到其他地区好吗？

在分散的工业生产和较轻的运输压力之间存在因果关系。

参考答案

01　there be 结构常作以下表示意愿的动词的宾语：expect、hate、intend、like、mean、prefer、want 等，这时候，通常用 there to be，所以正确的表达应该是：

People usually do not prefer there to be a long distance between living and working areas.

02　There is a casual relationship between scattered industrial production and less pressure on the transport system.

怪异的否定结构

口语部分

回答一个问题使用否定结构，雅思口语里常用的说法有哪些？

No, of course not！这是大家最容易想到的句子吧。我们在这一章就来为大家分析一下否定句的用法，以及如何花式表达否定。

首先我们把否定句分成全部否定和部分否定。如果句子中带有含 no, none, nobody, nothing, nowhere, neither, never 这样的词时，我们称之为绝对否定。所以，当有人问你 Do you like dancing? 或者 Do you like history? 时，你可以用很强烈的语气回答。比如：No way！Not a chance！

我们也可以把上面的词都套用一遍感受一下：

> None of my cells contain arty genes.（你喜欢艺术吗？）
> Nobody would believe it if I say yes.（你喜欢跳舞吗？）
> Nothing about sports can arouse my interests.（你喜欢运动吗？）
> I never like it, for even once.
> I like neither of live music or recorded music. I don't like music at all.（你喜欢音乐吗？）

类似的表达全部否定意义的，也可以用 all, often, wholly, always, entirely, each, every 加上否定词 not，比如：

> I can't entirely agree with it. 我不能完全接受。

当然，否定句也有一个更高级的搭配，叫作"双重否定表肯定"：

> I can't say no to it. 我没法不喜欢。（其实就是喜欢）
> It's impossible to say, "I don't like it." 说"我不喜欢。"是不可能的。
> I never think it has nothing to do with me. 我从来没觉得这事儿跟我没关系。

有时候我们想让否定意义更深刻，这个用法叫"追加否定句"：

> I don't have any interests in art, much less dancing. （更别说跳舞了）
> I don't like any kinds of sports, much less swimming. （更别说游泳了）
> It's difficult to understand history, much more the importance of history.

类似的几个用法，都表示更不用说，也可以用 let alone, to say nothing of, not to mention：

> I don't speak English very well, to say nothing of German or French or other languages.
> The young people will go crazy if they are cut off from Internet, let alone cut off from electricity. They will die. 年轻人要是断网就得疯，更别说断电了，他们会死的。

在翻译否定句的时候，要注意"否定结构的转移"，比如"我认为他说的不对"，这句话怎么翻译呢？

> I don't think what he said is right. <u>否定结构习惯放在第一个动词的前面</u>
> 我相信不付出努力我无法成功。
> I don't believe I'll be successful effortlessly.

还有一种比较复杂，要把否定结构从原因状语从句和不定式上拿到主语上。

> 我不是因为听说这里比较有名才来的。
> I didn't come here because I heard this place is famous.
>
> 他似乎不知道这件事。
> He didn't seem to know about it.
>
> 你不能光凭一件事儿就判断这个人好不好。
> You can't judge a person only by one thing he did.

所以，大家看到这里，对句子的主谓宾要特别敏感。知道"光凭"这个词，英语里肯定要用 by，所以是一个介词短语，要么作状语，要么作补语。句子的核心灵魂词还是"判断"，所以这个句子的否定结构，一定要放在核心动词前。

除此之外，我们还应该多了解一些特殊的否定结构，比如：

> no more than = only
> not more than = at most
> no more than three = three only
> not more than three = three at most

no more than 和 not more than 的区别是啥？比较一下下面这两个句子：

> Tom is no smarter than you. 你不聪明，汤姆也不聪明。
> Tom is not smarter than you. 汤姆不比你聪明。
> （俩人都聪明但是程度有差异）

所以这就是 no 和 not 的一个本质区别。no 的感情色彩很强，语气很强。

> I'm no swimmer. 我一点儿也不会游泳。
> I'm not a swimmer. 我会游，但是游的不像专业运动员那么好。
> I'm no philosopher. 哲学我一窍不通。
> I'm not a philosopher. 我懂哲学，但是没到哲学家这个级别。

另外还要注意 not a little 和 not a bit 的区别。

> I was not a little embarrassed. 我尴尬死了。（much embarrassed）
> I was not a bit embarrassed. 我一点儿也不尴尬。（not a bit = not at all）

再来一个比较难的否定式

> no other than/none other than（不是别人正是……）
> The new neighbor of mine is none other than Jacie. 我的新邻居不是别人正是杰西。
> The subject I'm studying is none other than art. 我选的专业不是别的，正是艺术。

但是如果只用 other than 就是另一个意思了，意思是"除了，而不是"。

> I chose English other than physics as my major is because English is a key to the door which turns to everything. It's an international language.

还需要注意几个限制级否定结构的用法。
none the worse/wiser for 表示并不是因为……（某原因）而……（更不行了）"，如：

> Old people are none the happier for they think most friends are dying. 老年人不是因为朋友都去世了才不开心的。
> I'm afraid I'm none the wiser for your explanation. 我恐怕您解释了，我也没明白。

none the less 表示"依然、仍然、不影响、就算这样",如:

> He has faults, none the less he is my best friend in my class.
> 他有缺点,但他依然是我在班里最好的朋友。

雅思口语考试中可能会用到的否定句如下:

> Definitely not! Not a chance! No way!
> I'm afraid I have to say no.
> I can't be dishonest to say I like it, because I truly don't.
> If a pig were to fly up, I would like it.

我们把这种说法叫作含蓄否定式,再给大家几个强烈语气的否定和反语:

> You catch me doing that. 你抓我去做这件事吧!(我自己可不会去)
> You tell me! Of course not! 你说呢?当然不去。
> I shall be hanged if I go there. 我死也不去那儿。
> I'm damned if I say yes. 我要喜欢就坏事儿了。
> Much I care! 我才不在乎呢!
> A fat lot you know! 您知道的真多!
> I'm anything but a scientist. 我什么都行,就是别跟我聊科学。
> He's anything but diligent. 他就是不努力,别的他什么都行。
> It's out of the question. 这绝不可能。
> That's the last thing I'll do. 我不会喜欢的。
> This is above my ability. 我不会做这件事。
> Being concentrated all the time is more than most people can insist on. 不是所有人都能一直坚持高度集中注意力。
> I'm far from being interested. 我一点儿也不感兴趣。

当然也有些句子用否定表示肯定。

> I can't get enough of him. 我看也看不厌,超喜欢。

练 习

01 改错:口语挑错

看看下面的句子有错吗?

Do you like going to museum?
No, I dislike the museum, much less history.
我认为这个说法是不对的
I think this opinion is not right.

02 大闯关：口语闯关

翻译下面的句子。

我更喜欢看电视而不是看报纸，主要因为报纸这东西和大街上的海报也没差多少，上面各种广告和过时的新闻，没有什么价值了。

参考答案

01 第一句其实是个省略句，后半句共用前半句的主语和谓语，那补全后就是 No, I dislike museum, I dislike history much less. 翻译过来就成了：不，我不喜欢博物馆，喜欢历史更多一些。和语境中想要表达的概念不一样了，所以正确说法应是 No, I dislike museum. much more history.
第二句否定结构有放在主句上的习惯，所以正确说法应为：I don't think this opinion is correct.

02 I prefer TV programs other than newspapers, mainly because newspapers which are full of advertisements and news that is out of date is no better than a poster and leaflets on the street, being completely useless.

写作部分

否定很好理解，句子里加 no 和 not 大家也都会，这一部分我只介绍几个特殊点供大家参考。

1 部分否定

当否定涉及表示全体意义的形容词（all, each, every 等）或副词（always, both, entirely, often, wholly 等）时，就是部分否定，主要在议论文中用于说明范围、列举事例，由于雅思议论文是正式文体，要求尽可能客观，世上没有绝对的事物，所以强调部分否定就十分有用。

说明范围的，比如：

2014 年 12 月 20 日　绘画课应该成为必修课吗？

Everyone cannot get the chance to pursue a career in arts or design.
不是每个人都有机会从事和艺术或设计相关的职业。

> **注意** 这里"everyone cannot"不是中文直译"每个人都不能"的意思,后者是全部否定,对应的英文是"no one can"。

说明例外的,比如:

> 2013 年 3 月 9 日　高学历和丰富经验哪个对年轻人发展更重要?

> A man of learning is not always a man of wisdom.
> 有学问的人不总是有智慧的人。

2　双重否定

否定之否定表示肯定,用于加强语气,比如:

> 2011 年 4 月 16 日　为什么很多人在保护环境上不作为?在推动个人行为上能够做什么?

> In environmental protection, nothing is nothing at all.
> 在环境保护上,没有一件事是微不足道的。

3　追加否定

追加否定是指"不……,更不……"这一表意适用于说明递进的否定关系。又有以下的表示方法:

(1) 用"much less"或"still less"来表示,比如:

> 2015 年 3 月 12 日　同意城镇空地植树比建住宅重要吗?

> Considering high land prices and low per capita living housing in cities, planners cannot leave too much space for infrastructure, much less for public green area.
> 考虑到城市的高地价和低人均居住面积,规划者们都不能保证给基础设施预留太多的空间,更别说公共绿地了。

(2) 用 "let alone、not to mention、not to speak of、to say nothing of" 来表示，比如：

> 2015 年 11 月 14 日 B 卷 自然资源高速消耗会导致什么问题？如何解决？
>
> Without sufficient energy supply, humanity cannot maintain the material conditions of survival, not to mention production and social orders.
> 失去了充足的能源供应，人类不能维持生存的基本物质条件，更别提生产和社会秩序了。

4 否定转移

谓语动词是 expect、fancy、feel、guess、imagine、suppose、think 等时，宾语等其他句子成分中的否定词应转移到句子的谓语动词上，叫"否定转移"，比如：I do not think I am a good man. 我觉得我不是个好人。

还有一种更复杂的转移否定，就是把原因状语从句中的否定词也转移到谓语动词上，比如：

> 2014 年 11 月 8 日 犯罪是因为后天原因还是先天原因？
>
> Most adult criminals did not break the law because people are basically evil.
> 大多数成年罪犯违法不是因为人性本恶。

句中中文的否定在原因状语从句中，但英文要把否定词提前。直译的话，中英文很难对应上，这一点我们必须注意。

类似的还有不定式以及介宾短语作定语、状语的转移否定，各举一例：

> 2015 年 8 月 8 日 同意经过监狱改过自新的人是给学生做犯罪教育最好的人选吗？
>
> Some ex-offenders do not seem to have the ability to clearly analyse and accurately introduce laws and regulations.
> 一些前罪犯看起来不具有清楚地分析、准确地介绍法律法规的能力。

> **2015 年 12 月 3 日** 同意面试不可靠，还有其他更好的方式吗？

> We cannot make an overall evaluation for a person's abilities by his or her performance in an interview only.
> 我们不能仅仅通过面试时的表现就对一个人的能力做出全面评价。

5 特殊的否定表达

（1）no other than 不是别的，正是……

> **2016 年 1 月 30 日** 用拥堵税减少交通流量是积极的还是消极的？

> The key point of solutions is none other than reducing traffic volume by compulsorily economic measures.
> 解决的关键不是别的，正是通过强制性的经济手段来减少车流量。

（2）other than 除了……

> **2013 年 5 月 11 日** 为什么大城市生活质量会下降？如何解决？

> The solution cannot be other than reasonably relocating social production and reduce population density.
> 解决办法只能是合理地重新布局社会生产、降低人口密度。

01 改错：写作挑错

看看下面的句子，你能找出错误吗？

2015 年 3 月 14 日 能给小孩最好照顾的是育儿所还是祖父母？

Grand parents are no more professional than caregivers in first aid, safety guiding and intelligence exploration.

在急救、安全护理和智力开发方面，祖父母不像保育员们那样专业。

02 大闯关：写作闯关

你能翻译出下面的句子吗？提示："并不因为……而……"英文的表达是：none + the 形

容词比较级 + for ...。

2011 年 5 月 14 日　应倡导传统价值以应对贪婪和自私的泛滥吗？

人们并不会因为空洞的道德说教而遵纪守法。

参考答案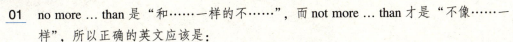

01　no more ... than 是"和……一样的不……"，而 not more ... than 才是"不像……一样"，所以正确的英文应该是：

Grand parents are not more professional than caregivers in first aid, safety guiding and intelligence exploration.

02　People could be none the more law-abiding for an ocean of moralization.

多变的比较结构

口语部分

比较级的使用体现了 critical thinking 的一种下意识。在对比火车和飞机的时候，要下意识把这样的句子 "I like the trains, because it's cheap" 改成："For it's cheaper and more comfortable, I fancy the train more."

大家在这一个知识点中最容易错的就是短单词的比较级形式，常见的错误比如：

> happy 的比较级是 happier
> healthy 的比较级是 healthier
> cosy 的比较级是 cosier
> fat 的比较级是 fatter
> clean 的比较级是 cleaner
> close 的比较是 closer

不容易错的是 younger, bigger, better, higher, taller 这样的常在教科书中出现的词。

同学们会下意识将"更"翻译为"more"，所以这就是我们需要适应的地方。可以把一些常见的容易出错的词总结出来，像看教科书一样多看几遍。除此之外还比较容易错的是 bad 的比较级是 worse，越来越差是 worse and worse，不是 badder and badder。

其实学好比较级，我们需要理解形容词的种类。一种是标明类别的，比如 chemical, final, local, northern 这样的，这些形容词不可以被 quite, very 之类的程度副词修饰，也没有级的变化。而另一种是用来说明事物的特征和性质的，比如 angry, good, heavy, young, 这些词是有级的变化的。

我们在比较级后面加上一个 than, 其后面通常是一个不完整的句子, 名词、代词、短语或者另一个从句, 有的时候还会跟副词或者形容词。有人把这类句子中的 than 看成关系代词, 可以起到主语的作用。如: She is healthier than ever.

怎么学好比较结构呢？在英语中比较两个事物时，基本可以分为三种情况来理解：超越、逊于和相等。

表示超越的结构有三个：

> better than/more than/superior to/还有 than + 关系代词的用法

这三个句子都有"优于、好于、超过"的意思。

> Doing is better than saying. 百说不如一做。
> She did more than she could. 她已经做了她能力范围内的事。
> His IQ is superior to his classmates. 他智商比同学们都高。
> He is a teacher than whom no man ever will be more knowledgeable. 他是一个再博学不过的老师。

表示不如、逊于的结构也有三个：

> inferior to/less than/lighter = less dark

前两个只是上面结构的反义词，第三个例子是反义转换的体现。

> My confidence grows higher and the morale gets less down. 我信心开始更强，斗志也没那么低落了。

在表示"相等"的这个概念里，需要掌握 7 个不同的结构：
（1） as...as... 如……一样
（2） as well as 和……一样
（3） the same as 像……一样
（4） such/so...as... 像……一样
（5） no sooner than 几乎同时
（6） no more than... 就像，不优于
（7） else than/other than 就是……

当然比较结构中还存在一种表示变化的说法（递增或递减），
最常见的是 more and more，如：

> Nowadays, more and more people like to send their kids to art schools.

这个句子也可以用 There is an increasing number of people...来替换。
一个特殊的用法，more than 可以放在动词前，表示"不但……，还有富余"，如：

> This machine can more than take photos.. 这机器不止可以拍照。

当然我们还要学会在比较级前面使用副词修饰语，这种用法叫强势比较结构，比如 far, much, a lot, a little, even, yet, no, still, some, any, considerably, rather, slightly 等。

> He is far better English speaker than me.
> He had become much more mature.
> You look a lot better.
> She is only a little bit taller than her sister.
> She is even lazier than me.
> This is bad, and that is yet worse.
> They'll become richer still.
> The book is no more expensive than that one.
> Would you like some more coffee?
> Is she any better today?

在形容词前加 even, still, yet 用于强调。用 no 强调事物属性是，不比另一件多或少，基本一致。一个类似的用法就是 no less than 或者 no fewer than。

> We won no less than $500 in a competition.（as much as）

疑问句和否定句就要用 any。

> Is that an any faster train?

有的时候 more 还可以当副词用，意为 very。

> I would say a more enjoyable experience that I had recently was when I was trying to buy a pair of new jogging shoes.

至于比较级的否定结构，只要记一个句子就可以了。

> She is more likely a soul mate than a girlfriend to me.
> 与其说她是我的女朋友，不如说是我的灵魂伴侣。

我们在雅思口语的考试中，专门有一类题目被称作对比题。常见的对比有喜欢住大房子还是小房子、你的家乡更适合年轻人还是老年人、你喜欢拥有几个朋友和一群朋友、喜欢现场音乐还是录制音乐、喜欢早上读书还是晚上、喜欢海里游泳还是游泳池里、喜欢公交还是的士、喜欢独立工作还是团队工作、喜欢晴天还是雨天、深色还是浅色、打字还是写字、室内运动还是室外运动。

关于社会现象的趋势就可以说

Nowadays, more and more/an increasing number of people like to…

The big house can accommodate more numbers of people.

大房子可以住更多人。

在强烈对比中就可以用强势比较结构

The atmosphere in the concert is far more vivid than that when you listen to on radios or MP3s.

It's a lot better.

在表示中立的时候可以说

The outside activities are no more better than the indoor activities to me.

除此之外，还可以使用 to the contrary, on the contrast, comparatively speaking 这样的连接词，来表示比较。

01 改错：口语挑错

看看下面的句子有错吗？

Do you prefer to live in a house or flat?

I prefer to live in a flat, because a flat can more than save money, besides a flat has less housework to do.

02 大闯关：口语闯关

翻译下列句子。

Do you prefer sending a text message or making phone calls?

我喜欢发短信，短信的附加功能比打电话多很多，比如表情、附件、照片。更重要的是，你可以在说话之前反复推敲揣摩你的语言，也不用担心打扰到对方。现在，电话功能已经越来越不常用了。如果你看我近几年的话费单，你会发现近几年花在打电话上的话费一直在降低。这是个强有力的证据。

参考答案

01　这是许多雅思考生在回答这类问题时经常会犯的一个错误，原句的意思想表达住公寓不止能省钱，还不用做太多家务。但是错在搞错了主语，flat 不能 save money, living in the flat 这个行为才能省钱。另外, flat 也不能 has less housework, 主语得是"我": 我不需要做太多家务, I don't need to do too much housework. 或者主语应该是 there be 的倒装结构, 家务活不多: there's less housework to do.

02　I prefer text message, for its functions are far more diverse than the functions of phone calls. For example, emojia, attachments, and photos. More importantly, you can think twice before sending it out without worrying about interrupting something important (disturbing the other party). Now, the phone function has been more and more uncommonly used. If you see my phone bill, you'll find the money I spent on calls plummets over the years. That's a solid proof.

写 作 部 分

比较结构用于对比, 在议论文和图表作文中都十分重要。根据比较双方的情况, 我们分成下面几组:

1　同级比较

就是比较的双方是一样的（as…as…, the same…as…）或者不一样的（not as…as…）, 不存在"更……"的关系。比如:

> 2015 年 9 月 3 日　犯罪是可以预防的还是让人无计可施的?
>
> After the community realizes the importance of education and social support, crime control and prevention would be not as difficult as people think.
> 在社区认识到教育和社会支持的重要性之后, 犯罪控制和预防将不会像人们想象的那么难。

图表作文中也可以使用:

> The proportion in Sweden displayed the same changes as the one in USA.
> 瑞典的比例展示了和美国一样的变化。

2　大范围比较

当比较的范围包含了大于等于三个对象时, 需要注意介词的使用, 地域范围用 in, 其他用 of, 即: the most…in/of…, 比如:

如何让文章的句子种类不再单一

> **2013年6月8日　鼓励消费是好还是坏？**

> Of all kinds of economic policies, stimulating consumption is not the only one ignoring the balance between supply and needs.
> 在所有种类的经济政策中，刺激消费并不是唯一忽略了供需关系的。
>
> Over-grazing became the most important reason for land degradation in the world with 35%.
> 过度放牧凭借着35%的数据成为了在世界范围内最重要的土地退化原因。

3　不同级比较 more...than... 的特殊词性

than 在这里可以充当关系代词，相当于 than what...，比如：

> **2014年1月9日　为解决交通阻塞提供免费公共交通是最好的选择吗？**

> Four decades ago, in the case of traffic reconstruction in Tokyo, the public transport system built by subways and buses was more effective than was expected.
> 四十年前，在东京交通重建的案例中，由地铁和公交车搭建的公共交通体系比预计的要有效得多。

4　特殊表达

（1）more than...和 more...than...

more than..."不仅……"，more...than..."不是……而是……"。各举一例。

> **2013年3月14日　同意建筑物的功能比外观重要吗？**

> In creating higher market value, improving the appearance of a building is more than an adjunctive means.
> 在创造更高的市场价值这一方面，改善建筑物的外观不仅仅是一种辅助性手段。

> **2012年8月4日　24小时电视播出是积极的还是消极的？**

> Most information transmitted by 24 hours TV programs seems more a waste

139

> of resource than a useful transmission, because they are high similarity, fatiguing and depressing.
> 　　24 小时电视节目播出的大部分信息不是一种有用的传播而是一种资源的浪费，因为它们高度重复，令人疲惫、沮丧。

more than 还有"多于"的意思，用于图表作文中；倍数和分数表达也属于特殊的不同级比较，在介词那一节已经介绍过了，也用于图表作文，大家必须掌握。

(2) no more...than... 和 not more...than...

no more...than... "两者都不……"，not more...than... "都……，……更……"。
注意下面这两句话的区别：

2013 年 2 月 16 日　处罚犯罪首选监狱还是社会服务等其他方式？

> Without necessary social support and behavior correction, public services are no more effective than imprisonment in reforming criminals.
> 　　没有必要的社会支持和行为纠正，社区服务和监禁在改造罪犯上一样无效。
> Public service is not more effective than imprisonment in achieving warning effects.
> 　　在更好的警告效应方面，社区服务和监禁都有效，但监禁更有效。

在图表作文中，no more than 是"仅仅"的意思，not more than 是"不超过"的意思。

> 　The time spent on mobiles was no more than 45 billion minutes at the beginning.
> 　　花在手机上的时间一开始仅仅有 450 亿分钟。(刚好 450 亿)
> 　The time spent on mobiles was not more than 45 billion minutes at the beginning.
> 　　花在手机上的时间一开始不超过 450 亿分钟。(少于 450 亿)

(3) rather than... 和 would rather than...

rather than... "而不是……"，would rather than... "宁愿……而不愿……"。比如：

2011 年 2 月 26 日　国家该努力实现食品生产的自力更生吗？

> Food supply is a national security issue rather than a pure marketing issue.
> 　　食品供给是个国家安全问题而不是单纯的市场问题。

2013 年 11 月 16 日　某些语言流行而另一些少人用是积极的还是消极的？

Most young people in developing countries would rather practice English than speak local language all the time for personal future development.
大多数发展中国家的年轻人为了个人未来发展宁愿练习英文也不愿终日只说方言。

练　习

01　改错：写作挑错

看看下面的句子，你能找出错误吗？

2012 年 1 月 12 日　政府为每座城镇兴建图书馆是必需的还是浪费钱？

In creating a quiet environment and providing convenient facilities, real libraries are superior than online ones.

在创造安静环境和提供便利的设施方面，实体图书馆远胜于线上图书馆。

02　大闯关：写作闯关

你能翻译出面的句子吗？

注意：no less than：多达……；not less than：不少于……。

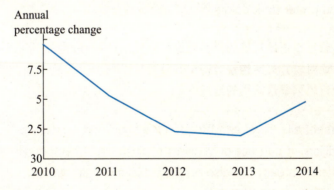

每年的变化总是不少于 2%。

参考答案

01　以 -ior 结尾的形容词（inferior, superior；minor, major；junior, senior 等）在表示比较叶后接 to 而不是 than，那正确的就应该是：

In creating a quiet environment and providing convenient facilities, real libraries are superior to online ones.

02　Annual change was always not less than 2%.

出彩的并列结构

口语部分

雅思口语考试涉及大量列举题目，比如你喜欢什么类型的音乐？周末喜欢做什么？旅游有哪些好处？我们把这些特殊疑问句开头的问题叫作列举题。那答题的时候，要有很多不同的答案，应该怎样讲才能逻辑清晰呢？

列举题：

> What are the benefits of traveling?
> What good qualities do you think good teachers should have?

对比题：

> Do you prefer fashionable hats or comfortable hats?
> Do you prefer dark colors or light colors?

这些问题是雅思口语最常见的需要用到列举技能的题目。我们回答这些问题的时候，需要做大量列举。这时候并列结构就显得十分重要！

下面是几个逻辑列举最常用的连接词：

> **For first of all**, travel can broaden the mind and enrich your knowledge.
> **In addition**, it can not only give people a great opportunity to try different food in different areas, but also drink the historical atmosphere, and experience the local culture and customs.
> **What's more**, traveling provides a great time for people to think and reflect on life.
> **More importantly**, you may meet more new friends during the trip and gain more useful information.

学好并列结构，最重要的是学好多样的连接词。比如：not only...but also...（不但……而且……）；both...and...；either...or...（要么……要么……）；neither...nor...，not...but...等。

> The outside activities can provide both exercise and social opportunities. （说好处）
>
> Going to the museum can not only extend the horizon, but also is a way of relaxation.
>
> I don't have a preference. I can either wear fashionable or comfortable hats. （做选择）
>
> In this information age, honestly, neither TV programs nor newspapers can arouse my interest.

我们在学习并列结构时需要区分两个概念：

1. 并列连词
2. 连接副词

并列连词保持两个分句意义上的对比、转折或者递进。而连接副词在结构上更松散一些，强调逻辑，不强调形式。比如 as well as；as much as；rather than；more than；no less than 等。比如以上我们答列举题的这些句子，看起来是两个句子，但其实也是连接副词连接的并列结构。这是口语考试中最常用到的并列结构！

这样的副词或词组还有：consequently, hence, so, therefore, thus, furthermore, what's more, however, nevertheless, nonetheless, still, also, besides, furthermore, in addition, moreover 等。

比如：

> I know it's very hard. Still, I wanna try. 我知道很难，但是我想试试。
>
> I don't like dancing at all; furthermore, I have no time. 我一点也不喜欢跳舞，再说，我也没时间。

了解了连接副词的概念，在你的定义里，并列结构的意义就应该更广泛一些了。

当然要学好并列结构中最需要注意的是，并列句两端内容要在逻辑上相关，词性上一致。

比如说在下面这个例子里，描述收到礼物后的心情复杂。

> If you saw my facial expression, you would know it was mixed with surprise, happiness and being moved.
>
> 如果你看到我的表情，你就会知道我脸上充满惊喜、幸福和感动。

and 前后连接的词都是名词，所以"感动"就要变成 being moved 这种名词结构。但是注意，有些同学在用 and 连接两个并列句时，需要了解 and 前后可以使用的词性。多数人会对形容词和动词短语的并列句比较熟悉：

> Fruit is full of water and rich in nutrition. 水果富含水和营养。
> I looked into her eyes and she looked down to the floor. 我看着她的眼睛，她低头看着地板。（道歉经历）

有哪些是大家不太熟练的并列结构呢？

1. and 介词短语之间的并列

This man walked across the street and into the underground station.

2. and 不定式之间的并列

I may decide to go abroad or to continue my job.

3. or else 表示选择

You could come and pick it up now or else we could leave it till the morning. 你可以现在来拿或者我们明天再说。（别人送的礼物）

4. yet 表示对比

She is a strange girl, yet you can't help liking her.

还有一个冠词重复原则，如果 and 前后连接的两个名词是同一个人或物，要重复不定冠词，但不重复定冠词，举个例子：

> My father is a teacher, a mentor and a friend to me. （常伴的家人）
> He is the commander and man in charge in our family.

01 改错：口语挑错

看看下面的句子有错吗？

Do you like history?

No, when I was in middle school, I never performed well in history tests. I felt really not confident. I haven't even had a second to like it.

02 大闯关：口语闯关

在经历题中，我们经常要描述一个人的连续动作，试着翻译下面的句子。

当时，我在机场看到一个老外，手里提个包，穿着风衣，系着红围巾，走进了大门，穿过了机场大厅，又到了咨询台，说了几句话以后感觉有些语言不通。

参考答案

01 连续性逻辑中一定需要连接词，正如这一题，成绩不好是不自信的原因，没自信造成不喜欢。所以，可以用这一章我们学习到的连接副词的知识来做一个改造。

No, when I was in middle school, by then, I never performed well in history tests, consequently/hence/there/thus, I felt really not confident, and therefore I haven't even got a second to like it.

02 At that time, I saw a foreigner at the airport, with a briefcase in hand, wearing a windcoat, as well as a red scarf, walking into the airport, across the hall and to the reception desk. He seemed to encounter some obstacles after saying some words.

写作部分

并列结构包括了以下几种：

1 平行关系

(1) …, …and…

这一种用法很简单，唯一要注意的就是，and 如果接并列的句子，大多数情况用句号和前一句隔开，单独的主谓宾结构一般独立成句。

> 2011 年 10 月 22 日　奥林匹克是盛事还是浪费？
>
> At local level, the spending creates employment and increases wages in related industries, expands local tax revenues and increases demand for related goods and services.
>
> 在地方层面上，这些花销可以在相关产业里创造就业、提升工资、增加地方税收、刺激对相关产品和服务的需求。

(2) both…and…

这种用法强调的是二者并列，前后的词性必须一致、而且不能是句子，比如：

> 2014 年 7 月 26 日　个人无力解决环境问题还是必须做出行动？
>
> Actions should be taken in both national level and in individual daily life.
>
> 必须在国家层面和个人日常生活中同时采取行动。

2 递进关系

(1) not only...but also...

这里 but also 后面是强调的重点，比如：

> 2012 年 4 月 28 日　同意停止杀戮动物获得产品吗？

> The increase of the number of some animals, such as the ferret, depends on not only protection but also domestication and artificial breeding for commercial purpose.
>
> 一些动物比如雪雕数量的增加不仅取决于保护，而且依赖于为了商业目的的驯养和人工繁育。

同时，not only...but also...还有个倒装用法，我们放在半倒装那一节再介绍。

(2) ...as well as...

前面是强调的重点，比如：

> 2016 年 4 月 21 日　如何解决增加的消费品生产对环境的危害？

> The priorities of final solutions are upgrading production techniques as well as adopting degradable materials.
>
> 最终解决的优先项是和采用可降解材料同样重要的升级生产技术。

3 选择关系

(1) neither...nor...

"既不……也不……"的意思，比如：

> 2011 年 8 月 27 日　为什么人们喜欢外国电影胜于本土电影？政府是否该为本土电影提供财务支持？

> Except view experience, most audiences care for neither producing countries nor ticket prices.
>
> 除了观影体验，大多数观众既不关心出品国、也不关心票价。

（2）…or…；either…or…

or 的用法和 and 的用法一样简单，但需要注意的是，表达否定意义时，常用 or 来连接，而不是 and，比如：

> 2015 年 2 月 12 日　同意提高最小驾驶年龄以促进驾驶安全吗？
>
> Due to immature physical and psychological conditions, anyone younger than 16 years old should never be permitted to operate heavy machinery or drive motor vehicles.
> 由于不成熟的身心状态，任何小于 16 岁的年轻人都不应该被允许操作重型机械或驾驶机动车辆。

either…or…是 or 的加强版，表示"要么……要么……"，可以用来连接句子，比如：

> 2015 年 4 月 11 日　年长者和年轻人竞争职位会导致什么问题？如何解决？
>
> Either a family starves or a young man lose the chance to start career life.
> 要么一个家庭挨饿，要么一个年轻人失去开始职业生涯的机会。

4　转折关系

but（但是）、while（却）、whereas（反之）、yet（然而）等连接反转的内容，比如：

> 2011 年 4 月 30 日　该对外国游客收取高于本地人的费用吗？
>
> Slightly higher admission fees would not impact overseas tourists' enthusiasm, but it would be an extra help to improve travelling spots' financial conditions.
> 稍高的门票不会影响海外游客的热情，但对改善景点的财务状况而言却是额外的帮助。

转折结构也常见于图表作文，用于数据或趋势比较，提供两个句式供大家参考：

> As revealed by the graph, there was / were 特殊变化（名词）in 某一单项 during the period, while others showed 大多数的变化（名词）.
> 如图所示，某一单项展示了某种与众不同变化，同时其余的项目均显示了另外的变化。

比如：

As revealed by the graph, there was a stable increase in the quality by pipeline during

the period, while others showed fluctuations.
如图所示，管道运输的量在区间内展示了稳定的上升，同时其余的项目均显示了波动。

> The one displayed the largest number was 数值最大的单项 with 最大的数值, whereas the smallest one, 最小的数值, showed in 数值最小的单项. The others distributed between the two extremes.
> 展示最大数字的是拥有某一数值的某一单项，而最小的数字，某一数值，出现在某一单项。其余的数值散布其间。

比如：
◇ The one displayed the most proportion was Turkey with nearly one third, whereas the smallest one, only a half of the former, showed in Sweden. The others distributed between the two extremes.
展示最大比例的是接近三分之一的土耳其，而最小的比例，只有前者的一半，出现在瑞典。其余的散布于两者之间。

练 习

01 改错：写作挑错

看看下面的句子，你能找出错误吗？

2013 年 7 月 27 日 保护古建筑的钱应用于建设新房屋和道路吗？

Either the constructure of infrastructures or the development of real estate should not become the excuse for cultural destruction.
基础设施的建设和房地产的发展都不应该成为文化破坏的借口。

02 大闯关：写作闯关

你能翻译出下面的句子吗？提示：nor 用于否定含义之后、表示否定也适用于之后的内容时，需要倒装。

2016 年 1 月 9 日 A 卷 政府该为理科而不是其他科目投入更多吗？

如果关系到社会公正的社会科学不该得到资助，那限制在技术层面的自然科学也不该得到。

参考答案

01 并列项目的否定形式不用"either ... or ... not ..."，而用"neither ... nor ..."，所以应改为：

Neither the constructure of infrastructures nor the development of real estate should become the excuse for cultural destruction.

02 If social science about justice should not get financial support, then nor should natural science which is limited in technical level.

如何只用一句话
提升全文的语法格调

常被忽略的部分倒装

口语部分

提到倒装句这三个字，很多人可能很难把它和口语应用联系起来。我们在什么时候才会讲倒装句呢？其实 there be 就是一个倒装结构，there 没有什么实际意思，be 是谓语动词，后面出现的才是主语。比如：

> There was a drop in the temperature.
> 正常的语序应该是：A drop in the temperature was there.（最近降温了）

倒装体现了英国人特别重视逻辑结构的特点，先说逻辑的，再说内容的。大家最熟悉的倒装结构应该是 here/there 开头的句子结构，如：

> Here comes our headmaster. 我们校长来了。

但是这个结构有一个要求，就是主语不能是代词，如果是代词就不能完全倒装，如：

> Here it is.
> Here you are.
> Here is your key.

除此之外，完全倒装的第二个常见用法是承上启下，如：

> He is the member of the student's union and so am I.

在口语中特别适合用于讲你和另外一人的共同之处。比如聊到共同爱好：

> She is the fan of the Big Bang and so am I.

再比如聊到第一天上学见面的场景：

> She went to school 1 hour before class and so did I, so we met and talked with each other.

在这个结构中，只要用对系动词和助动词就可以了。当然否定结构中要把 so 换成 neither。

> He is not a fan of history class and neither am I. So, one day we skipped the class and played basketball together.

一个比较类似的倒装是由句首为 now, then, soon 或 thus 的句子，如：

> Now comes your turn.
> Soon came another upsurge of the revolution.
> Thus began the game.

总的来说，在英文中完全倒装分为 4 种。除了以上所说的承上启下的作用，我们也可以先从句子结构来理解一下倒装。

上面说到的是副词的倒装。还有分词和不定式的倒装，如：

> Buried in the sands was an ancient village.（污染之地）
> Gone are the days when I was carefree every day.（童年趣事）
> Standing beside him was his wife.（同朋友吃饭）
> Facing the house is a beautiful lake.（未来的房子）
> To be carefully considered are the following questions.（分析问题）

倒装的主要目的是为了强调，但也为了保持句子平衡或者上下文衔接紧密。

状语、表语和主语补语也可以提句首倒装，常出现在描述中：

> Among these people was his friend Jim.
> By the window sat a young man with a magazine in his hand.
> On your left is the river.
> Above is what I can think of about the benefits of traveling.
> Below is the blue ocean.

还有一种用法比较少见，是地点副词 away, down, in, off, out, over, round, up 这些词放在句首，后面用倒装。这种倒装的目的是为了渲染气氛，使描写更生动。如：

> Down came the rain and up went the umbrellas.
> Round and round flew the plane.
> The door opened and in came Mr. Smith.

英语修辞有一个尾重头轻的感觉，最复杂的结构往往都在句尾。所以如果句子特别复杂，常规套路：Millions of visitors came to this historical place with interests and curiosity to watch how amazing the Terra Cotta warriors are.

修辞套路：To this historical place came millions of visitors with interest and curiosity to watch how amazing the Terra Cotta warriors are.

再比如说在环境法这个描述里，

常规套路：Some rubbish just lay on the ground, beside the rubbish bins.

修辞套路：On the ground lay some rubbish, just beside the rubbish bins.

这个用法是状语或表语提到句首的倒装。

总的来说，完全倒装有 4 个公式：副词、地点副词、状语、主语补语、不定式和分词。倒装结构要多套用在实际的人物描述、地点描述中，以便更好地掌握。

以表语开头的句子，有时为了把较长的主语放在后面，需要将表语和谓语都提到主语前。

> Such would be my home in the future.（未来想住的房子）

不过也要分清楚什么是前置，什么是倒装。

除了状语外，英语的词序是相对固定的。不过有时候出于修辞原因，也会把宾语、主语补语或宾语补语前置，并且不引起倒装。如：

> A very good lesson I had at that time.（忘事儿）
> A horrible mess they've made it.（童年趣事）
> Whether she really feels sorry I don't quite know.（道歉经历）
> A very reliable person he is.（最好的朋友）
> A shame I call it.

但是以 not a single, nothing, nobody, no one, many 引出的宾语前置就得用倒装结构，如：

> Not a single word did Mary say the whole evening.

01 改错：口语挑错

看看下面的句子有错吗？

Do you think people should make most of the weekends?

Well, definitely. So important is the weekend to people that many complain about forcing employees to work over-time cruel. It has become more and more precious, because people are having anxiety today in weekends especially when the errands to run are over occupied.

02 大闯关：口语闯关

试着翻译下面的句子。

人物描述：第一次见到她是在一次面试时，她坐在桌子对面看着我，手里边握着笔，脸上戴着粉色眼镜，嘴里边声音一出来，我就被迷倒了。

参考答案

01 刚开始，学着使用倒装句的同学往往会感到恐惧。因为句子一倒装语序就乱了。但英语的句型还是不离主谓宾，这句话的基本意思是"周末太重要了"，后面的 that 可以翻译为"以至于"，合起来是 so that 结果状语从句的用法，但是把 so 提前然后倒装，起到了强调感受的作用。所以后半句翻译就可以了，So important the weekend is to people that many complain about forcing employees to work over-time is cruel.

02 The first time I met her was in an interview, she was sitting in front of me by the table, in her hand was a pen, on her face was a pair of glasses, out of mouth came out her voice, I was completely enchanted.

写作部分

完全倒装就是句子的每一个主要成分的位置都和正常语序相反。这一节还是列举几个可以在实战中应用的用法供大家参考。

1 so … that …；such…that…

这两个词组是"如此……以至于……"的意思，so 后面的半句可以完全倒装，我们把用法公式化，就是：

> So ＋ 形容词 ＋ be ＋ 主语 that 主语 ＋ 谓语 ＋ 宾语.
> Such ＋ 形容词 ＋ 宾语 ＋ be ＋ 主语 that 主语 ＋ 谓语 ＋ 宾语.

具体的讲解我们后面在结果状语从句中还会涉及，这里只简单举个例子。比如：

> 2014 年 4 月 12 日　教育的意义在于使人对社会有用还是实现个人目标？

> 如果论点是"Social environment decides education effects."：
> So important is individual social attributes that the future of everyone is molded by the whole socioeconomic level.
> 个人的社会属性是如此重要，以至每个人的前途都被整体社会经济水平所决定。

2 Now is the time to …

是"是时候去做……了"的意思,正常语序是:The time to … is now. 常用于提出解决方式的建议或者发出号召,比如:

> 2014 年 9 月 6 日　城市快速发展给年轻人带来的问题?如何解决?

> Now is the time to correct the abnormal development of the real-estate industry to release the financial pressure from mortgage.
> 是时候去纠正畸形发展的房地产业以减轻来自房贷的经济压力了。

3 方位状语位于居首

地点和方向状语可以提前到句首,全句用倒装,常见的副词包括:away、back、down、in、of、off、out、over、round、up 等。比如:

> 2014 年 2 月 22 日　国家为孩子支付教育费用的好处多于坏处吗?

> Out of every penny spent on the education for next generation comes the bright future of the whole country.
> 整个国家的光明前途来自于在下一代教育上花的每一分钱。

这一用法在图表作文中也常用,特别是地图题,比如:

> In the north part of Stewart district sits a hotel.
> 一个旅馆坐落于斯图尔特区的北部。

4 表示强调:表语 + 系动词 + 主语

主系表结构强调表语时可以完全倒装,比如:

> 2016 年 6 月 4 日　训练年轻人竞争而不是合作的好处大于坏处吗?

> Critical to everyone's future development is having high integrity and healthy winning attitude.
> 高度合作精神和竞争精神对每一个人的未来发展都是关键的。

5 长主语后移

主语过长（包括包含过长的定语或定语从句的情况），而宾语或表语比较简单时，可以采用完全倒装。比如：

> 2012 年 10 月 20 日　便捷的国际旅行是积极的还是消极的？

> Intolerable is the pressure that extraneous foreigners and visitors put on local service industry, including transport, food and accommodation.
> 过多的外国人和游客给包括交通、食宿在内的地方服务业带来的压力是不堪承受的。

6 非谓语动词提前

为了表示对动作或状态的强调，现在分词、过去分词、动词不定式这些非谓动词可以提前到句首，全句用倒装，比如：

> 2011 年 7 月 28 日　为什么女性倾向学文而男性倾向学理？该改变它吗？

> To be completely analyzed are the influences of hormone and traditional social training.
> 荷尔蒙和传统的社会训练的影响要全面分析。

01 改错：写作挑错

看看下面的句子，你能找出错误吗？

Then, a year of a nosedive from 0.85 to 0.35 followed.
然后是紧跟着一年的从 0.85 到 0.35 的突降。

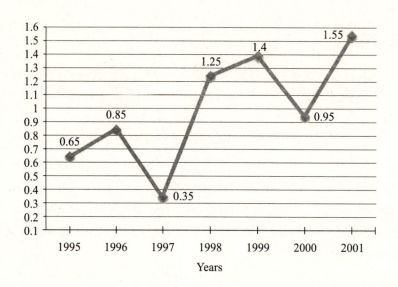

02 大闯关:写作闯关

你能随手翻译出下面的句子吗?注意:完全倒装时要小心主谓单复数要一致。

2012年6月16日　为什么人们不认识邻居?如何解决?

社区更少的公共空间和线上社交流行的结果就是这样。

参考答案

01　now、then、thus 位于句首时,句子要完全倒装,常见的谓语动词有:be, begin, come, end, follow 等。

Then followed a year of a nosedive from 0.85 to 0.35.

02　Such are the results of less public space in community and the popularization of online communication.

被完全遗忘的完全倒装

口语部分

什么叫部分倒装？部分倒装是为了修辞目的把助动词或者情态动词丢前边，动词自己不变位置。

> Do you prefer eating at home or restaurant?

想表达"我很少出去吃饭"，用英文可以这样说：I seldom go out eating. 这是正常语序。Seldom do I go out eating. 是倒装语气，强调 seldom，表达真的很少出去吃。

观察一下这个句子的用法，是不是表否定的词放最前面，助动词或情态动词放在动词前面，动词不变位置。

公式一：否定副词位于句首时句子用倒装：never、seldom、rarely、little、hardly、scarcely、no sooner、no longer、nowhere 等。

> Never shall I do a job without job satisfaction.（要工作满意度还是高薪）
> Seldom do I travel with friends.（一个人旅行还是和别人一起旅行）
> Hardly do I have time to have fun, let alone dancing.（是否喜欢跳舞）

当然，口语中还有一个特别常见的用倒装结构的词就是 not until，它位于句首也要用倒装结构，如：

> Not until I went back home did I realize how worse the situation was. 没到回家我都没意识到事态有多严重。（忘事儿经历）
> Not until Steven taught me did I know how to speak English naturally and authentically. 直到史蒂芬教我，我才知道该怎么把口语说得地道、正宗。

之前我一直鼓励大家用使用目的来记忆语法。所以我们来一起用表达感情的方式记住这句话，表达做某事特别后悔：

> At that time, I was thinking: "Under no circumstances will I ever dance in front of people any more."（否定词在前，后面使用部分倒装结构）

但有一个短语是特例，就是 in no time，这个短语放句首，句子不使用倒装。

> In no time, I figured this problem out. 没过多久我就想明白了。

还有一个场景大家可以想象一下，在一个惊喜的场景中，表达直到他看到礼物，他才忽然明白他的朋友想要给他一个惊喜。我们在这个句子里想要强调时间状语，怎么讲对这个句子呢？

> Only when he saw the gift did he realise that his friends prepared a big surprise for him.

或者在谈未来的题目中，表达我只有出了国才有机会去做这些事，强调条件的话，怎么讲对这个句子呢？模仿一下上面的句子。

> Only if I successfully go abroad will I have the chance to do all of these things.

所以这里我们来记一个关于时间状语提前的第二个部分倒装公式。

公式二： Only +状语位于句首的倒装（often/many a time 表示时间的状语也可以）

> Only then did he realize that was wrong. 直到那时他才意识到错了。
> Only when returned home did he realize what has happened.
> 直到到家他才意识到发生了什么。
> Only by begging was he able to make himself survived. 只有靠乞讨，他才能活下来。
> Often did I warn him not to do so. 我经常警告他别这么干。
> Many a time has David given me advice. 大卫经常给我建议。

在所有表达感受的句子里，一定不能忘了 so that 这个短语。

在口语考试中，经常有对人、地点、物品的感叹。有时候为了强调效果，会把 so 后面的部分提前，而后面就要使用部分倒装。

> A concert is so vivid and interactive that we all have to stand up, wave our hands and scream.

这句话要是想强调感受，就可以使用倒装：

> So vivid and interactive is a concert that we all have to stand up, wave our hands and scream.

公式三：so + *adj.* / *adv.* 位于句首的倒装

> So cold was the weather that we had to stay at home. 天气冷得只能待在家里。
>
> So fast does light travel that we can hardly imagine its speed. 光速快到我们难以想象其速度。

除此之外，not only 放句首，句子需要倒装。

公式四：not only 倒装，but also 不倒装

> Not only is he a teacher, but he is also a guitarist. 他不但是个老师还是个吉他手。
>
> Not only did he speak English more quickly, but he spoke more beautifully. 他的英语讲得又快又优美。

公式五：虚拟条件句的省略与倒装

> Had you come last night, you would have seen him. 你要是昨晚来了，就能见到他了。
>
> Should you require anything, leave me a line. 要是需要我做什么，就留个言。
>
> Were it not for your help, I would still be a stupid boy. 要不是你帮我，我现在还是个二愣子。
>
> Had I money, I would buy it. 要是我有钱，我就买了。

所以，你记住了吗？否定词、Only、so that、not only, but also、虚拟条件句 5 个部分倒装结构。

01 改错：口语挑错

看看下面的句子有错吗？

（天气改变计划）Unfortunately, on the next day, it started to rain. My friend found it first and I was then woken up by her phone. Not until that time I didn't realized why her phone was coming this early.

很不幸，第二天，开始下雨了。我朋友先发现的，然后我被她的电话吵醒了，在这之前我也不知道她为什么这么早打电话来。

02 大闯关：口语闯关

翻译下列句子。

我这辈子都不会再和别人一起旅游了。

我现在很少运动了。

参考答案

01 not until 作部分倒装句，提前到句首时，助动词要和主语倒装。所以正确说法应该为：Not until that time did I realize why her phone was coming.

02 No longer will I go traveling with other people again.
Seldom do I play sports now.

写 作 部 分

使用部分倒装好处很多，如果在考场上出其不意使用一下就可以收到意想不到的效果。下面我们来认识几个好用的部分倒装句式：

1 only 位于句首

（1）only by ... can sb. ...

这一句是比较简单的倒装句式，情态动词 can 提前。

Only by / through ...（名词 / 动名词词组）can / could sb. ...（动词词组）.

只有通过……某人/某事才能……

比如：

> 2016年1月30日 通过拥堵税减少交通流量是积极的还是消极的？
>
> In fact, only by upgrading transport facilities and strengthening traffic control rather than taxing in disguise can the causes of congestion be solved fundamentally.
>
> 事实上，只有通过升级交通设施和加强交通管理，而不是变相收费，才能从根本上解决拥堵问题。

逻辑上，这一句既可用于论据分析，也可用于举例子。上面是论据分析，下面我们再看个举例子体会一下用法：

> **2016年6月18日　同意教育孩子良好的行为习惯也是学校的责任吗？**
>
> Only through the observation of teaching staff could we get an objective appraisal of a child's real characters in daily life.
> 只有通过教职员工的观察，我们才能对一个孩子在日常生活中的真正品行做出客观评价。

(2) Only + 时间状语（从句）/ 条件状语（从句）+ 半倒装句子

时间状语从句：

> **2014年3月8日　同意全职学习要持续到18岁吗？**
>
> Only when the number of labors with high quality could social production develop accelerately.
> 只有当高素质的劳动力的数量得到保证之后，社会生产才会加速发展。

条件状语从句：

> **2015年7月23日　健康还是其他重要领域该优先得到政府投资？**
>
> Only if public health and the right to survival have been fully guaranteed could social members start to pursue a higher quality of life.
> 只有当公众健康和生存权得到了充分的保证，社会成员才能开始追求更高的生活质量。

2　否定副词提前至句首表示强调

适用这一点的常见否定词包括：at no time、at no point、by no means、few、hardly、in no case、in no sense、in no way、little、merely、never、no more、no longer、no sooner、nor、not、not until、nowhere、on no condition、rarely、scarcely、seldom 等。当它们位于句首时，其后用部分倒装。

2012 年 4 月 21 日　计划未来不如专注当前吗？

Never should a man desiring success take blind action without clear aims and practical plan.

一个渴望成功的人永远也不应该在没有明确目标和可行计划时盲目行动。

为了更容易掌握还是将这句公式化：

否定副词 + 情态动词／助动词 + 主语 + 谓语／系动词 + (宾语)。

3　neither、nor 或 so 位于句首

在这种情况下，neither、nor 是"也不"的意思；so 是"也"的意思。比如：

2014 年 2 月 15 日　成功靠努力和决心还是金钱外貌等其他因素？

It is not money, nor is it good looks that could amplify a person's talent.

扩展一个人才能的，既不是金钱也不是美貌。

2015 年 6 月 27 日　缺乏安全感的原因和解决方法

The authorities should advertise real security conditions to rebuild public confidence, and so should non-government organizations.

当局应该宣传真实的治安状况以重建公众信心，民间组织也该这么做。

01　改错：写作挑错

看看下面的句子，你能找出错误吗？

2014 年 9 月 27 日　单独居住的原因和影响

Dissatisfied though are some living conditions sometimes, people yet avoid the unnecessary interference from other family members.

虽然某些生活条件有时不让人满意，人们仍然可以避免来自其他家庭成员的不必要的干扰。

02 大闯关：写作闯关

你能翻译出下面的句子吗？注意语序。

2015年11月19日A卷　机器人对人类未来很重要还是有负面影响？

很少有现代产品脱离自动化生产线纯手工生产的。

参考答案

01　用as、though的让步状语从句，可用部分倒装语序，不过需要把句末提前、其余句子成分不变，所以应该是：

　　Dissatisfied though some living conditions are sometimes, people yet avoid the unnecessary interference from other family members.

02　Seldom is a modern product produced by pure hand without an automatic production line.

中文没有的强调结构

口 语 部 分

强调句型,可以算是雅思口语考试中最常用、几乎在三个部分都会出现的句型,用来表达观点、讲故事、举例子。

在 Part 1 中问你是否喜欢科学:

> It's worth mentioning that I'm a science student. 值得一提的是我是个理科生。

在 Part 2 中讲个别人送的衣服

> It's surprising that she gave gray pajamas. 我好惊讶她居然给了我一件灰色的睡衣。

到了 Part 3 句型一下就多:

> It's reported that/clear that/well known that...据报道……/要确信……/众所周知……

所以,要想学会强调句型,我们先来熟悉一下它的基本构成。

> It is(was)+ 被强调部分(通常是主语、宾语或状语)+that/who...

强调句型可以强调句子里任何一个需要被强调的成分
比如我们崇拜一个人:

> I admire his courage and persistence, because that's what I lack.

这句话可以改成几个版本的强调句呢?

强调宾语:

It's his courage and persistence that I admire, because that's what I lack. 他的勇气和

坚持是我所崇拜的，因为这正是我缺少的。

强调状语：

It's because that's what I lack, that I admire his courage and persistence. 正因为我缺少，所以我很欣赏他的勇气和坚持。

或者改变一点意思

It's because courage and persistence are what I lack that I admire him. 正因为勇气和坚持都是我缺少的，我才那么欣赏他。

强调主语：

It's that I admire his courage and persistence, because that's what I lack. 是我欣赏他的勇气和坚持，因为我缺少。

这几个说法在语法中都是对的。大家需要多总结在口语中哪些地方可以用到这些句型？我用得最多的一句是 It's worth mentioning that... 值得一提的是……比如说，很多人很喜欢讲自己的专业，被问到"Do you like music?"时，就可以答 It's worth mentioning that I've been studying piano for over 15 years.

在 Part 2 描述一个人的事迹时，可以说：

> It's worth mentioning that he used to be the badminton champion in his school.

这算是一个比较万能的用法了，可以熟记。

还有一个特别好用的套路：It's *adj. /n.* that... 用来表达感受：

> It's really fantastic that I saw the sunrise. 好赞的是我看到日出了。
> It's really a pity that I didn't see the sunrise. 好遗憾我没看到日出。

我们为什么要用强调句？我以前看 Sky 电视台的 An Idiot Abroad 节目时，当时制片人讲了一句话：

> I've been to many exotic places, I genuinely think travel broadens the mind.

当时我就学到了，genuinely/truly/really/do 放在 think 前可以加强语气。

强调结构的作用在口语 Part 2 考试中体现较明显，比如有的同学在讲近水之地这个题喜欢重复简单句型：

> You can go swimming. You can have delicious seafood. You can see a lot of girls in bikinis lying on the beach.

这些连续性信息会给听者特别杂乱的感觉。所以语句上要有提炼信息的感觉：

> Actually, there're lots of things you can do here, like swimming, having delicious seafood, but what I enjoy the most is to watch those girls in bikinis lying on the beach.

这样说的话就有主次之分了，可以做很多事，但最喜欢的是什么，主语从句在这里也有强调的作用。

学习强调结构，至少要知道还有哪些句型有强调作用：

1. 比较状语从句：Nobody likes here more than I do.
2. 双重否定：Doing exercise is never wrong.

最后我们来记一下以下这个常用句型：

- It is not until that…
- It is clear (obvious/certain/true/possible…) that…
- It is important (necessary, right, strange, natural) that…
- It is said (reported/learned/well known) that…
- It is suggested (ordered) that…
- It is about time that…
- It is the first time that…
- It is …when…
- It is …before…
- It happens/seems/looks/appears that…
- It takes thousands of people many years to build the Great Wall.
- It is no good learning English without speaking English.
- It doesn't matter if you're not beautiful.
- It's kind of you to say so.
- It looks as if he is ill.
- It was not until his wife came back that he went to sleep.

01 改错：口语挑错

看看下面的句子有错吗？

呼吸新鲜空气是我每天晚上去公园跑步的原因。（用强调句型造句）

It's the fresh air I can breathe that I'd like to go jogging every evening.

02 大闯关：口语闯关

Do you like going to the park?
超舒服，那种坐在椅子上看着湖面什么都不想的感觉。

参考答案

01 强调句型是一个比较容易掌握的句型，因为句子成分都可以放在强调部分。但是唯一要注意的就是句子逻辑，在这个例子中提前的状语，是一个原因状语，所以全部提前应该是 for the fresh air，或者把 for 放在句尾。
It's the fresh air I can breathe that I'd like to go jogging every evening for.

02 It's so comfortable that I feel when I sit on a bench, and stare at the lake, thinking about nothing.

写作部分

句子中要强调的内容不同，采用的方法也不同，常用的有下面几种：

1 助动词 do 提前表示强调

就是把助动词 do 单独列于谓语动词前，表示强调，相当于中文加入"确实"的意思。需要注意的是，这里助动词 do 的单复数必须和主语一致。比如：

> 2013 年 11 月 21 日　应该鼓励去其他国家学习其语言和文化吗？
>
> Presently, the divergence about whether youngsters should be encouraged to study overseas does raise public awareness for its role in education globalization.
> 当下，关于年轻人是否应该被鼓励去留学海外以得到更好的教育的分歧确实唤醒了公众对于其在教育全球化上的作用的注意。

这一句可以放在文章的首段用来引题，它的句式主干公式化就是：

> Presently, the discussion about 主要论题（whether、why 等引导的从句）does draw 相关人群's attention to 讨论意义（名词词组）。
> 当下，关于主要论题这一问题的讨论确实引起了相关人群对于相关领域的关注。

表达这一语义的并列选项可以总结为下表：

当下，	关于……的讨论	主要论题	确实引起了相关人士对……的关注	相关领域
Currently, Nowadays, Presently, These days,	the analysis about the disagreement about the discussion about the divergence about	whether、why 等引导的从句	does attract sb. 's interest in does draw sb. 's attention to does raise sb. 's awareness for does trigger sb. 's concern with	名词 / 动名词词组

2 双重否定表示强调

双重否定表示肯定，但语气远强于直白的肯定，适合于议论文中下结论、提建议、发号召。比如：

> **2014 年 12 月 13 日　应该禁止店铺出售不健康的饮食吗?**
>
> It is by no means pointless for public health authorities to popularize nutrition knowledge and make people recognize the harms of junk food and reduce the intake consciously.
> 公共健康部门普及营养知识、使人们认识到垃圾食品的危害并自觉减少摄入量就绝不是无意义的。

其主干可以表达为：

> It is by no means pointless for sb（相关人群）to 采取某种措施（动词词组）.
> 相关人群采取某种措施绝不是无意义的。

再如：

> **2014 年 12 月 6 日　高楼型城建和低层型城建哪个更好?**
>
> It is by no means pointless for municipalities to adopt different kinds of layout based on their own population and urban functions.
> 市政当局根据它们自己的人口和城市功能采用不同的布局绝不是无意义的。

3 强调句式

强调句子的某一部分（可以是主语、宾语、状语等）时，可以用以下的句式：
It is/was + 强调的句子部分 + that/who 句子其他部分.
下面列举几个例子：

> 2012 年 3 月 10 日　对未来人口老龄化的评价
>
> It is longer life expectancy and an aging society that would take effect in hitting the pocket of tax payers.
> 更长的生命预期以及老龄化社会在加重纳税人负担上会产生一定的影响。

这是针对主语的强调句式。

> 2015 年 3 月 14 日　育儿所和祖父母在照顾小孩上哪个能做到最好？
>
> It is very close relatives who young parents can totally trust.
> 年轻的父母能够完全相信的就是近亲。

这是针对宾语的强调句式。

> 2012 年 2 月 18 日　为了使生活变简单人们要摒弃使用科技吗？
>
> It is in raising living standards that appropriate application of technology mainly plays a role.
> 适宜的应用科技的主要作用就体现在提高生活水平上。

这是针对状语的强调句式。

01 改错：写作挑错

看看下面的句子，你能找出错误吗？

2012 年 4 月 21 日　计划未来不如专注当前吗？

That makes life and careers fruitless is the want of motive.

令生活和事业无所成就的就是漫无目的。

02 大闯关：写作闯关

试着翻译下面的句子，注意其中复杂的定语。

2013 年 7 月 13 日　同意流行服饰等商品互相模仿吗？

当下，对于互相模仿的趋势的厌恶确实引起了公众对于时尚产业的健康发展的关注。

参考答案

01　what 引导的主语从句用来强调主语，而不是 that，所以这一句应是：
What makes life and careers fruitless is the want of motive.

02　Nowadays, the adverseness for the tendency of copying does trigger a community's concern with the sound development of the fashion industry.

高大上地巧妙
运用从句

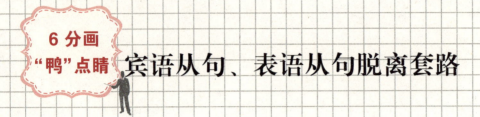

宾语从句、表语从句脱离套路

口语部分

从上一章大家可以感觉到英语的组句要领是分清楚句子成分和表达作用，并且弄清楚定语、状语、补语、同位语的位置。在这一章，我们来讲一下句子成分的升级版——从句。从句就是作句子成分的不是一个单词而是整个句子。

当然我们这里首先要讲的是名词性的从句，和状语从句区分开。名词性从句和状语从句的两个大类。所谓名词性从句，就是整个从句的语法作用和一个名词是一样的。

能充当名词从句的一共有5种：

> 1. that 从句：You need to make sure that everything is checked before sending it out.
> 2. wh-从句：You can't be certain of what's going to happen.
> 3. how-从句：I couldn't understand how he managed to do it.
> 4. 同位语从句：I have a feeling that we're followed.
> 5. if/whether 从句：I don't know if you know about this.

我们先来看宾语从句，首先要弄清楚宾语的位置，然后就知道怎么替换了。宾语常见的位置有4种：

1. 动词后面

比如在 make sure, make up my mind, keep in mind 等动词短语后面，think, believe, ponder, reckon, hate, envy, learn, suggest, explain, agree, wonder, prove, mean, state, feel, hold, take, owe, have, lend, offer, pass, pay, post, read, show, teach, tell 等动词后面。

2. 形容词后面

比如在 sure, certain, glad, please, happy, sorry, afraid, satisfied, surprised 等形容词后面。

3. 介词后面

比如 whether, except, but, besides 等介词后面跟 that 从句。

4. 人称代词宾格后面

比如 me, him, her, you, them, us 等人称代词后面。

下面我们来造句：

> Before we leave, we need to make sure that everything is in the bag.
> I'm sure that you'll like it.
> I like the product you sent to me except that it's a little scratched.
> I was told nothing about how to get there.
> He told me that he would leave Dalian Airport at 8 o'clock.

学会宾语从句的第一步是搞清楚宾语从句的组建模式，**表示下决心做某事，表示说的、想的、羡慕的、提供的、教的、告诉的、建议的，都是表达跟交流有关的动词，后面常跟宾语从句**。这是宾语从句的第一个模式。

另外一个例子是有宾语补足语的时候宾语从句的位置：

> I think it wrong that he told a lie to everyone.
> I think that I wronged him and that I thought he told a lie to everyone.

第二个模式是表达感受

> I'm sure that you'll make it.
> I'm sure that everything will be fine.
> I'm glad that you like it.
> I'm sorry that you lost your cat.
> I'm satisfied that you think of me all the time.
> I'm surprised that my bestie bought me a ship.

whether 和 if 前面通常出现的动词都和怀疑有关，比如：know, ask, care, wonder, find out, leave, put, discuss, doubt 等。当然也有一个特殊的词 depend on 是这样用的，如：

> My life depends on whether I can pass this exam.

第三个模式是在虚拟语气后用宾语从句

当表示：建议（suggest, advise, propose）、要求（demand, desire, request）、决定（decide）、命令（order, command, require）、坚决主张（insist）时，后接宾语从句，用"（should）+动词原形"结构。如：

> I suggested that you (should) study hard.
> He ordered that we should go out at once.

在使用宾语从句时需要注意经常用错的几个点：语序错误、形式宾语错误、否定词位置错误。这些在英语中的使用习惯，都和中文表达习惯有差异，是雅思考生常见的出错点。

1. 语序错误：He is wondering why am I coming.
   正确：He is wondering why I'm coming. （宾语从句用陈述语气）
2. 不用形式宾语：I thought that he could get 6 in speaking test impossible.
   正确：I thought it impossible that he could get 6 in speaking test. （先短后长）
   再看一例：He left whether I could pass the exam to my judgment.
   正确：He left it to my judgment whether I could pass the exam.
3. 否定词应放主句：I think he doesn't like the English teacher. （不地道）
   正确：I don't think he likes the English teacher.

难点分析：

什么时候宾语从句的引导词 that 不能省略？
1. 当 it 作形式宾语时；
2. 当宾语从句前置时；
3. 有两个或两个以上宾语从句时，第一个 that 可省，其他 that 不能省略。

来看例子：

> I think it impossible that Ma Rong has betrayed Wang Baoqiang.
> That I will win her heart, I believe.
> I believe (that) you have done your best and that things will be fine.

whether 和 if，哪个用来引导宾语从句？
1. whether 后可以直接跟 to，但 if 不可以；
2. whether 可以放在介词后，但 if 不可以；
3. whether 可以和 or not 连用，但 if 不可以。

来看例子：

> You can decide whether to go out eating tonight/we should go out eating tonight.
> I'm thinking of whether I should ask him to return my book..
> I can't say whether or not you are still my friend.

if 可引导否定概念，whether 不可以

> He asked if I didn't send him the email yesterday.

雅思口语考试中最常见的应用：

> I don't know if you know about it.
> My answer depends on whether it's a topic about clothes or general things.
> It occurs to me that…
> Can you imagine how exciting it was?
> I highly doubt that…
> I'm sure that…
> He told me a lot about how this was going to influence my life.
> I heard that…
> I was told that…

表语从句与宾语从句的原理类似，只不过表语从句的动词是系动词。表示说明问题的讲法多一些。

> The question is when I can figure out this problem.
> The question is whether you still love me.
> The problem is how we can get started.
> What I clearly remember is that there was a time, we had a trip together, she looked after me day and night, which moved me a lot.

表语从句经常放在句尾表示总结：

> That's how I feel.
> That's basically what I think.

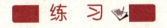

01 改错：口语挑错

看看下面的句子有错吗？

At that time, I was thinking why is she so beautiful?
I can't say if or not you are still trust worthy.

02 大闯关：口语闯关

试着翻译下面的汉语句子。

Do you like doing outdoor activities?
我的答案取决于我现在是复习阶段，还是休假阶段。

参考答案

01 这是宾语从句的常见错误，宾语从句中语序不能再是疑问句语序，而要换成陈述语序。所以正确说法应该是：At that time, I was thinking why she is so beautiful.
whether 是唯一可以和 or not 连用的词，if 不可以，所以正确说法是 I can't say whether or not you are still trust worthy.

02 My answer depends on whether I'm in the situation of reviewing or on vacation.

写作部分

宾语和表语我们前面的章节讲过了，这两种句子成分如果以分句的形式出现，就构成了宾语从句和表语从句。下面我们简单介绍一下使用时的注意事项，并分别提供一个在实战中可以模仿的简单例子。

1 宾语从句

宾语从句常用的引导词包括：
连词：if、that（常省略）、whether
代词：what、which、who、whose
副词：how、when、where、why
下面是一个可以参考的简单的宾语从句：

> 2014 年 8 月 2 日　青少年犯罪的原因和处罚
>
> The problem results from that in the interest of audience ratings, media portray a lot of vices which teenagers quickly pick up.
> 问题源自于，为了博收视率，媒体展示了很多不良行为，然后孩子们很快就学会了。

这一句的语法拿分点在 that 引导的复杂的宾语从句；逻辑拿分点为交代论据、进行解释。句式主干可以公式化为：

> The problem results from 宾语从句.
> 问题源自于某一原因。

这一句式还可以参看以下例句：

> **2014 年 8 月 21 日　国际旅游和商务导致和外国人接触增多的影响**
>
> This threat comes from that local culture and traditions take a backseat, because local residents may tend to follow foreign lifestyles more.
> 　威胁来自于地方文化和传统的地位将会下降，因为当地居民会倾向于接受外国的生活方式。

这一句表意的并列选项可以总结为下表：

这一问题	源于	原因	基于	论据
The condition The issue The problem The situation	comes from originates from results from	宾语从句	现在分词 accompanying with coming from originating from stemming from 过去分词 based on brought by caused by derived from placed by 介词 by by means of through via	名词词组

2 表语从句

表语从句常用的引导词有：
连词：as if、as though、that（常省略）、whether
代词：what、whatever、when、where、why、which、who、whoever、whose
副词：how、when、where、why
下面是一个可以参考的简单的表语从句：

> **2014 年 5 月 15 日　该为优秀雇员们每年放 4 周假吗？**

> A frustrating fact is that long annual leave could pose a threat to the continuity of working process because of the absence of employees in some positions.
> 一个令人沮丧的事实是长年假可能会给工作流程的持续性带来威胁，因为一些岗位上的雇员可能缺席。

这一句的语法拿分点在 that 引导的含有原因状语从句的复杂的表语从句；逻辑拿分点为交代论据、进行解释。

句式主干可以公式化为：

> An encouraging / frustrating fact is that it could offer an advantage to / pose a threat to 第二个相反观点（名词词组）because of 论据（名词词组）.
> 一个令人鼓舞／沮丧的事实是它可能会带来某种好处／威胁，因为某一原因。

这一句式还可以参看以下例句：

> **2016 年 6 月 16 日　年轻人上大学是对国家有益还是会造成大量失业？**

> A key point is that it would create an impassable barrier to keep a low unemployment rate, because the expansion of higher education does not mean the expansion of job market.
> 一个关键点是因为高校扩招不等于就业市场的扩张，它会为保持低失业率制造障碍。

这一句各句子成分的并列选项如下表：

一个关键点是	它能给……带来好处／坏处	观点	因为	论据
An encouraging / frustrating fact is that A key point is that A merit / demerit is that An important thing is that A strong point / side-effect is that	it could bring positive / negative changes in it could offer an advantage to / pose a threat to it would bring convenience / trouble to it would lead to	名词词组	because of due to	名词词组
	it would create an opportunity / obstacle to	动词词组	as because since	接从句

01 改错：写作挑错

看看下面的句子，你能找出错误吗？

2012年5月12日 同意和监狱相比，教育可以更好地预防犯罪吗？

The possibility for changing the fates of low social class mostly depends on that the government has done in generalizing public education.

低社会阶层改变命运的可能性取决于政府在推广公立教育上的所作所为。

02 大闯关：写作闯关

试着翻译下面的句子，注意其中的状语。

2013年7月18日 网络使人们不再需要直接交流的优缺点

另外一个缺点是因为缺乏机会去锻炼社交技能，它会对正常的人际交往带来麻烦。

参考答案

01 宾语从句引导词 that 和 what 的区别在于：what——从句缺成分，what 不可省略，"……的东西"的意思；that——从句不缺成分，what 可省略，无实际含义。所以应该是：

The possibility for changing the fates of low social class mostly depends on what the government has done in generalizing public education.

02 Another demerit is that it could bring trouble to normal interpersonal interaction because of lack of chances to practice social skills.

定语从句烂俗写出新意

口语部分

定语从句是一种关系从句,从句中的先行词在从句中作成分。**为了让大家分清这个概念**,我们先来说说什么叫关系副词、什么叫关系代词。

> I'd like to talk about Zhongshan Park, which is located in the city centre.

在这个从句中 which 直接连接了 is,在从句中作主语,代替了 park,拆开是:I'd like to talk about Zhongshan Park. The park is located in the city centre. 在含定语从句的句子中 which 直接代替了 the park,作了它的代词。这时候 which 就是一个关系代词。

> I'd like to talk about Zhongshan Park, where you can see beautiful trees and flowers.

在这个从句中,where 连接了 you can see,where 并没有成为主语。那它代替的部分是什么呢?这句话可以拆成: I'd like to talk about Zhongshan Park. In the park you can see beautiful trees and flowers. 这样看就清晰了,where 代替的是 in the park,是一个状语成分,所以我们把 where 叫关系副词。

在定语从句中选定先行词时,需要判断它是关系代词还是关系副词:
比如:

> (错)This is the mountain where I visited last year.(where 是"在那里"的意思)
> (正)This is the mountain that I visited last year.(that 指代我去过的那座山)

那定语从句在雅思口语考试可以用在哪里呢?
基本信息题:

> The major I'm studying is English, which is a promising major.
> I come from a city called Yinchuan, which is the capital of Ningxia Hui Autonomous Region.

> I'm currently living in a very nice apartment, where there're lots of restaurants around.

定语从句通常起限定修饰和解释说明两种作用。什么是限定修饰：什么时间认识的、什么时间去的，which 在从句中充当宾语而非主语。如：

> I would say a person that I had known about two years ago. 我想说一个我两年前认识的人。

"两年前认识的"，就是限定用法的定语。
什么是解释说明：描述型的、形容词的、评价的。如：

> It's called Sanya, which is a beautiful coastal city located at the southern part of China, with warm sunshine and beautiful sea views.

定语从句后是形容词，地点，描述就是解释说明用法的定语。
那什么时候需要解释说明呢？我们来看几个在雅思口语考试中的实际例子：
对事件、方法、数据、功能的定义解释说明：

1. （休闲）My favourite way of relaxation is cupping therapy or taking a hot bath, which are very old-fashioned and very traditional but genuinely useful for me to release my pressure.
2. （健康）Statistics also show a high rate of death from over work, which kind of makes a sense and a warning for modern people to care more about their leisure and life.
3. （手机）My phone provides me a "Hey, Siri" function which allows me to organize my timetable by directly talking to Siri, and make the direct order.
4. （周末）I assume the day I adore the most in a week is Friday, which is the end of the week.
5. （运动）I tend to play some highly tactical games which can actually burn my blood in fires, my morale, my desire of winning and competition. That's why I put my passion in to badminton, which is a kind of sport that requires both agility and a strategic mind.

对人的行为、关系的解释说明：

1. （朋友）I assume normal friends tend to be just acquaintances who seldom call or care but will greet you when you run into each other and they sometimes help you but not always.

2.（周末）My Saturday has been totally devoted to my boss who pays me to do so.

表示限定关系的定语也非常好记，通常是表示时间、地点、方位的信息。常出现在 Part 2 的第一段里，或者在表示最喜欢的某物时，或者是赞美某人时。如：

> The person that I had known in my high school.
> The experience that I had two years ago.
> The room that I adore the most.
> This is the most outstanding leader that I've ever seen in my life.
> This is the most enjoyable moment that I've ever had in my life.

当然，定语从句还可以由"介词+关系代词"引导，作介词宾语。

> They tried to think of a method by which they could solve the problem.
> The person to whom this letter was addressed left this house five years ago.
> This is something I'm very proud of.
> I wanted to do the job I'd been trained for.

作从句紧接宾语时，要注意不要漏掉介词 to 或 for。

定语从句中还有一种非限定性定语从句，既不表示限定，也不表示修饰，而表示补充说明。比如：

> He didn't win the competition, which was exactly what I wanted.

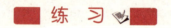

01 改错：口语挑错

看看下面的句子有错吗？

The reason why I think this is a good place which is full of flowers and trees is because the environment is beautiful.

02 大闯关：口语闯关

试着翻译下面的句子。

我下班有时候心烦就喜欢去公园，那儿听不到汽车鸣笛，只能听到虫鸣鸟叫，十分惬意，是个放松、休息、散心的好地方。

参考答案

01　刚学习定语从句的同学，有硬造从句的坏毛病。一个简单的检测办法，就是把自已造的句子按句子逻辑翻译一下。那上面的句子就是：我之所以觉得这个充满花和树的地方是个好地方是因为它环境优美。这是句子想表达的意思吗？主线逻辑应该是之所以喜欢这个地方，是因为环境好，有树和花。所以定语从句出现的位置就错了，定语从句起限定和修饰作用，这里所说的"这个地方"，不应该由"有花有树的地方"作限定。正确说法：The reason why I think this is a good place is because the environment is beautiful, full of flowers and trees.

02　Sometimes, after work, I feel depressed. Then, I like to go to the park, where I can hear the birds singing but cars' beeping. It's a good place to relax, rest and empty my mind.
注意，中文表达习惯里，有时候会有连续的动词，我下班，心烦，去公园。这些意群概念，在中文中直接堆在一起就可以达意，但英文句子非得分出个主谓宾才行，这是中英文组句最大的差异。学英语的同志们要格外注意。

写作部分

我们前面讲过定语，定语以从句的形式出现就是定语从句，放在它所修饰的名词、代词之后，引导定语从句的关联词为关系代词和关系副词。下面我们就简单示范一下定语从句在考试中的用法：

1　关系代词引导的定语从句

关系代词包括 which、who、whom、whose、that 等。比如：

> 2014 年 9 月 6 日　城市快速发展后年轻人面对的问题及解决方法
>
> 　　With hindsight, intense competition and high unemployment rates accompanying with urbanized and populated development patterns showed a tremendous impact on the youth who do not have advanced degrees or come from lower classes.
> 　　事后来看，伴随城市化和人口密集化的发展模式而来的激烈竞争和高失业率对没有高学历或者来自于低社会阶层的年轻人影响巨大。

这句话包含了一个 who 引导的定语从句，我们可以公式化得出以下句式：
With hindsight, 某一分论点（名词或动名词词组）showed a tremendous impact on 某一相关人群 who 定语从句.
事后来看，某一作用对某些人的巨大影响是十分明显的。
它还有很多备选表达方式：

事实证明，	某一分论点	对……产生了巨大影响	受影响的对象
Based on fact, Grounded on factual analysis, With hindsight,	名词 或动名词 词组	exerted a strong influence on had a great effect on made a huge difference to produced an enormous impact on presented an immense effect on showed a tremendous impact on	某一相关人群 who 引导的定语从句.

这一句适用于文章主体部分，用这一句开始分述各分论点，强调这一点对某些人群的巨大影响。

2 关系副词引导的定语从句

关系副词包括 when、where、why 等。比如：

> 2012年8月11日　青年毕业即失业会导致什么问题？如何解决？

> For graduates, work is the only place where hope and career development lies.
> 对大学毕业生来讲，工作是希望和职业发展的唯一所在。

这一句我们可以公式化并推而广之：

对相关人群来讲，	相关事项是	唯一的 最重要的	时间/地点/原因	
For sb.,	... is/are 或 ... was/were	the most crucial the most important the only	time when .... place where ... lies. reason why	……的时刻。 ……所在。 ……的原因。

这里表意的重点在于强调相关事项在某一方面的重要性，和上一个选项一样，适用于提出分论点。

3 限定性定语从句和非限定性定语从句

这两者的区别可总结成下面的表格：

	和修饰词间隔	和修饰词关系	可否省略	特殊点
限定性定语从句	无分隔	限定	不可省略	专有名词必须用
非限定性定语从句	逗号隔开	补充说明	可省略	非限定性定语从句

下面我们针对同一道题各举一例，体会一下二者的区别：

> **2014 年 1 月 9 日　为解决交通阻塞提供免费公共交通是最好的选择吗？**

> 限定性定语从句：
> Compared with other measures like rebuilding road systems, free public transport would bring about unreasonable burden on the tax payers who seldom use public transport.
> 与像重建道路系统这样的方法相比，免费公共交通会给很少利用公交系统的纳税人带来不合理的负担。

这一句里的 who seldom use public transport 限定前面 the tax payers 的内容，省略后会使句子表意不清。

> 非限定性定语从句：
> Compared with other measures like rebuilding road systems, free public transport would bring about unreasonable burden on the tax payers living in sparsely populated areas, who do not have chances to take buses or subways.
> 与像重建道路系统这样的方法相比，免费公共交通会给人烟稀少地区的纳税人带来不合理的负担，他们没机会搭乘公交车或地铁。

这一句里的 who do not have chances to take buses or subways 补充说明前面 the tax payers 的内容，省略后会使句子基本表意不受影响。

4　涉及比较的定语从句

as 和 than 也可以引导定语从句，说明比较的对象，各举一例。
as 引导的定语从句：

> **2015 年 2 月 28 日　大学前间隔年好处多于坏处吗？**

> After one year of work or travel, the youngsters will be not same ones as they just graduate from high school without too much understanding about the world and themselves.
> 在一年的工作或游历后，年轻人将不同于刚刚毕业、对社会和他们自己都没有太多理解的那些人。

than 引导的定语从句：

> 2012 年 2 月 4 日　年轻人该遵循传统还是特立独行？

> Breaking outdated traditional views, people will have the capability to create more opportunities than they could find.
> 打破过时的传统观念，人们将会有能力去创造比他们能找到的多得多的机会。

01　改错：写作挑错

看看下面的句子，你能找出错误吗？

2016 年 6 月 4 日　训练年轻人竞争而不是合作的好处大于坏处吗？

Cooperation is the means which openness, trust and safety feeling could be built up.
合作是开放、信任和安全感得以建立的方式。

02　大闯关：写作闯关

试着翻译下面的句子，注意：but 也可以引导定语从句，相当于 "… not …" 的意思。

2011 年 9 月 3 日　高等教育培养不出人们成功的素质吗？

没人能仅靠在学术教育中学到的知识成功。

参考答案

01　当限定说明的词需要用介词时，定语从句之前要带上相应的介词，所以应该是：
Cooperation is the means by which openness, trust and safety feeling could be built up.

02　There is no man that can be successful with the knowledge learned in academic education only.

7分群"鸭"有首

主语从句出手保证不错

口语部分

毫不夸张地说雅思口语里最常使用的从句就是主语从句。几乎每道题都可以用,贯穿 Part 1、Part 2 和 Part 3,绝对是口语的高分句型。口语评分标准里是这样写的:

3分: 尝试使用基本句型,但准确度有限,或依赖预先背诵的几句话。除预先背诵的内容外,错误很多。
(也就是说你不会组句)

4分: 能使用基本句型并正确使用一些简单句型,但极少使用从句。常出现错误,且会造成误解。
(什么叫极少?就是只有一两句,通常大多数考生都会用的从句是状语从句,when I was young,由 because,but 引导的从句之类的)

5分: 能使用基本的句型,且具有合理的准确性。使用有限的复杂句式结构,但通常会出错切会造成某些理解困难。
(什么叫有限?就是除了状语从句,你还会用一两个其他的从句,比如常见的定语从句 who,which 和宾语从句 I think that)

6分: 结合使用简单句和复杂句,但灵活性有限,使用复杂结构时经常出现错误,尽管这些错误极少造成理解困难。
(什么叫结合使用?就是使用频率更高了。有简单句就会出现复杂句,那么你要问自己了,除了状语、定语、宾语从句外,你还会用什么从句?在哪里?怎么用?)

7分: 较灵活的使用一系列复杂语法结构,虽然反复出现一些语法错误,但语句通常正确无误。
(什么叫一系列?至少得5种从句以上,都要体现出来)

雅思口语对于从句的要求其实并不算高,因为强调使用性,就算经常、反复出现一些语法错误,在评分标准中,也能体现出 6-7 分的高分来。

那么我们来看从句出现的位置。

> Do you like traveling?
> Yes, of course. I like traveling, because traveling is very relaxing. I can see many sights, and eat lots of different foods.

一般4分的人也就写到这里了。我学了从句应该怎么用呢？往哪用呢？

在这里我简单解读一下口语考试的考点，雅思口语考核考生回应信息的能力、列举理由的能力、举例的能力、对比的能力以及总结的能力。所以回应→列举→举例→对比→总结就是我们回答每一个问题的基本思维结构。

如果你要想达到，流利与词汇6-7分要求的"详尽"讨论的标准，你就需要学会如何举例子。

还是这个题 Do you like traveling?

回应：Definitely, yes！I like traveling.

列举理由：可以是功利的 Traveling can enrich my knowledge and broaden my mind. 旅游可以使我增长知识开阔视野。可以是感性的 I'm a great fan of traveling. I like the feeling to escape from hustle and bustle 我喜欢逃离喧嚣。可以是习惯：I almost go traveling every year as long as I have a holiday.

举例：可以使用主语从句来组句：

What I often like to do is to ...
a) go to the beaches to enjoy the sunbath
b) go abroad to experience different cultures
c) group some friends and travel together

我喜欢做的事就是去沙滩、去国外、搭伙儿旅游等。这就是主语从句最常出现在口语考试中的位置。

同理，在 Part 2 中，描述一个人，描述一个地点，描述一个场景，描述一个物品，都可以在细节信息部分，提炼信息，表达一种强调，比如：

What impressed me the most is … 给我留下最深刻印象的是……
What I'm saying is… 我想要说的是……
What attracted me the most is …最吸引我的一点是……
It's worth mentioning that… 值得一提的是……

下面我们就来看一下，什么是主语从句。主语从句在口语中常出现的一种结构是这样表述的：

What（特殊疑问词） + 主+谓+（宾）

主语从句是一种名词性结构。因为英语的语言风格是一种主谓中心式风格，充当主语的必须是一个名词性质的东西。但如果主语是一句话，则中文和英文表达就会出现偏差。

看上面这个句子，"我最喜欢做的事是去沙滩上晒太阳"。在这个句子中，"我最喜欢做的事"是主语，"是"是系动词，"去沙滩上晒太阳"是表语。那怎么翻译"我最喜欢做的事儿"呢？语法不好的同学就会说：I most like to do thing is，在这句话中，"I"是第一个出现的名词，所以按照英国人的理解方式，就变成了"我是个……去太阳"，就混乱了。而且句子里，"like""is"都是动词，就容易产生句子结构混乱，造成理解困难。语法稍微好一点的同学，可能会把"事儿"翻译成"The thing"：

> The thing I like to do the most is to go to the beaches and enjoy sunbathing.

这个句子是说的通的，因为 the thing 是一个名词，I like to do the most 作了后置定语，相当于 the thing（which）I like to do the most，这样这一大块，就可以作具有名词性质的主语了。

在主语从句中，我们用 what 来代替 the thing，也能够表达同样的意思，作为名词性结构出现在主语的位置上。

> <u>What I like to do the most</u>（名词性结构）is to go shopping.

同理，把这个名词性结构放在表语的位置上，就成了表语从句，放在宾语位置上就成了宾语从句：

> Going shopping（名词性质的主语）is <u>what I like to do the most</u>（名词性结构的表语）.
> I don't know（谓语动词）<u>what I should do</u>（名词性结构宾语）.

在举例的时候去讲 what I often like to do：

> （Friends）What I often like to do is to hang out with them in a karaoke bar.
> （Film）What I often like to watch is an American blockbuster.
> （Reading）What I often like to read is a novel.
> （Weekends）What I often like to do is to invite some friends home and have a big dinner.

说的再简单一点，所有主谓结构都可以用主语从句改造。比如：

> I can get more information from TV.
> ＝What I can do is to get more information from TV.
> I want to be a doctor in the future
> ＝What I want to be in the future is a doctor.
> He told me,"You must go to Canada."
> ＝What he told me was "You must go to Canada."

练 习

01 改错：口语挑错

看看下面的句子有错吗？

Do you like watching films?

Yes, as long as I have free time, what I like to do is watch action films, especially something like *Fast and Furious*, *Avengers* or something like that.

02 大闯关：口语闯关

翻译 Describe a Wedding 中的片段。

所有她的亲戚朋友都被邀请了，婚礼开始的时候新娘从旋转台阶上出现，就好像童话里的公主。整个婚礼给我留下最深刻印象的是新郎新娘交换戒指的瞬间，让我觉得特别感动。

参考答案

01　这是在上课时经常听到的一个错误，主语从句 what I like to do is to go shopping，这个结构的核心点是要做正确的动词和名词的匹配，如果前半句用的是 do，后半句则是动词短语。题目中的错误就是后半句匹配了名词，翻译过来就有歧义了：我最爱做的事是动作片。正确说法是我最喜欢的是动作片，或者是我喜欢做的事儿是叫上几个朋友一起看动作片。另外单复数也有错误，正确说法应该是：What I like are action films，或 What I like to watch is an action film，或 What I like to do at weekends is to call some friends and watch some action films.

02　All of her relatives and friends were invited. When the wedding started, the bride showed up on the spinning stair, looking like a princess in a fairy tale. During the entire wedding, what impressed me the most was the moment when the newly-wed couple exchanged their rings, which made me so moved.

写作部分

2013年1月12日的题目是"孩子们学习时间过长是积极还是消极的？"。我们编个励志故事：屠呦呦刻苦努力、缩短了学习时间、加速了事业成功，比如"她在两年里完成了高中三年的学习任务给很多老师留下了深刻的印象"。

我们翻译成：

> She completed all three years' study tasks in only two years and surprised many teachers.

高大上地巧妙运用从句

这是我们最常犯的错误之一，在中文中，句子是可以直接作主语的，比如"我爸爸昨晚打我绝对是个错误"，这里面"我爸爸昨晚打我"就是个句子，就如同"我在两年里完成了高中三年的学习任务"一样，作主语没问题。在英文中，这样的句子可不能直接作主语，句子作主语叫"主语从句"，最常见的是三种用法：

1 That 引导

像上面那句，得改成：

> That she completed all three years' study tasks in only two years surprised many teachers.

这里的 that 什么意思也没有，中文里没有对应的语意，所以我们写句子的时候经常会忘记它。

2 疑问词引导

可以用来提问题的句子都可以，包括：how、what、when、whenever、where、wherever、which、who、whoever、whom、whose、why 等。比如：

> 2012 年 2 月 25 日　大学生除学习外参与其他活动必要吗？

> What youngsters learned from community engagements afforded them an in-depth understanding of the important interpersonal skills.
> 年轻人从社会活动中学到的东西让他们对于重要的人际交往技巧有一个深入的了解。

再比如，还是这道题，换个疑问词：

> How to use time properly is the key for final outcome.
> 如何合理地安排时间是决定最终成效的关键。

3 it 做形式主语，后置的主语从句

这种用法有点难以理解，因为中文里并没有相应的概念。可以这样理解，前面作主语的那句话太长了，写出来不好看，比如前面那句：

> That Ms. Tu completed all three years' study tasks in only two years surprised many teachers.

主语相当于一句话的脸，长这么长不修图怎么发朋友圈？怎么办？放后面，前面用 it 作形式主语，变成：

> It surprised many teachers that Ms. Tu completed all three years' study tasks in only two years.

这里面后置的主语从句不一定非得是 that 引导，第 2 条提过的疑问词都可以引导。比如：

2012 年 11 月 24 日　同意手书会被现代通信技术替代吗？

> It doesn't matter whether the message is written on a piece of paper or is shown on the screen. What matters is who wrote it and what it contains. To me, the content far outweighs the form.
>
> 信息写在纸上还是展示在屏幕上并不重要。重要的是谁写的、写了些什么。对我来讲，内容大于形式。

这里后置的主语从句是 whether the message is written on a piece of paper or is shown on the screen，引导词就是 whether。

记住这段话，只要题目是关于两件事的比较，比如 "2014 年 12 月 4 日　语言学习是大班好还是小班好？" "2014 年 4 月 26 日　线上工作和学习的方式取代现实的方式好不好？" 等等，都可以回答：It does not matter whether … or …. What matters is …. To me, … far outweighs ….

再看：

2013 年 6 月 8 日　政府应该鼓励消费吗？

> Actually, it has been totally ignored that easy credit would make financial risks become higher.
>
> 事实上，宽松的信贷会升高金融风险被完全忽略了。

在写作中，模仿上面这句就可以把这个拿分点固化下来，拿到主语从句的分数。从下面这个表格中抽出一句，写文章时，当写到举例子的时候，不用 "for example" 这种传统的说法，换成背好的这个东西，例子在后面照常写，分数就来了。

事实上，	以下事例能够证明这一点	举例子
Actually, As a matter of fact, Indeed, In fact, In reality,	it is a strong support that it is an powerful explanation that it could be cited as a supporting evidence that it could be seemed as an outstanding footnote that it could be used as a typical example that	从句

01 改错：写作挑错

看看下面这两句话，你能找出来哪里不对吗？

1）2015 年 10 月 31 日　对艺术创作的资助该来源于政府还是其他渠道？

If the government supplies more support in artistic field or not is not the crux of the matter.
政府是否在艺术领域提供更多的支持并不是问题的关键。

2）2016 年 4 月 16 日　同意公共公园比购物中心重要吗？

Where should the limited public resources be allocated depends on local residents' needs.
有限的公共资源应该被用于何处取决于当地居民的需求。

02 大闯关：写作闯关

你能翻译出下面的句子吗？注意从句中的句子结构有点复杂。

2013 年 11 月 30 日　人们为什么追逐名牌？它是积极的还是消极的？

实际上，以下事例能够作为证据：在一些公共社交场合，名牌服饰能够帮助其拥有者轻易地获取陌生人的关注。

参考答案

01 1）if 和 whether 都有"是否"的意思，不过 if 不可以用于句首的主语从句，这里应该把 if 改成 whether。

Whether the government supplies more support in artistic fields or not is not the crux of the matter.

it 作形式主语，后置的主语从句用 if 引导就没问题。

2）这句和上一句一样，是雅思写作里针对政府投资类题目的，可以当作万能句用，不过写错了。要注意的是，疑问词引导的主语从句用的是陈述句语序，助动词 should 不需要提前。应改为：

Where the limited public funds should be allocated depends on local residents' needs.

02 In fact, it could be cited as supporting evidence that in some public social occasions, brand name clothing could help the owners draw strangers' attention easily.

同位语从句复杂但不臃肿

口语部分

很多人不太懂什么是同位语从句。在前几章我们讲过同位语，That man over there, the man in black T-shirt is my English teacher. 前半句没说完，后半句作补充说明，两个名词都占了主语的位置，就叫同位语。那同位语从句呢，就是说前半句是个词，后半句是个句子，两个成分都是名词性质，表达同样的内容，后者对前者作补充说明。在词汇：decision, proposal, hope, feeling, opinion, evidence, advice, announcement, argument, belief, claim, conclusion, decision, explanation, fact, idea, impression, information, knowledge, message, news, opinion, order, probability, promise, reply, saying, statement, suggestion, thought, threat, warning, wish, word 这些转述词后面常会出现同位语从句。

比如说在 Part 3 里探讨科技问题，可以说：

> Nowadays, there is a solid evidence that global warming is happening.
> We can draw the conclusion that happiness is not directly related with money.
> I got this idea that probably I could try this.

句子乍一看还有点像定语从句，但是并不是，两个同位语成分是平行的，又不是表示解释说明的表语从句，或者补语从句，所以这是同位语从句。再来一个特别常见的吧！

> Have you any ideas what time it is?

前面说到了 idea 是一个名词，后面又用了从句 what time it is。如果说 Do you know what time it is? 就成宾语从句了。只不过重复了 idea 和从句，这个句子就变身成为同位语从句了。

找到点感觉了吗？再看一个例句：

> I have a small doubt whether she still loves me. 我有点怀疑她是不是还爱我。

宾语从句：I doubt for a while whether she still loves me.

动词变名词，句子成分就完全变了。

那么我们套用以上公式：

> I have a feeling that there's someone watching me. 我感觉有人在看我，feel 变 feeling
>
> There is little hope that I could get a 7 on this exam. 考 7 分好像没什么希望了。
>
> He made a proposal that we break up right now. 他提议我们马上分手。

动词变名词，宾语从句变同位语从句。你学会了吗？

当然同位语从句也可以加在主语上，一般就如同下面这样的了：

> The idea that you are always right is totally wrong.

在描述领导的第一印象时可以用到：

> The impression that he always talks quickly really scared me at first.

博物馆题可以用到的句型：

> The question whether the museum should be free needs to be answered by the government.

但是还是要注意辨析一下同位语从句和定语从句，我们来学习两个句子：

> The fact that he kissed her really impressed me a lot.
>
> The fact that you are talking about it impressed me a lot.

这两个句子，第一句中包含同位语从句，从句有完整的主谓宾，he kissed her，说明说的是一件事儿，和前面的 fact 是同位语。

第二句从句没说完，that you are talking about 你说的什么什么，所以这个成分是用来限定修饰前面 fact 的，你说的事实让我印象深刻。翻译的时候也要带上"白勺的"。所以是定语从句，千万不要混淆了哟。

01 改错：口语挑错

看看题目《Describe a Creative Person》中的这些句子有错吗？

1) The fact he was so versatile and full of creative ideas truly impressed me a lot.

2) Although I was attracted by this drama, the fact that drinking the soup of smelly tofu mixed with durian became punishment of the game because we lost it still surprised me.

02 大闯关：口语闯关

试着翻译下面这个能在 Part 3 用到的句子。

每次我坐地铁，我就有个感觉，现在大多数人都沉迷于手机。这大概是这个时代的主流休闲方式吧。

参考答案

01 1) 乍一看没什么问题，但是请记住，同位语从句中的 that 不可省略。

2) 本题没有错误，同位语从句的基本结构就是，名词 + 引导词 + 简单句。这个题目中的句意是：虽然我被这闹剧吸引，这事儿，因为我们输了游戏要喝臭豆腐汁和榴梿作为惩罚还是很让我意外。

02 Every time when I take the underground, I get this idea that nowadays most people are indulging in mobile phones. This probably is the main way of relaxation.

写作部分

同位语我们在前面讲过了，就是一个名词紧跟在另外一个名词或代词后面，用来说明后者。同位语从句就是把名词性的同位语换成了从句的形式，用来说明前面紧挨着的那个名词。可引导同位语从句的有 that、whether、what、who、how、when、where 等，其中 that 最为常见，这里我们主要示范 that 引导的同位语从句在议论文中的用法。

> 2014 年 1 月 9 日　免费公共交通是避免交通阻塞的最好选择吗？

如果主旨段第一句的论点是 "be a suboptimal choice because of inconvenience"，则第二句可以解释为：

> It could be interpreted as the fact that most people living in far suburbs or working in fixed hours cannot give up cars because of the limitation of the present routines and set schedule.
>
> 这可以被解释为因为现有的路线和既定的时刻表的局限，大多数居住在远郊或者在固定时间工作的人还是不能放弃使用私家车。

这里 that 引导的从句是前面 the fact 的同位语从句，这一句公式化可以变成：

> It could be interpreted as that 解释（句子），since 深入解释（句子）.
> 这可以被解释为某一原因，因为在其背后的深层原因。

　　这一句适用于针对论点的论据解释部分，同时，这一解释部分还包括了一个原因状语从句，这样就可以就论据再进行更深一步的论述。
　　再看个类似的例子：

> 2014年1月11日　为什么年轻人换工作及对其评价

　　如果论点是"be better fit with progressing skills, strengths and career aspirations"，则第二句可解释为：

> It is realized by the fact that without promotion, changing jobs is a chance to break the ceiling of career, because with experience, workers deserve more.
> 这是由以下事实决定的，在没有升职的情况下，换工作是突破职业瓶颈的一个机会，因为在掌握经验后，工人们理应得到更多。

　　这一句的备选句子成分可以总结为下表：

它可以被解释为	具体原因，	因为	深入解释
It could be explained by the fact that It could be illustrated by the fact that It could be interpreted as the fact that It is easy to understand the fact that It is realized by the fact that	从句，	因为 + 从句 because since as	从句
		因为 + 名词 because of driven by due to for	名词/ 动名词词组

　　语法上需要注意的是同位语从句和定语从句的区别，同位语从句中的that不充当句子成分，比如上面句式中的that不充当任何句子成分，但是不可以省略，而定语从句中的that是作句子成分但可以省略的。我们可以通过下面的例子来体会两者的区别：

> 2014年2月1日　缩小贫富差距是最好的创造更幸福的社会的途径吗？

> The fact that the yearning for a better life could push individuals to contribute their energy to work is known to all.
> 众所周知，对更好生活的向往能推动人们为工作贡献自己的精力。

这一句里面 that the yearning for a better life could push individuals to contribute their energy to work 中的 that 不作句子成分，但是不能省略，这一从句是前面主语 the fact 的同位语从句。

> 2016 年 5 月 21 日　国家互助是义务还是经援根本送不到需要的人手中？

> The fact that international aid organizations worry about is known to all.
> 众所周知，国际援助组织担忧这一事实。

这一句里 that international aid organizations worry about 中的 that 充当成分，作 worry about 的宾语，可以省略，这一从句是前面 the fact 的定语从句。

同位语的其他引导词和 that 的用法一致，比如：

> 2015 年 11 月 21 日　为什么父母在教育中扮演不同角色？将来会如何发展？

> The question how parents of different genders play the role in the personality formations of children is still not clear.
> 不同性别的父母在孩子性格形成中如何起作用的问题还没有答案。

练 习

01　改错：写作挑错

看看下面的句子有错吗？

2014 年 5 月 15 日　该为雇员们每年至少放 4 周的假期吗？

如果论点是 "hinder continuity of work process"，则第二句可解释为：

We must carefully consider a problem if periodic staff shortages would beset some employers because of the difficulty in finding 4-week' fillers-in.

我们必须审慎地考虑一个问题，就是周期性的人员短缺是否将会困扰很多雇主，因为很难找到 4 周的暂代者。

02　大闯关：写作闯关

试着翻译下面的句子，注意同位语从句的运用。

2014 年 5 月 17 日　该鼓励孩子们在家和在校规律地看电视吗？

如果论点是"boost the intelligence development of children",则第二句可解释为:

它可以被解释为,归功于有趣的描述和生动的场景,规律性地收看教育节目能让孩子们保持心灵活跃。

参考答案

01　if 不能引导同位语从句,必须换成 whether。

We must carefully consider a problem whether periodic staff shortages would beset some employers because of the difficulty in finding 4-week' fillers-in.

02　It could be interpreted as the fact that watching educational programs regularly can keep children's minds active thanks to interesting description and tableau vivant.

6分来"鸭"去脉　原因状语从句老调换词新弹

口语部分

状语从句部分许多考生会觉得掌握起来比较轻松，因为这些句子和中文的语序并没有什么差别。当然，也会有考生误以为状语从句就是个标准的五分句型，在口语使用的十大语法现象中（状从、定从、主从、宾从、表从、被动语态、虚拟语气、时态、强调与倒装、独立主格结构），从句表达越丰富的，往往越容易获得考官对语法评分项的青睐。但是误以为状语从句不重要的那就打错特错了！

首先，既然状语从句和中文语序那么相近，就说明这是最好修成的从句功利，不同人讲出的感觉也是不一样的。先举一个例子：

> Do you like sports?
> A 同学：Yes, I like sports, because I think it's very important to keep me healthy.
> B 同学：Well, kind of, in that sports are important to keep me healthy.

有人说，这两句话的区别就是把 because 换成 in that 这个连接词，很简单。其实，语言能力讲究的是精准表达，in 在这里的含义是"在……方面"，它往往有一些限制作用，多只由于某一方面的原因或理由。

我们比较一下逻辑，中文说你喜欢运动吗，答我喜欢，因为我认为运动对健康很重要。我们从语气上来分析一下，这句话有什么缺失？喜欢运动可以有很多理由，可以是喜欢运动完浑身轻松的感觉、喜欢发泄、喜欢竞技、喜欢合作、喜欢战胜别人、喜欢自己被人崇拜的样子、在运动中找到了自己的天赋、看到自己喜欢的球星就忍不住想练练、喜欢健身塑形的感觉、喜欢自己大汗淋漓给身体充电的感觉。在那么多理由当中，A 同学只回答了一个理由，因为运动对健康重要，是一个很功利的理由，在这个句子里听不到任何的感受甚至情绪。不禁让人怀疑，是真的喜欢吗？我见过那么多喜欢运动的人，表述可不是这样的。所以，如果没那么喜欢，在用词上就应该更敏感一些。就像 B 同学说的：还好，你看运动对健康挺重要嘛，in that 就是一个非常非常精准到位的连接词。

所以，in that 大概表达了一种"仅因为，就是因为"的意思，有限制意味。使用时，更多用于否定的原因、典型的原因，常见于 Part 3 的原因分析题中。

> Why do some old people only remember happy things?
>
> Some old people only remember happy things in that they can't get used to this fast changeable society.

> Do you like reading newspapers?
>
> No, I don't, in that newspapers today are flooded with media hype and scandals instead of some newsworthy events, I seldom waste my time on it.

再来看第二个连接词 since，这个词有"自从"的意思，在原因状语从句中表示"既然"。通常它既表示原因，又表示时间，表示已经存在的情况，所以不能乱用。比如：
I like eating bananas, since they are very delicious. 这个讲法就非常别扭。
正确的语境应该是：

> Since lack of sleep caused so many health problems, like allergies and chronic fatigue, it is fair to say sleep is very important.

我们再看几个常见词的区别：

1）as 和 for

for 通常出现在书面语中，不表示直接原因，只能用于句末，表示对前文的附带说明：

> I want to be an engineer, for it's my dream.

as 所表示的原因通常是对方知道的：

> My weekend is very boring, as I'm a student and I need study for my exams.

2）now that 和 since

now that 表示由于新出现的情况而促成了某事的发生：

> Hey, Steven, I heard the flight ticket to Santorini is very cheap recently. Now that you are free from school work, why don't we go there together?

since 表示原先已经存在的情况：

> I want to travel around the world, since I have saved some money.

3) since 和 seeing that，considering that 意思差不多，带有"鉴于""考虑到"的意味

> She is very smart at the time, considering she is only a high school student.

再说一个原因状语从句的加强语气用法，我们可以在 because 前面加上 simply，just，merely，mainly 来加强语气。as 的前面也可以加上 especially，particularly。

当然，原因状语从句里还有两个特别的连接词，一个是 inasmuch as，一个是 insofar as，通常用于表示"既然"和"鉴于"，有点像 now that，但是只出现在正式文体中：

> Inasmuch as the debtor has no property, I abandon my claim.
> Insofar as it is not my fault, I don't care.

这两个词比较少见一些。下面列举一下在口语话题中的使用原则：

since/seeing that 表示已有的情况：

> 因为我住在海边，所以我非常喜欢吃海鲜。(小吃)
> Since I live near the coast, I very much enjoy eating seafood.
>
> 因为我爸爸是个工程师，所以我未来也想和他做一样的事情。(工作)
> Seeing that my father is an engineer, I want to do what he is doing in the future.
>
> 因为我数学好，所以我才学了计算机。(专业)
> Since I was good at math, I chose computer science as my major.
>
> 因为山西的面食特别有名，还有很多古城，所以每年数以百万的人都喜欢来旅游。(家乡)
> Seeing that noodles and ancient city in Shanxi Province are very reputable, every year as many as millions of people like to pay a visit here.

as 表示显而易见

> 鉴于我是个学生，我周末过得很紧张。(周末)
> As I'm a student, I have very tense weekends.
>
> 因为现在中国人富了，越来越多的人开始喜欢国际旅行。(旅游)
> As Chinese people become rich, more and more people start to like traveling abroad.

我很喜欢去博物馆，因为这地方特长见识。(博物馆)
I'm very fond of going to the museum, as this place extends my horizon.

我很喜欢我的卧室，因为这对我来说是个独立的空间。(居住)
I adore my bedroom, as this is an independent space for me.

我喜欢大房子，因为大房子大，可以让很多人一起住。(居住)
I'm really into a big house, as it's spacious enough to accommodate many people.

我喜欢现场音乐，因为现场氛围好。(音乐)
I have a great passion for live music, as the atmosphere is fantastic.

now that 表示目前的状况

既然你现在有时间，咱们一起去玩吧！(近水之地)
Now that you have free time, let's go and play together.

鉴于飞机票价越来越低了，我觉得越来越多的人开始喜欢坐飞机了。(常坐飞机的人)
I suppose more and more people are becoming fancy for taking planes, now that the price goes down gradually.

既然你了解这些，你一定会感兴趣。(长途车旅行)
Now that you know these, you must be interested.

for/considering that 作补充说明

我上学第一天特别紧张，因为所有环境对我来说都是陌生的。(上学)
I felt really nervous on the first day I went to school, for everything in the surroundings was unfamiliar to me.

我非常喜欢我的家乡，因为这里有我的亲人和好朋友。(家乡)
I'm deeply attached to my hometown, considering this place houses my relatives and friends.

我喜欢晚上学习，因为白天干扰太多了。(学习效率)
I'm partial to evening study, for the distractions are too many in the day time.

in that 特殊理由

> 我喜欢音乐，因为音乐是治疗悲伤的良药。(音乐)
> I can't say no to music, in that music is a cure to sadness.

最后还要注意一点，在英文中，出现了 because，就不能再用 so 了！

01 改错：口语挑错

看看下面的句子有错吗？

Do you think it's important for children to learn how to swim?
For swimming is a basic life skill, it's very important to learn swimming. My father asked me to learn it simply since I can save myself if a flood is coming.

02 大闯关：口语闯关

试着翻译一下 *Describe a gift You bought for others* 中的句子：

你知道我爸是个摄影迷吗，我买这个航拍器就是为了投其所好。既然这是目前最先进的拍摄技术之一，而且还不算贵，我当然要买来给他。

参考答案

01 for 作因为讲时从不放句首，语气没有那么强烈。另外除了 because 可以和副词连用成为 simply because，其他原因状语连接词习惯上不与副词连用。另外，since 往往出现在句首，译为"既然"，as 表示显而易见的原因。使用时要注意区分。应改为：Since swimming is a basic life skill, it's very important to learn swimming. My father asked me to learn it simply because I can save myself if a flood is coming.

02 You know, my father is a camera fan. I bought this drone just in order to cater to his pleasure. Now that this is the most advanced technology in video and it's not very expensive, of course I will buy it for him.

写作部分

这一部分的连词我们在"第八招 连词"里面讲过了，原因状语从句可以由以下词引导：for、because、since、as、now that、considering、in that 等。

因果关系相对简单，这一节的重点在于如何建立合理的论述结构。因果关系主要用于议论文的论据分析部分，我们要写出这样的层次来：论点 — 论据解释 — 深入解释（包含举例子）。在这个逻辑分析的层次中，论述跑偏是低分的一个重要原因。比如：

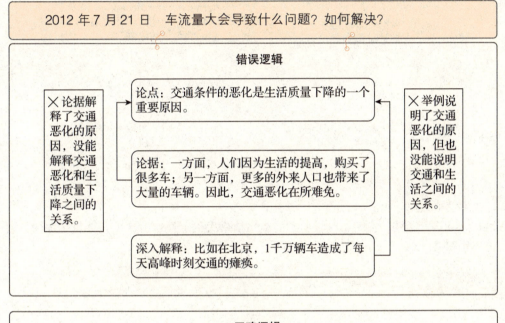

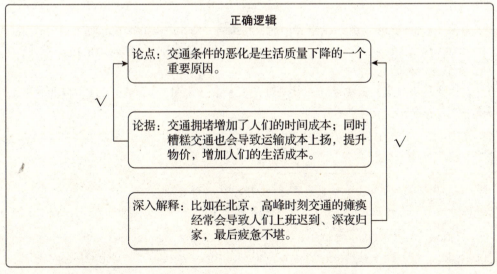

再看一个例子：

> **2014 年 10 月 11 日　因为使用手机和网络，人们正在丧失沟通能力吗？**
>
> 立场：不同意
>
> 论点：the convenience and low costs　　　　　high efficiency
> 　　　便捷、低成本　　　　　　　　　　　　　高效
> 　　　　　↓　　　　　　　　　　　　　　　　　↓
> 论据：The instant communication in virtual　Individuals could expand community
> 　　　world save mush time and effort　　　　quickly and be freed from space and
> 　　　　　　　　　　　　　　　　　　　　　　quantitative restrictions
> 　　　虚拟世界里的即时沟通节　　　　　　　　人们可以快速扩大社交圈，摆脱
> 　　　省了大量时间和精力　　　　　　　　　　空间和数量的限制
> 　　　　　↓　　　　　　　　　　　　　　　　　↓
> 深入解释：because it overcomes the barrier　because Online technology integrates
> 　　　　　in physical distance.　　　　　　　resources and realizes instant
> 　　　　　　　　　　　　　　　　　　　　　　information exchange
> 　　　　　因为它克服了距离的障碍　　　　　　因为线上科技整合了资源并实现了
> 　　　　　　　　　　　　　　　　　　　　　　信息的即时交换

　　上面的论据和深入解释部分之间就使用的原因状语从句，接下来我们再看 because, since, now that, as, in that 具体使用时的区别。

　　because 语气最强，在句首时，引导的分句结束后用逗号与主句隔开；放在主句后时它的前面不加逗号。

> **2014 年 5 月 24 日　为什么年轻人对学校不满及如何鼓励他们学习？**
>
> 　　As for solutions, the most important step should be motivating children to have learning interests of their own, because it is the only way to drive children to learn actively.
>
> 　　至于解决方案，最重要的一步应该是鼓励孩子们自发的学习兴趣，因为这是唯一能让孩子们主动学习的动力。

since 放于句首，表示已知的情况，翻译为"既然"。

> **2012 年 7 月 21 日　车流量大成为问题的原因和解决办法**
>
> 　　Since traffic systems have become a determinative element for city's operation, it is necessary for the government to evaluate the impacts of traffic congestion.
>
> 　　既然交通系统已经成为城市运营的决定性因素，政府必须评估交通阻塞的影响。

now that 放于句首,也是"既然"的意思,与 since 的区别在于,now that 引出的原因是以前未出现的新情况,而 since 则没有这一要求。

> **2012 年 11 月 8 日   计算机课是否应成为基础教育的第四个主要部分?**
>
> Now that computers are becoming an imperative part for daily life, educators must face the issue whether it should be upgraded to the fourth main subject.
>
> 鉴于计算机正成为日常生活必不可少的一部分,教育工作者必须面对着是否将它升级为第四门主课的问题。

as 语气最弱,表示双方都知道或者众所周知的情况,放在主句前后均可。

> **2016 年 3 月 16 日   同意停止为人类牟利而杀戮动物吗?**
>
> Animal experiments could accelerate the development of medical technology, as only the related tests can ensure the safety of medicines and products.
>
> 动物实验能够加速医疗技术的发展,因为只有相关测试才能确保医药和产品的安全性。

in that 用于主句后面,前面不加逗号,表示因为。

> **2014 年 12 月 20 日   绘画课应该成为必修课吗?**
>
> Students focusing on colleges may be disturbed by the learning of these subjects in that they are examined by the contents from textbooks only.
>
> 那些专注于考大学的人会被这些科目的学习所干扰,因为考核他们的只是教科书的内容。

01 改错:写作挑错

看看下面的句子有错吗?

2014 年 4 月 24 日　该控制针对孩子们的广告吗？

Because advertising is becoming an important method in achieving marketing goals through affecting children's thoughts, so some parents worry about that and call for strict regulations to control it.

因为广告正在通过影响孩子们的想法而成为一种重要的实现市场目标的方法，所以一些家长开始担心并要求以严格的规章限制它。

02 大闯关：写作闯关

翻译下面的句子，注意句子中包含的从句：

2014 年 5 月 15 日　该为雇员们每年至少放 4 周假吗？

既然带薪年假已经成为一种流行的工作激励方法，那就是时候去探讨是否应该把它的长度延长到 4 周了。

参考答案

01　在中文中，因为和所以是关联使用的，但在英文中，because 和 so 不可以同时出现在一句话中，我们只留下 because，后面的主句前面不加任何连词。

Because advertising is becoming an important method in achieving marketing goals through affecting children's thoughts, some parents worry about that and call for strict regulations to control it.

02　Since annual leave has become a popular method of work motivation, it is time to delve into whether the length should be extended to 4 weeks.

结果状语从句换个表达顺序

口语部分

结果状语从句要跟目的状语从句进行区分，结果状语指的是两个动作是连续的，一个是另一个的结果。比如：他气得说不出话来了。He was so angry that he couldn't speak. 在中文中它表达这样一种意思："太……以至于……"正好可以在口语考试中用于"喜欢"的话题。

> I'm such a big fan of swimming that I almost go there every week.（游泳）
> I'm such a book worm that I read about 1 hour every day.（读书）
> I'm such a night owl that I almost never sleep before 2 o'clock.（熬夜）
> I'm so crazy about my idol that I even have a diary which I use to write something to him and imagine he can read it.（偶像）
> I'm so crazy about ice cream that I really can't stop myself after eating 8 or 9 of them until my mother threatens me that I may get cancer because of it.（零食）

当然这个句子也可以不用 I 来起句，只表示某一动作单一地产生了某个结果。当然，多数还是在描述情绪，比如担心、心跳、累、紧张、困、感动等。

> She worried to be blamed so that she cried in front of me.（道歉经历）
> My heart beat so fast that I could hardly breathe.（第一次用外语）
> I was so tired/nervous that I could hardly stand.（极限运动）
> She was so moved by the sight that she began to burst into tears.（收到礼物）

也可以倒装表达对感受的强调：

> So sleepy was I that I could hardly keep my eyes open.（早起的经历）

这个句型还可以用来描述"无法用言语描述景色之美"：

> It was so spectacular that I could hardly use any language to describe it.

形容天气也是好句型：

> It was so cold that my hands couldn't stop trembling．（看天经历）
> It was such a foggy day that we could hardly see the road．（天气改变计划）
> The rain was so heavy that the cars could hardly move forward.
> The wind was so strong that some trees were almost blown down.
> It's so hot that most people wanted to go swimming．（游泳）
> The weather was such that I could not go out.

用来描述不良情绪也是绝配：

> I was so ill that I couldn't even stand by myself．（难受的经历）
> I was so regretful that I almost wanted to kill myself．（忘事儿）

为了更好地掌握这个句型，我们再收集一些常用语境：

> 1. 我学习特别努力，以至于我喜欢的女孩终于开始注意我了。
>   I studied so hard that the girl I liked finally noticed me.
> 2. 我起得很早以便能赶上火车。
>   I got up so early that I could catch up the train.
> 3. 乔布斯工作太努力了，结果病倒了。（钱重要还是满意度重要）
>   Steve Jobs worked so hard that he became badly ill.
> 4. 他有那么多钱，后半辈子都不用愁了。（钱的重要性）
>   He was so rich that he doesn't need to worry about anything for the rest of his life.
> 5. 社会发展速度太快了，以至于不学习就会被淘汰。（学习的重要性）
>   The speed of social development is so fast that people will be replaced and knocked out without endeavoring in study.
> 6. 他说得太快了，我完全没听懂。（第一次用外语）
>   He spoke so fast that I totally didn't understand.
> 7. 人口增长得太快了，就会造成粮食短缺。
>   The population grows so fast that a shortage of grains will occur.
> 8. 他对我那么好，我不能怪他呀！（道歉经历）
>   He was so nice to me that I couldn't blame him.
> 9. 这东西太贵了，我攒三年工资也买不起。（满意的购买）
>   This stuff is so expensive that I couldn't afford it after saving for three years.
> 10. 这衣服太好看了，我不停照镜子。（别人给的衣服）
>   These clothes are so beautiful that I can't stop looking at the mirror.

总之，下次为了提醒自己用对这个句型，就记得所有描述情绪的形容词，无论是积极的还是消极的；所有描述样貌的形容词，好看或不好看；所有描述程度的，快或慢，多或少，早或晚，努力不努力，好还是不好；所有描述天气的，好或者不好；所有描述美食的，好吃或者不好吃，香或者臭；所有描述娱乐的，好玩或者无聊，都可以使用结果状语从句，来表示一种夸张。当然，也可以表示严重后果：

> 这个药太毒了，伤肝。
> The medicine is so noxious that it hurts my liver.
> 他病得太厉害，死了/该休息了。
> He was so sick that he died (had to rest).
> 高三生活太压抑，小明跳楼了。
> His life was so depressing in Grade Three that Xiao Ming jumped off the building.

除了 so that，结果状语从句还有其他引导词。在描述一个好朋友时，可以说：

> He was so kind as to help me with the homework.

在描述一次天气改变计划的经历里，可以说：

> The weather was so bad as to make the planned trip hard to proceed.

结果状语从句主要用来表达感受，所以在各种内心戏中都可以用这个句型：

> I was thinking, "How could I be so stupid as to forget it!"（忘事儿经历）
> I was thinking, "How could you be so considerate as to prepare gifts for me!"（别人送的衣服）
> I was thinking, "How could this place be so polluted as to generate such a disgusting smell!"（被污染的地方）
> I was thinking, "How could you be so mean as to borrow everything from others!"（借物经历）
> I was thinking, "How could I be so clever as to solve this problem that nobody has any ideas about!"（想象力的经历）
> I was thinking, "How could this place be so crowded as to make everything hard to get close and even see clearly."（不喜欢的旅行）

不过，要注意的是这个句型只能在主句和从句的主语一致的情况下使用，像上面高三生活压抑那句，从句用的是小明作主语，就无法用 so as to 了，只能说 so as to cause Xiao

Ming' suicide。还有一个细节要注意的是否定句，如果从句是否定句，那主句就不能再用 so，而要用 too，举个例子：

> I was too angry that I didn't want to talk with him.（生气的经历）

口语中对于这个句型还有一个省略式就是 *adj.* + enough：

> I was busy enough to think about anything.（忙碌的经历）

01 改错：口语挑错

在题目 Describe a time you helped someone 中，分析下下面的句子有错吗？

I was thinking, "They are so little luggage that I could carry six once. It's a wonderful time to show off my strength."

02 大闯关：口语闯关

试着把题目 Do you think leisure is important 中的这个句子翻译成英文：

现在的孩子的作业太多了以至于完全没有休闲时间，甚至很多人眼神都成了那种机器人的样子，没有一点灵气。

参考答案

01 so that 结构中不应该出现名词，否则应该改成 such 而不是 so，所以应该去掉名词，名词 luggage 和主语 they 意义比较重复，保留一个就行，应该改成：I was thinking, "The luggage are so little that I could carry six once. It's a wonderful time to show off my strength."

02 Nowadays, there are so much homework for kids that they totally have no leisure time. Many kids even look like robots in their eyes, with no inspiration.

写作部分

结果状语从句的连词包括：so that、so...that...、such...that...。

1. so that 在结果状语从句里是"因此"的意思，后面引导结果，可以连接论述的论据解释和深入解释。例如：

> **2016年1月9日B卷 世界各地的文化娱乐雷同好处多于坏处吗?**

> Cooperation worldwide creates more chances for people to contact with new social attitudes and lifestyles so that it becomes the key to realize continuing cultural prosperity.
>
> 世界范围内的合作为人们接触新的社会观念和生活方式创造了更多的机会，因此它成了实现文化持续繁荣的关键。

2. so...that... 是"如此……以至于……"的意思，比如:

> Mr. Trump was so popular that he was a hair's breadth away from the White House.
>
> 特朗普先生太受欢迎了，以至于他离白宫仅仅一步之遥。

这一句简化成公式就是:

> 主语+be/动词+so 形容词/副词+that 主谓宾/主系表.

这一句还可用倒装的方式表达:

> So popular is Mr. Trump that he was a hair's breadth away from the white house.

同样用法公式化，就是:

> So+形容词/副词+be/动词+主语+that 主谓宾/主系表.

同样是表达"如此……以至于……"的意思。这句话包含了一个因果关系，"如此……"是因，"以至于……"是果。这句话正好可以用来说明论据和进行深入解释。比如:

> **2014年12月4日 语言教学小班型效果好吗?**

> So important are individualized guidance and correction that more opportunities to practice in small learning groups could bring about better effects.
>
> 个性化的指导和纠错是如此的重要，以至于在小的学习小组里更多的练习机会能带来更好的效果。

3. such...that...也是"如此……以至于……"的意思。它和 so...that...的区别在于，so 是副词，后面需要接形容词或副词；而 such 是形容词，后面要接名词词组。比如：

> Hillary Clinton is such a nice lady that many housewives will vote for her.
> 希拉里·克林顿是一个那么可爱的女士，以至于好多主妇都会投票给她。

这一句用 so...that...表达就是：

> Hillary Clinton is so nice of a lady that many housewives will vote for her.

同 so...that...一样，such...that...也有倒装结构：

> Such a nice lady is Hillary Clinton that many housewives will vote for her.

再来看一道真题：

> 2014 年 5 月 17 日　该鼓励孩子们在家和在校规律地看电视吗？

> Educational programs contain such interesting descriptions and lively scenes that watching regularly definitely can keep children's minds active.
> 教育节目包含了如此有趣的描述和生动的场景以至于规律性地收看能绝对让孩子们保持头脑活跃。

练　习

01　改错：写作挑错

看看下面的句子有错吗？

2015 年 9 月 26 日　为什么一些国家废物回收量不足？如何鼓励回收？

The prices of non-recyclable materials like plastic are cheap enough so that it is hard for customers to choose expensive environmental materials.

塑料等不可回收材料的价格低到足以让用户难以选择昂贵的环保材料。

02　大闯关：写作闯关

翻译下面的句子，注意倒装结构。

2014年4月24日　针对孩子的广告应该被控制吗?

儿童，作为一个特殊的顾客群，其市场位置是如此重要，以至于对于针对儿童的广告的任何禁令都将严重伤及上游企业。

> **参考答案**
>
> 01　这一句的结构应该是：主语 + be + 形容词 + enough + that 结果状语从句。当主句的结尾是 enough 时，结果状语从句用 that 即可。
> The prices of non-recyclable materials like plastic are cheap enough that it is hard for customers to choose expensive environmental materials.
>
> 02　So important is the marketing position of children, as a special customer group, that any ban on advertisement targeting children would hurt upstream business seriously.

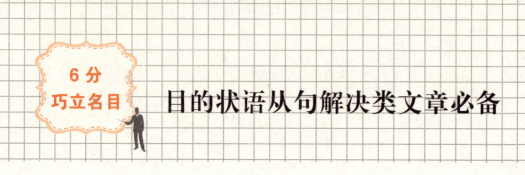

目的状语从句解决类文章必备

口语部分

"以至于"和"以便能"是两个概念,这就是为什么上一章我们说要分清结果状语和目的状语,因为 so that 确实都可以引导这两个从句。

区分两个句子:

> I studied so hard that she eventually noticed me.
> I studied very hard so that she could notice me.

目的状语从句总是在表示一种"为了能"的意思。所以,为了能练好这个句型,我们先认真思考一下,从小到大我们到底有多少伟大的目标与梦想:

1) 为了能有时间玩……In order to have time to play…
2) 为了能让老师喜欢…… In order that the teacher could notice me and like me…
3) 为了能考个好成绩…… So I can have a good result in the exam…
4) 为了下周能有好精神…… So that I can be working efficiently in the next week…
5) 为了能提高效率……in case I have no efficiency…
6) 为了能保持清醒…… …for fear that I will lose my concentration.
7) 为了能吃上冰淇淋…… …so that I can eat the ice cream.
8) 为了能得到老爸表扬…… In order to get praise from my dad…
9) 为了能得到女神青睐……In order that my goddess could fall in love with me…
10) 为了能赢得比赛……In order to win the game…
11) 为了能考上清华…… …so that I can go to study in Tsinghua University.
12) 为了能多挣点钱……In order to make more money…
13) 为了能有更好的工作…… …so that I can have a better in the future.
14) 为了能给你幸福…… Just in order to make you happy…
15) 为了能远离疾病…… In case I might get ill…
16) 为了能改掉坏习惯…… …in case I can't get rid of my bad habits.
17) 为了能打发时间…… …so that I can kill the time.
18) 为了能睡个好觉…… Lest I can't sleep well…
19) 为了能获得好的教育…… …for the purpose that I could have a better education.

20）为了能充实精神生活……In order to enrich my spiritual life...
21）为了能有更好的未来……So much so that I could have a better future...
22）为了能给孩子做个好榜样……So much so that I could be a good role model to my child...
23）为了能支付得起体面的生活……So as to afford my decent life...
24）为了能赶上火车……In order to catch the train...
25）为了能跟朋友交流……In order that I can communicate with my friends in these topics...
26）为了能长长见识……In order to enrich my knowledge...

而这些就是我们经常使用目的状语从句的地方，大家会发现 in order that 在语气上目的性最强烈，for fear that 和 in case 表达的是以防、以免，lest 多用于书面语，for the purpose that 表示为……目的

当然除了我们以上讲的 26 个人生目的以外，口语表达中还有很多很小的目的，比如为了第二天能骑自行车，为了能锻炼孩子动手能力（手工），为了能更好地理解世界（科学），为了能得到观众尖叫（运动），为了能补充维生素（水果）等等。

在雅思口语考试中，这个用法常出现在 Part 2 经历题的描述中，通常经历题的第二问都要求阐述做某事的目的。

- 比如描述一个早起的经历：
  For fear that I would miss the train on the next day, I decided to go to bed early.
- 帮助别人的经历：
  I gave him some more money so that he could buy a train ticket to get back home.
- 第一次使用外语的经历：
  In order that she could understand, I talked with her really slowly and clearly.
- 使用想象力的经历：
  So much so that we could get out in time, we worked in a group and allocated the task.
- 忙碌的经历：
  In case I couldn't pass the exam, I burned the midnight oil every day.
- 有些物品题中也可以这样用：
  In case he doesn't like it, I searched the Internet again and again.（送给别人的礼物）

- 还有一些跟未来目的和打算有关的题：
  ◇ I want to work in this company so that I can get the opportunity to talk with the moist versatile and talented and innovative genius in this area. （想去工作的大公司）
  ◇ I wish to work in this country so as to put myself in an atmosphere of diligent working and innovation. （想去工作的国家）
  ◇ I'm eager to learn this course so as to gain a skill and competitiveness in my future career prospects. （想学的课程）

这样的话题还有想吃的食物、目标、想住的房子、想做的工作，想买的东西等等。在 Part 3 中，使用这个从句的地方也有很多。尤其在解决办法类问题中：

Nowadays, a lot of young people don't like to go to the historical places. Do you have any good methods to solve this problem?

Well, I think a useful method is to invite some movie stars and pop stars to the historical places so that young people who are usually big fans of them will come with great enthusiasm. Then the culture of historical buildings can be spreaded successfully.

你可以用上面的从句试试回答下列题目：

如何解决交通问题
如何解决景区乱扔垃圾的问题
如何让中国年轻人更快加入到全球化大环境当中
如何让不喜欢学习的孩子重新爱上学习

另外一个需要注意的就是时态和情态动词的搭配：

主语时态	从句时态
一般现在时 现在完成时 一般将来时	may/shall/can/will + 动词原形 （shall 少用）
各种过去时态	might/should/could/would + 动词原形

而从句是一定要有情态动词的！

练 习

01 改错：口语挑错

看看下面的句子有错吗？

It's not strongly recommended that we should work at weekends, so that we could feel unhealthy at the end because of overtime working.

02 大闯关：口语闯关

试着应用目的状语从句来翻译下面的句子。

1) 我妈总说一定要多吃水果，以防得病。

2) 为了能考个好成绩，我每天都学习到晚上12点。

参考答案

01 目的状语从句和结果状语从句很容易分不清楚。题目中的句子翻译成汉语是：强烈不推荐我们应该在周末工作，以便到最后因为过劳而不健康。这个意思是不是就很奇怪？我们是为了不健康才工作的。造成这个错误的原因是情态动词的误用，上面的从句表达的很明显是结果不是目的，所以不该用情态动词！另外 so that 中间要有形容词 It's not strongly recommended that we work so hard at weekends as to feel unhealthy at the end because of overtime working.

01 1) My mother always said, "You must eat more fruits in case you get ill."

2) In order that I can get good marks, I study to 12 o'clock p. m. every day.

写作部分

目的状语从句的连词包括：以便（so that、in order that）、以防（lest、in case、for fear that）。需要注意的是，在议论文写作中，目的状语从句部分一般是对还未发生的事情的推断，需要用 can、will、could、would、may、might 等情态动词。

1. so that 和 in order that 在目的状语从句中是"以便"的意思，后面引导从句说明目的，在议论文中可以连接解决措施和实现目标。

当面对要求分析原因（What are the causes?）以及提出解决办法（What measures should be taken to solve the problem?）的问题时，回答解决措施时要注意两个要点：

（1）解决措施不能过于笼统，仅仅在方向上提出空洞的口号是缺乏说服力的。比如：分析儿童不如从前健康的原因并提出解决意见。

分析原因为 "unhealthy diet"；提出的解决措施是 "promoting healthy eating" 就不行，太过笼统，不具备可操作性，也就没有说服力，逻辑单项会失分。

具体的解决方案不仅要求提供方向性的指南，还需指明相应的具体的措施，比如 "popularizing dietary knowledge and providing nourishing food service in schools"。

再比如年轻人不愿选择基础科学专业的解决措施，仅仅说明 "improving material conditions" 是不够的，应该说明如何实现这一点，如 "raising science researchers' average income by dispensing more grants"。

（2）解决措施还可以写出层次来，以提高说服力。

这个层次可以包括：具体的措施、这一措施预期要达到的目的。比如：

2016 年 2 月 18 日　环境破坏是无药可救了还是尚有可为？

具体措施
adopt the tougher industrial standards in the emission of carbon and other wastes
在碳排量和其他废物排出上设定更严格的工业标准

预期目的
The producers would be pushed to invest more on the exploration of new energy and accelerate technological innovation.
迫使生产者们在新能源的开发上投入更多并加强技术革新。

这两项之间就可以用目的状语从句：

> As for solutions, to adopt the tougher industrial standards in the emission of carbon and other wastes should be the first choice so that the producers would be pushed to invest more on the exploration of new energy and accelerate technological innovation.

这一句的句式骨架就是：

As for solutions, 某一措施（n./Ving/to v.）should be the first choice, so that 实现某一预期目的（句子）.

还有很多同义词替换来表达同样的意思：

为了解决这一问题，	某一具体措施	占有优先权	实现某种预期目的
Aiming at solving the trouble, As for solutions, To address the issue, To counteract the problem, To fix the paradoxical situation,	名词/ 动名词/ 不定式 词组	is a preference should be an optimal choice should take the priority would be an effective means would be an efficient method	so that ... in order that ....

2. for fear that、in case、lest 都是"以防"的意思，在议论文中也可以用于说明解决措施的部分，只不过后面目的状语从句的逻辑内容需要变成相应发生的后果。和上一类的区别在于，so that 等引导的是要实现的目的，是积极的，而 for fear that 等引导的是要避免的问题，是消极的。

可以把上一条里面的例子变一变：

> 具体措施
> adopt the tougher industrial standards in the emission of carbon and other wastes
> 在碳排量和其他废物排出上设定更严格的工业标准
> 要预防的后果
> Greenhouse effect extends and influences other industries such as agriculture.
> 温室气体效应加剧并影响农业等其他产业。

> 连起来就是
> As for solutions, to adopt the tougher industrial standards in the emission of carbon and other wastes should be the first choice, lest greenhouse effect extends and influences other industries such as agriculture.

句式骨架就变成了：

As for solutions, 某一措施 (n./Ving/to v.) should be the first choice, lest 某一需要预防的后果.

表格也可以变成：

为了解决这一问题，	具体措施	占有优先权	以防某一后果
Aiming at solving the trouble, As for solutions, To address the issue, To counteract the problem, To fix the paradoxical situation,	名词/ 动名词/ 不定式词组	is a preference should be an optimal choice should take the priority would be an effective means would be an efficient method	for fear that.... in case.... lest....

图表作文中目的状语从句一般用于流程图中，用来说明加工的目的：

> 原料 is 加工过程（动词被动语态）by a 设备 so that 加工目的（句子）.
> 原料将由某种设备进行某种处理，以便得到某种结果。

比如：

> The mixed powder of clay and limestone are heated in a rotating heater so that they could form small particles.
> 黏土和石英石的混合粉末在一个旋转加热器中被加热，以便形成小颗粒。

01 改错：写作挑错

看看下面的句子有错吗？

2013 年 3 月 2 日　远距离学习的好处大于坏处吗？

Online education suppliers are strengthening supervision in case some people will swindle degrees by academic frauds.

线上教育正在加强监管，以防一些人以学术欺诈的方式骗取学位。

02 大闯关：写作闯关

翻译下面这句话，注意其中既有表达目的的状语，也有目的状语从句。

2013 年 10 月 26 日　城乡差距的危害和解决方法

为了解决这个问题，加强农村基础建设应该是个有效的办法，以便吸引更多的人口和商业投资流向这些地区。

参考答案

01　表达"以防"的从句中不用将来时态，而用一般现在时，虽然要防止的事情还没有发生。

Online education suppliers are strengthening supervision in case some people swindle degrees by academic frauds.

02　To counteract the problem, strengthening the infrastructure in rural areas would be an effective means so that more population and business investment would flow to these regions.

6分 恰逢其时 时间状语从句注意少见用法

口语部分

时间状语从句是最常用的一个状语从句，因为每个话题拓展信息都需要从 why, what, when, where, how 这几个角度进行，我们之前一直在说场景，说到休闲、周末、运动、音乐都会用到时间状语，比如：

> When I have free time, for example in holidays or on weekends, I like to...
> When I was in high school, I used to like...but after I graduated...
> When I feel upset or down, what I like the most is to play some music, like...
> When I do my homework, or before sleep, I like to put on my earphones.
> When I feel exhausted about work or study, I like to go traveling...
> When the weather is not lousy...
> When I was a child...
> Before I sleep...
> After I graduate...

这个句型在口语考试中非常常用，几乎可以用在任何一个 Part 1 题目中，而且非常简单。只是许多考生在短时间内做不出反应，所以在 Part 1 常规训练中，往往都会加入一些场景细节信息拓展训练，举个例子：

> Do you like park?

> Well, yeah, I like parks. It's a peaceful place to think and relax.（形容词）
> When I have free time, for example after dinner,（场景）
> what I like to do the most is to walk in the park with my family
> talk about some trifles in a day, share what's new in our lives.
> Sometimes to see the sunset and enjoy the view and the cosy feeling after a whole day work or study.
> It's genuinely a fantastic place.

再如：

> Do you like science?

> Yeah, I'm a big fan of science.
> When I was young, I was really addicted to quantum physics. I used to read *A Brief History of Time*, in which I learned how amazing the world I'm living is. That book taught me what's black hole and what is the theory of relaticety, by a story that two twin brothers, one goes to space, 50 years later he came back and found his brother already 60 years old but he was still young. That's when I found science truly enchanting.

when 引导从句是时间状语从句中比较简单的一种，当然也最需要我们熟练使用，当然，英语中还有很多引导时间状语从句的用法，比如：

> As soon as/the moment/immediately/the instant/no sooner than/hardly when…

"刚……就……" 通常都是出现于机场，见面之类的场景。如：

> I had hardly sat down when he stepped in.（别人向你道歉的经历）
> Hardly had I seen the lightning, when I heard a loud thundering.（天气改变计划）

另外一个很特殊的时间状语从句是 By the time（到……时候，就……）通常都是指完成目标的场景，常用于将来时态的考题如未来想要的房子，未来想做的工作，未来的目标，未来的打算，未来的一次特殊之旅。这个句型使用后，主句通常是 will have done 将来完成时，译为：到那时，我肯定得（变成）……

将来时态在口语考试中的应用场景非常有限，精心设计一定会有意想不到的效果。如：

> What's your plan for the future? 和 Do you prefer to live in a house or apartment?
> I always think, "By the time I graduate, I will have become a master."
> By the time I could afford this house, I will have become a successful person.

Whenever, every time when… 也常用于场景构建

> Whenever I have free time, I'd like to go to the cinema with my friends.（电影）
> Every time when I flee boring I call my friends and ask them out.（休闲）

看一个完整的例子：

> **Do you like shopping?**

> Yeah, definitely. Every time when I feel upset, I like shopping, because it's a kind of good way to release my pressure. Sometimes only surfing the shopping website can make me feel content as the process gives me great stimulation.

not...until... 直到……才……，这个句型用于讲述发现一个事实的感受，在 Part 2 Describe a time you forgot to do something. 和 Describe a time you learned from making a mistake.（忘事儿、旅游）中常用：

> Until I knew this, I didn't realize how stupid I was.

时间状语从句的主要难点在于时态的搭配，比如 since 和完成时的连用：

> I have been in Beijing since I graduated.

还有 when 和 while 的区别，后者要描写的动作得是延续性的或者同时发生的。when 则是一个时点。如：

> While he read, I cooked the dinner.
> What were you doing while he was getting the drinks?

在题目 Describe a time you used your imagination 中，就可以用含延续性动作的时间状语来描述玩密室逃脱过程中忽然的主意：

> While we were confused, I suddenly got the idea to turn off all the lights and I found the password was shown on the wall in luminous color.

when 还有几个特殊用法，可用来表示一件突然的、意料之外的事情：

> I was taking a walk when I came across him.（帮助他人）
> I was just getting into the subway station when he came to me and said…

另一种结构是与 be about to 或 be on the point of 连用。
早起的经历 Describe a time you got extremely early.

> I was about to go to sleep, when there was a knock on the window.

帮助他人的经历 Describe a time you helped someone：

> I was on the point of leaving when he showed such a helpless look.

是非常实用的 Part 2 黄金句，在事件经历题中作故事铺垫。
when 还有 at which time 或 and then 的意思，表示"然后"：

> I expect to be there two days or so, when I shall return.
> I was a student until the 2008 Olympic Games, when I trained as a translator.

这个句型可以在面签的或者旅游过边境时使用。在雅思口语考试当中，这个句型倒并不是很实用，不过通过这些与平时表达习惯不相同的句子，我们也了解一下真正地道的句子是怎样说的，多多收集，有一天你也一定能够地道口语脱口而出！

练 习

01 改错：口语挑错

看看下面的句子有错吗？
You should have the pills when the water is still hot.

02 大闯关：口语闯关

试着应用时间状语从句来翻译下面的句子。
我就要亲到她的时候她电话响了。

参考答案

01　正确说法为：You should have the pills while the water is still hot. 使用时间状语从句的一个难点就是分清什么是瞬时动作，什么是延续性动作，水热不是一个瞬间，所以这里应该用 while 而不是 when。翻译过来就是：趁着水还热乎，你应该把药吃了。

02　I was about to kiss her, when her phone rang. 大部分同学是不是想说成：When I almost kissed her, her phone started ringing. 严格意义上来说这并不算错，因为比较直译。时间状语中的时间点是：我就要亲到她的时刻是手机响的时刻。但是记住本章我们说到的另一个用法，be about to 表示将要，马上要做某事了。when 在这表示"就在这时"。在语境上有那种非常不合时宜出现的感觉。

写作部分

时间状语从句的引导词有很多：when、whenever、while、before、after、since、once、until 等等，因为雅思写作容量太小，TASK 1 和 2 总共只有 400 字，我们要在这么点字数内展示多变的语法技巧，那么时间状语从句只能出现 1-2 次，下面我就重点介绍几个可以模仿的实战用法。

议论文中时间状语的应用：

1 when 引导的时间状语从句

when 是"当……时"的意思，这一句可以用在议论文的开头第一句，用来说明全篇讨论涉及的背景意义。例如：

> 2013 年 8 月 13 日　政府该为大学生付学费吗？

> When we think of the public welfare in education, the thing that springs to mind is whether governments should supply free higher education.
> 当谈到教育领域内公众福利的时候，我立即想起的事就是政府是否应该提供免费的高等教育。

那么把这一句公式化就变成：

When we think of 相关领域（名词词组），the thing that springs immediately to mind is 主要论题（whether、why 等引导的从句，复述题目）．

当我们考虑某一领域内的某种局势的时候，第一件想起的事就是主要论题这一问题。

这一句式的语法拿分点是 when 引导的时间状语从句，以及 that 引导的主语的定语从句。逻辑上，此句的难点在于相关领域必须切题。

> 2013 年 12 月 12 日　购买更多的家电是积极还是消极的？

> When it comes to the application of technology in daily life, the matter of prime importance is whether higher owning rate of domestic appliances is a positive phenomenon.
> 当提及科技在日常生活中的应用时，最重要的问题是家用电器更高的拥有率是否是一个积极的现象。

表达这一语义的并列选项可以总结为下表：

当考虑……的时候	相关领域，	第一件需要关注的事就是	主要论题
When it comes to When we think of When we are analyzing When mentioning When discussing about	名词词组，	the thing that needs to be addressed is the thing that springs to mind is the issue that takes priority for consideration is the matter of prime importance is 相关人群 have to pay close attention to 相关人群 must confront the question	whether、why 等引导的从句

需要注意的是：当主句的主语和时间状语从句的主语一致的时候，从句中的主语是可以省略的，比如上表中最下边一栏的内容"When mentioning 和 When discussing about"，后面主句的主语一定是人。

而最常见的相关人群包括：

> 教育类：educators 教育工作者
> 社会类：sociologists 社会学家
> 科技类：scientists 科学家
> 生活类：the public 公众，individuals 人们
> 环保类：environment engineers 环境工程师
> 犯罪类：legal experts 法律专家
> 经济类：economists 经济学家

2　whenever、every time、anytime 引导的时间状语从句

whenever 和 every time 是"每当"的意思，在议论文中应用的场景不如 when 广泛，但可以用来强调事物的重要性，"每当某一时刻，这个事情的重要性就显现出来了"。例如：

> **2012 年 4 月 21 日　同意计划未来不如专注当前吗?**
>
> Whenever people can see if they are likely to face a problem with the help of careful planning, they can avoid or prepare well, rather than to deal with the crisis when it comes unexpected.
>
> 每当在详细计划的帮助下，人们能够预见到他们是否会遇到什么问题时，他们就能进行规避或者做好准备，而不是在危机不期而至时匆忙应对。

还可以用来假设事情的后果，例如：

> 2014 年 6 月 21 日　人们为什么换职业？它是积极还是消极的？

> Every time individuals change their careers, they may have to waste time and energy on orienting themselves in unfamiliar work surroundings.
> 每当人们改变职业，他们都可能不得不浪费时间和精力来适应新的工作环境。

3　the moment 的用法

the moment 是"……的时候就……"的意思。可以用来表示某事的意义，一旦做了这事，就意味着……。
例如：

> 2015 年 4 月 30 日　年轻人和父母同住的好处大于坏处吗？

> A young man begins to become independent the moment he moves out from his parents' home and learns to take care of himself.
> 年轻人搬离父母家并学着照顾自己的时候，就是他开始变得独立的时候。

4　until 的用法

until 是"直到"的意思，在议论文里，我们可以用 keep doing … until …来在文章的结尾发出号召，我们需要一直在某方面努力，直到实现了某个目标，例如：

> 2014 年 11 月 13 日　该禁止某些食物广告以防过度饮食造成健康危害吗？

> In addition, supervisory authorities and watchdogs should keep guiding the contents of advertisements until a perfect supervising system has been built up.
> 另外，监管部门和监督组织应该一直指导广告的内容直到一个完善的系统被建立起来。

其主干可以表示为：
In addition, sb.（相关人群）should keep 采取某种措施（动词现在分词词组）until 实现某一结果（从句）.
另外，相关人群应该一直采取某种措施直到某一结果能够被实现。

再如：

> **2014 年 4 月 26 日　线上工作和学习取代现实方式好不好？**
>
> In addition, online education suppliers should keep improving their teaching methods until the quality of education they provide could be guaranteed.
>
> 另外，线上教育提供者应该持续改善他们的教学方式直到他们提供的教学质量得到保障。

图表题中时间状语的应用：

1. as、while、before、after 的用法。

as、while：与……同时；before：在……之前；after：在……之后。这些词侧重表达的是简单时间的顺序，多用于线性图和多时间点的柱状图，我们可以用来对比各单项的变化：

> As revealed by the graph, there was／were 特殊变化（名词）in 特殊变化的单项名称 during the period, while others showed 大多数的变化（名词）.
>
> 如图所示，特殊变化的项目展示了某种变化，同时其余的项目均显示了不一样的变化。

比如：

> **2014 年 2 月 1 日**
>
>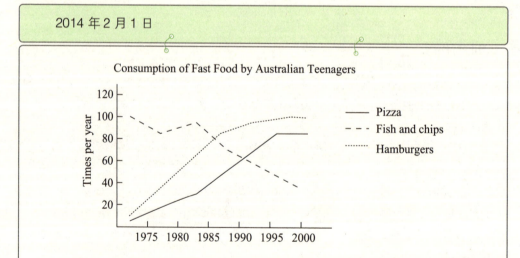
>
> As revealed by the graph, the times of fish and chips dropped stably in the later period, while others both showed increase in similar degrees.
>
> 如图所示，鱼薯店的次数在后期稳定地下降，同时其余的项目均显示了出类似程度的上升。

before 和 after 的用法比较简单，还是根据上图，我们来看两个例子：

> Before the times of pizza and hamburgers kept stable in the last 4 years, they both experienced moderate growth.
> 在比萨和汉堡的次数在最后 4 年保持恒定之前，它们都经历了中速的上升。
> The number of fish and chips started to rebound after it reached the bottom at 80 times in 1977.
> 在 1977 年触底达到 80 次以后，鱼薯店的数值开始回升。

2. since、once、until 的用法

since 是"自从"；once "一旦"；until 是"直到……"。需要注意的是：since 自从……以来，主句表示的是从这个时刻到后来一个时间段内的状态，用完成时，可以用来描述一段时间内发生的变化。

> The number of hamburgers has increased by 70 times since it started to climb in 1975.
> 自从汉堡从 1975 年开始爬升以来，它的数值已经升高了 70 次。

once 一旦……，从句表示的是某一个时间点之前的事，用完成时，可以用于流程图中，例如：

Once the last step has been done, 原材料 is/are sent to a 器械 for 加工细节（现在分词）in order to 加工目的（动词词组）.

当上一步被完成之后，原材料被送到某一机械处进行某种加工，以便达到某一加工目的。

比如：

> Once the last step has been done, the cleaned bottles are sent to a furnace for heating and melting in order to change them into recycled liquid glass.
> 当上一步被完成之后，洗净的玻璃瓶被送到一个熔炉进行加热和融化，以便把它们变成循环的液态玻璃。

until 可以用于交代一段变化的终点：

单项名称 displayed 某种变化（形容词 + 名词）in 某一时段, then turned to 下一种变化（动词原形 + 副词）until it reached at 终点数值 in 终点时间.

在某一时段内，某一单项展示了某种变化，后转变为下一种变化，直到在某一时间达到了某一数值。

比如前面的线形图：

> The number of fish and chips displayed a slow decline in the first 5 years, then turned to increase until it reach at 95 times in 1985.
>
> 在前五年，鱼薯店的数字展示了一段缓慢的下降，然后转变为上升，直到在 1985 年达到 95 次。

练习

01 改错

看看下面的句子有错吗？

2012 年 8 月 11 日　青年毕业即失业的影响和解决

By the time many youths graduate, they still do not prepare enough to handle daily work independently.

很多年轻人直到毕业的时候都还没做好独立应对日常工作的准备。

02 大闯关：写作闯关

翻译下面的句子，注意句首和句尾的两个从句。

2013 年 9 月 7 日　核能是最好的能源吗？

当我们审视能源危机的解决方案的时候，第一件需要被定位的就是核能是否是最优的替代能源。

参考答案

01　by the time 是 "到……时为止" 的意思，一般从句用一般过去时，主句用一般过去时或过去完成时。

By the time many youths graduated, they still did not prepare enough to handle daily work independently.

02　When we check up the solutions for power crisis, the thing that needs to be addressed is whether nuclear power is the best alternative resource.

7分 辨物居方 条件状语从句显得客观学术

口语部分

条件状语从句是许多雅思考生都喜欢的从句，也是高分的常见策略。对于逻辑思维好的同学，都会下意识给题目分层。Do you like sunny days? 你喜欢晴天吗？Well, if it's not too hot. What's your favourite color? Hmm, if you are talking about clothes, maybe black.

对于雅思口语来说，分层和给出限定条件是基本方法。除了 usually, generally speaking 和 from a general level 这样的层次，再细分就要用到时间状语和条件状语了。比如说我们常考的列举题：

> What do you like to do for relaxation?
> What do you like to do at weekends?
> What do you like to do with friends?
> What do you like to do in the evenings?

在答题的时候就可以分为，If I'm not very busy 和 but now 这样的两个层次。

> Usually, I like to watch some films or play computer games, but if I'm not very busy, say if it's during the holidays, what I like to do the most is to group some friends and organise a barbeque party or picnic outside in the suburbs. But now, my life is a little running around the o'clock, so the only thing I do is to study.

另外一个常见条件状语的地方，是对过去的回忆，在 Part 1, Part 2 中经常会出现回忆题。比如 Part 2 人物题常有的 How do you know this person, 以及 Part 1 里的 What did you do last weekend? How was the first day in your school?

那回答的时候就可以带上 Honestly, If I remember well/If my memory serves me well, the first time I met him was in an ice-breaking party on the first day of school. He was very distinctive, talking elegantly to everyone present, wearing blue jeans and a white shirt, looking like a golden boy.

当然如果时态换成将来时，What's your plan for the future? 回答也可以说，Hopefully, if everything goes smooth, I'd like to further my study in the UK first.

if 从句放句首很多时候可以用来表达一种不确定的、保守的、谦虚的语气。

在表达个人选择时：

> If I have a choice, I guess an apartment takes a better chance to win my preference. 如果我能选的话，我觉得公寓更有可能是我喜欢的类型。
>
> If I must say, I believe eating out is more likely to be my preference. 如果一定要说的话，我觉得在外面吃更符合我的偏好。

在表达对数字的估算时：

> If my math isn't wrong, it needs at least 2 hours to transport. 如果我数学没错，至少要 2 小时的车程。

在表达虚拟语气时：

> If I were him, I wouldn't be this sober. 如果我是他，我不会这么淡定。
>
> If the pigs were to fly up, I would like to go to the museums. 如果猪会飞，我就会喜欢去博物馆。

当然我们传统意义上的条件句，可能是真实条件句。类似于：

> If you work hard, you are bound to be successful. 如果你努力就一定会成功！（努力是成功的条件，这是条件句的真实面貌：有了条件，就一定会导致结果）

当然条件状语从句不止 if 一个连接词，我们还要学会 unless/supposing that/assuming that/presuming that/let's say/given that/only if/so long as/provided/providing that/on condition that/in case 这些连接词。

unless 表示除非，意思相当于 "if...not..."。如：

> I won't like museums unless it is in a theme of Japanese manga. 我不喜欢博物馆，除非是日本动漫主题的。

supposing/presuming that 通常是祈使语气，表达对未来的猜想和设想。如：

> Supposing that in the future, human jobs are all replaced by artificial intelligence, what shall we do?

Let's say 有时候也可以表假设，这个说法就非常口语化。

Let's say I have a girlfriend, what would I buy her on her birthday?
假如我有个女朋友，我该在她生日买点啥？

providing/provided 强调在满足一定条件下才可以做某事，如果强调一件事的必要条件可以用 only if，比如说要去 UCL 必须要雅思 7 分，在考试中的情景可能是这样的：

> Next year, if everything goes smoothly, I'll go to study in UCL providing I have a band score of 7 on this test. 如果我雅思 7 的话，如果一切顺利，明年我会去伦敦大学学院读书。

更常用的一个条件状语从句是 as long as 表示只要，在 Part 1 的所有场景题中，除了我们上一章说到的 when I have more free time，也可以用条件状语从句 As long as I'm not busy，就可以丰富这个表达了。

不过需要强调的一点是，if 引导的真实条件句往往是考生最喜欢使用的从句，因为英语语序与汉语无异。所以考生使用这个从句的频率会非常高，有时就会略显啰唆，比如：

> What is the most popular way of relaxation for Chinese?

学生常见啰唆表达：

> Well, it really depends. For different age groups, people have different preferences. If the question is for young people, probably they like playing basketball, because they are young and energetic. If the question is for old people, probably they will say dancing in the square is what they like.

英语表达有从简原则，这样故意复杂化问题，但实质上表达内容非常有限对得分并没有任何帮助，需要引以为戒。有些中国考生会喜欢用这种结构对称的报告式语气，十分不地道，不口语化。

其实讲一个 if 就行：

> Well, if you look at the last decade, the biggest change is that an increasing number of people are relying their lives on the Internet, as well as amusement. Nowadays, more and more people like computer games, trendy Internet clips and social network sites.

练 习

01 改错：口语挑错

看看下面的句子有错吗？

What's your favorite color?

If I must say, my favorite color is green.

02 大闯关：口语闯关

试着用 supposing/presuming that；let's say 来翻译下面的句子。

假如未来有一天世界末日了，钱能给你带来什么？真正能让你幸福的是有人不离不弃，保护着你。(Part 3 你觉得钱和幸福有直接关系吗？)

参考答案

01　答句翻译过来是：如果我必须得说，我最喜欢的颜色是绿色。我们考虑一下语境，如果我必须得说的潜台词是我不愿意说，或我说不出来，通常前面得有情绪铺垫比如 Well, it's really hard to say. 或者 I don't know, I have never thought about it, but if I must say. 这句话里的另外一个常见错误是 must 情态动词后必须用动词原形。

02　Presuming that one day it's doomsday, what can money give you? It's the person who never leaves you, but always protects you and makes you happy.

写作部分

条件状语从句是用来限定主句的前提条件的，比如：

> If we have enough money, we can solve any problem.
> 只要有钱，我们就能解决任何问题。

这里，从句里的有钱就是条件，没钱就什么都是问题，有钱就什么都不是问题。
在议论文中，我们可以参考两种含义的用法：

1 assuming、provided、if、in case 引导的条件状语从句

这些词汇在条件状语从句中都表示"如果、假如"的意思。if 在前面的虚拟语气部分已经说过了，我们来看看其他几个词的使用：

> **2011 年 3 月 12 日　勇于竞争如何影响个人？**

Fierce competition may result in hostility among workers assuming a "win at all costs" attitude becomes popular in the workplace.

假如不惜一切代价获胜的态度在工作场合流行，残酷的竞争就可能会导致雇员们互相敌对。

> **2014 年 11 月 22 日　线上购物取代实体店购物是积极的吗？**

It is hard for individuals to be on their own with tendency for over consumption, provided there are no peers standing with them.

假如没有同伴和他们在一起，人们很难依赖自己来应对过度消费的倾向。

> **2014 年 11 月 1 日　失业比有工作但不喜欢强吗？**

In case some people are very proud of living self-sufficiently, unemployment benefits can be embarrassing and may be viewed as a hand-out.

如果人们特别自豪于自给自足的生活方式，那失业救济金就可能是令人尴尬的并可能被视为一种施舍。

2　if only（或 only if）、as long as 引导的条件状语从句

它们都是"只要的意思"，可以用来强调前提的重要性。

> **2011 年 12 月 3 日　为什么食物千里运输？它是积极的还是消极的？**

Food imports will not become a menace to public security if only the local government pays close attention to local food-supplies and avoids over reliance on other areas.

只要地方政府密切关注地方食品供应和避免过度依赖于其他地区，食物输入就不会成为对公众安全的威胁。

> **2015 年 5 月 9 日　该因为环境问题弃用科技还是科技会解决这一问题？**
>
> Humanity will possess more force to put the wrongs right as long as technology develops continually.
> 只要科技持续发展，人类就会拥有更强大的纠错能力。

图表作文中条件状语从句可以用于工作流程图。工作流程图主要描述人员工作的流程，比如考驾照、面试等，它比加工流程图难度更大，因为其中一些步骤有成功和失败两个分支、需要分别交代。那么在交代分支的时候，我们就可以用"如果……，就要……。否则，就得……"这样的表达。

下面的句式可以参考：

- The next step would be 流程（名词／动名词词组） if the result of the last one was pass, so that 目的（句子）.
  如果上一步通过了，下一步将会是某一流程，以便达到某一目的。
- 参与人员 would not get the chance to 进行下一步的流程（动词词组） for 实现的工作目的（动名词词组） unless they pass the last step.
  除非通过了上一步，否则参与人员没机会进行下一步的流程以实现某一目的。
- As long as 参与人员完成了上一步（动词词组）, they are qualified to 进行下一步的流程.
  只要参与人员完成了上一步，他们就有资格进行下一步。

这里涉及了 unless 引导的条件状语从句，unless 是"除非"的意思，可以用于强调前提条件的不可或缺性。

我们用 2013 年 4 月 13 日的这个考取驾照的工作流程图来示范一下这几个句式的用法：

The Process of Driving Test

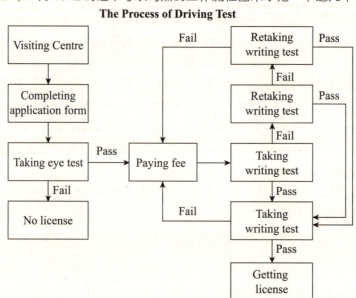

- The next step would be a writing test if the result of the last one was a pass, so that the examinees' traffic knowledge could be examined.
  如果上一步通过了，下一步将会是一个笔试，以便测试申请者的交通知识。
- The candidates would not get the chance to take a driving test for proving their driving skills unless they pass the last step.
  除非通过了上一步，否则考生没机会进行路考以证明他们的驾驶技能。
- As long as the applicants pass the driving test, they are qualified to get their driving licenses.
  只要申请人完成了路考，他们就有资格得到驾照了。

练习

01 改错：写作挑错

看看下面的句子有错吗？

2013 年 2 月 2 日　看电视对孩子绝无好处吗？

If children sit in front of screens too long time, their vision usually will become impaired.
如果孩子们过长时间端坐在屏幕前，他们的视力通常会受损。

02 大闯关：写作闯关

翻译下面这句话，注意除了条件状语从句之外，还涉及 not only...but also...的用法。

2016 年 5 月 7 日　不同能力的孩子一起受教育还是因材分开施教？

只要学校能够提供充足的选修课来确保天才儿童发展特长，统一的教育就不仅不会阻碍其智力发育，而且会更好地培养其社交技能。

参考答案

01　if 引导的条件状语从句，如果说明的是常识或者经常发生的动作，那么从句和主句都用一般现在时。

If children sit in front of screens too long time, their vision usually is impaired.

02　As long as schools could set sufficient elective courses for gifted children to develop their talents, unified education will not only foster their intelligence development, but also can more finely train their social skills.

7分 见贤思齐 比较状语从句为分析提供参照

口语部分

到了比较状语这个概念，有些同学可能就要犯糊涂了。什么是比较状语从句？谁和谁比较？怎么比较？如果你熟悉下面这个句型，可能会恍然大悟。这是我学过的第一个比较状语从句：

> Nobody likes grapes more than I do. 没有人比我更喜欢葡萄。
> （选自2001年《李阳疯狂英语自学卡》）

当初学这个句子就觉得挺实用，"没有人比我更……"，不就是一种强烈的表达情绪感受的方式吗？那如果表达自己狂热地喜欢音乐、画画、唱歌，也可以用到这个句型：

> Nobody likes singing more than I do.

than 后面是 I do，完整的主谓结构，是状语从句。

> She is taller than me.
> She looks more beautiful than he looks.

我们在第十七招也提到过比较结构的7种形式。有的时候比较状语从句和比较结构也没有那么清晰的界限，因为在口语表达中会有省略。比如：Eating at home is more comfortable than (eating at) restaurants (is). 句子结构学的比较好的同学应该能看出这个句子的完整结构来。

那我们既然明白了原理，这一章还是训练大家对这个句型敏感度的使用。
来讲几个平时不容易想到的比较结构。
我们在什么时候会用到比较？形容人、形容吃的、形容场景。

> 他就是个普通的不能再普通的人。
> He is no more than a normal person.
> 他对我来说不只是一个朋友。
> He is much more than a friend to me.

> 我可没有你那么疯狂。
> I'm not any more mad than you are.

描述内心戏的时候，比如抱怨：

> 这不过是一次失败嘛。
> It's nothing more than a failure.
> 我数学不好，物理也差不多。
> My math is poor, and I know no more physics than I know math.

再说到场景，我可以说我旅游的时候，看到的景象和我想象的完全不一样。

> It's not as good as what I had expected. 真没我期待得那么好。

as...as 句型表示"和什么一样多"。这个句子经常会出现在数据使用时！这里列举几个雅思口语考试中特别容易出现数据的考题：

> What is the most popular mean of transportation in China?
> What is the most popular way of relaxation for Chinese?
> What is the most popular travel destination for Chinese people?
> Train. According to the statistics, every year during the Spring Festival, as many as 290 million people are using trains to go back home.
> Internet, from data, you can easily see that many trendy TV programs have a great number of audiences, as many as tens or hundreds of millions of people who are relying on the leisure from online entertainment shows. Game players are even no less than these coach potatoes.

as many as 在这两个例句里就可以翻译为"多达"。我们在提到价格的题目里，也可以说到这个句型。比如送给别人的礼物，或者未来想买的房子，未来想买的车。都可以说：

> It's really expensive indeed, as expensive as an iPhone 7.
> 这其实挺贵的，和一部 iPhone 7 一样贵了。
> It's really pricy, the price is as much as 5 million RMB.
> 这个相当贵，价格高达 500 万人民币。

还有一个比较状语从句相当经典，就是 the more, the more 句型，翻译过来就是"越怎样……，越怎样……"比如：

> The more efforts you pay, the more harvest you will get.

当然，这一句型常出现于各种"建议性"考题，常见于 Part 3，比如：
孩子该不该学早学英语，就可以说：

> The earlier kids study English, the better language sense and memory skills they will get in the future.

该不该熬夜，也可以说：

> The old people always say that the earlier you go to bed, the more energetic you'll be the next day.

父母应该和孩子怎么沟通，就可以说：

> The more parents communicate with kids, the less contradiction there will be.

比较状语从句经常会出现一些省略让大家看起来特别费解，这里有两句话特别经典，值得背诵。比如：

> Last year I went to the Great Wall; the number of tourists was more than was reported.

有同学可能会问，more than 后面怎么又有一个 is？这是因为比较状语从句经常省略主语，原句应该是这样的：

> Last year I went to the Great Wall; the number of tourists was more than (what) was reported.

我们可以模仿这个句型造一些高级的句子了。比如考官问你未来什么打算，或者签证官问你去英国准备待几天。你可以说：

> I decide to stay no longer than is necessary. 我决定需要待多久就待多久。
> （潜台词是决不多待一天）

我们再看几个句子：

> Don't drink more than is good for you. 别喝太多，适量就好。
> I've done more than is asked, but still there is no promotion. Then I guess it's already the time to go. 我已经做了比给我要求的更多的事情了，但是还没升职，那我觉得就该走了吧。

在家乡题或旅游题里，说这个城市比其他地方的文化氛围要好：

> This city offers better cultural advantages than has generally supposed.

01 改错：口语挑错

看看下面的句子有错吗？

Do you always believe in news?

Well, not always. For example, every time when there is a gas explosion or an earthquake, the casualties should be more than reported. I seldom believe that.

02 大闯关：口语闯关

试着用 the more, the more 句型翻译下面的句子。

有时候家长越是逼孩子学习，孩子就越叛逆，这样反倒起不到作用。

参考答案

01 more than 是比较状语从句和比较结构的连接词，需要注意的是前后比较的内容需要在意义上、结构上、词性上保持一致。比较的是死亡人数 casualty 和报道的死亡人数，后面的 reported 显然就在词性上不对了。应该是 what is reported，变成名词性的结构，或者 is reported，省略主语。所以正确说法是：Well, not always. For example, every time when there is a gas explosion or an earthquake, the casualties should be more than what is reported. I seldom believe that.

02 Sometimes, the more parents enforce their children to study hard, the more rebellious they will become. This, on the contrary, can't give any better effects.

写作部分

比较状语从句包括了简单的 than、复杂一些的 as *adj.* as...以及涉及部分倒装的 the more...the more...句式，我们一个个来分析。

1 than 引导的比较状语从句

实际上句子的结构应该是：

主语 + 系动词/谓语 + 形容词比较级/副词比较级 + than ....

比如：

> 2015 年 10 月 31 日　对艺术创作的资助该源于政府还是其他渠道？

> In view of the longer investment cycle in cultural industries, there needs to be public financial support to implement a benign cycle more than other industries.
> 鉴于其更长的投资回报周期，文化产业比其他行业更加需要公共资助来确立一个良性循环。

再比如对于建议类题目，我们可以用比较的方式提出评论：

> 2015 年 12 月 19 日　用文化传统吸引游客赚钱是种破坏还是其唯一得到保存的办法？

> To consume and reserve traditions in commercial operations is better than to leave them to fade away in time.
> 在商业运营中消费并保留传统比弃之不顾并任其随时间而逝更好。

这也可以用来对比曲线变化，比如：

> The quality of the pipeline increased more stably than others.
> 运输管道的量上升的比其他项目更平稳。

2　as...as 表达

as...as 是"如同……一样"的意思，注意两个 as 之间填入的是形容词或副词。

> A man can be as beautiful as a woman.
> 男人能像女人一样漂亮。

来看一个复杂一些的真题例子：

> 2015 年 9 月 3 日　犯罪可以被预防还是无法可想？

> Low education level and poor ability in making a living are as crucial as the defects of human nature.
> 低教育水平和糟糕的谋生能力和人性的缺陷一样关键。

这里的否定形式是 not as...as，比如：

> 2014 年 11 月 22 日　评价线上购物取代实体店购物

> Real stores supply commodity information not as efficiently as online ones.
> 实体店提供商品信息不像网店那么高效。

3　the more ..., the more ...句式

the more ..., the more ...是"越……越……"的意思，需要注意的是，这里的 more 指代的是形容词或副词的比较级。

> 2013 年 12 月 21 日　不健康的运动应该被禁止还是人们有权去选择它们？

> The longer time people participate in sedentary entertainment like Mahjong, the more likely they are to suffer from some sudden illnesses such as heart attack and stroke.
> 人们参与像麻将这样久坐的娱乐的时间越长，就越可能得上突发的疾病，比如心梗和中风。

我们把这一句式用法公式化，就是：
The + 形容词比较级 +（名词）+ 主语 + 系动词／谓语（一般现在时），the + 形容词比较级 +（名词）+ 主语 + 系动词／谓语（一般将来时）。

比如上面的例句：
The　longer　time　people　participate in　sedentary entertainment　like Mahjong,
　　形容词比较级 名词　主语　　谓语　　　　　宾语　　　　　　　定语
the more likely　they　are　to suffer from some sudden illnesses　such as heart attack
形容词比较级　　 主语 系动词　　　状语　　　　　　　　　　　　　定语
and stroke.

这一句式语法上要注意的是时态：从句（第一处 the more 从句）的时态常用一般现在时或一般过去时；如果主句（第二处 the more 从句）的谓语动词用一般将来时，从句的谓语动词要用一般现在时表示将来。

逻辑上这一句可以作为举例子出现，说明一种常态，最常见的错误是重复论点，而不是更深一步地提供细节来论述论点。比如：

> 2014 年 5 月 10 日　男性应该帮女性做家务吗？

如果论点归因于"strengthen marriage bonds"，那么第三句写成下面这样是无效的，

245

因为和论点一样,没有说出任何新东西:

> The more housework husbands do, the stronger marriage bonds would be.

实际上,我们可做如下解释:

> The more housework husbands do, the more respect for what their spouse brings to the family they could show.
> 男性所做的家务活越多,他们所能表达出的对于配偶所作家庭贡献的感激就越多。

01 改错:写作挑错

看看下面的句子有错吗?

The starting point of road transportation was nearly twice as much as the one of water transportation.

公路运输的起点几乎是水路运输的两倍。

02 大闯关:写作闯关

翻译下面这句话,注意 the more..., the more... 的用法。

2015年5月21日 为什么人们晚要小孩?对社会和家庭有什么影响?

实际上,年轻人在进入社会后的日子里不能处理的问题越多,他们对于维持原有的家庭计划的自信将会越少。

参考答案

01 在数据图表中,表达倍数关系需要用 as…as;一般来讲,倍数表示为:数字 + times as … as。比如:

The money in Jack Ma's pocket is 300 billion times as much as mine.
马云兜里的钱是我的3000亿倍。

表达倍数比较特殊的词汇有:twice *adv.* 两倍
            triple *adj. n.* 三倍的量

那么正确的表达应该是:

The starting point of road transportation was nearly twice as many as the one of water transportation.

02 In fact, the more issues young men cannot handle in the days they just come into the real world, the less confidence there would be left for them to keep their original family plans.

让步状语从句突显思维缜密

口语部分

　　让步状语从句在口语中的体现是最简单的，就两个词 though，还有 although，跟中文表达的语序也并没有太大差别，表达"虽然"的意义。唯一要注意的是汉语表达习惯中会同时出现"虽然""但是"这两个词，英文中只要出现一半就好了，或者"虽然"，或者"但是"，不需要重复。从句只能有一个连接词。比如，翻译"虽然我妈总说街摊儿零食很不卫生，但是我控制不住我自己。"在这句中，没有但是，很多人会在造句中有不舒服感，不如用 still 试着：

> Although my mother always says, "Don't eat street snacks, they're very dirty.", I still can't control myself.

让步结构在辩论性话题中经常会出现，尤其是在做比较时：

> Do you prefer traveling alone or with other people?
>
> Well, although traveling with others is fun, I still like traveling alone, because it gives me more freedom.

这样的话题雅思口语考试中有很多。

Part 1 中有：

- Do you prefer taking a bus or taxi?
- Do you prefer live music or recorded music?
- Do you prefer to study in the morning or in the evening?
- Do you prefer outdoor activities or indoor activities?
- Do you prefer a hat or cap?
- Do you prefer working alone or with other people?
- Do you prefer handwriting or typing?
- Do you prefer dark colour or light colour?

我们都可以用这个句型：Well, although taking a taxi sounds more comfortable, I still think bus is more likely to be my preference.

Part 3 中也有经典的对比问题，比如：

> **男女对比问题/古今对比问题：**
>
> 在选择休闲方式、运动方式、购物方式、玩具上，男女有哪些不同？
> What are the differences between men and women in choosing different sports?
>
> Although some girls today are more and more sporty, most girls are still afraid of being sunburned or hurt. So, in my experience, they never have a liking for outdoor sports.

让步状语从句的另一个经典用法就是：no matter how/where/what。无论前路多么艰难，条件多么苛刻，都要克服困难。

用英语来说就是：No matter where you are, I'll find you. No matter how old you are, I'll marry you.

这也是一种让步状语从句。在雅思口语 Part 1 中，表达情感就可以代入这个句型。比如聊起户外运动：

> No matter how bad the weather is, my passion about badminton never has worn out.

在 Part 2 中讲到礼物题，也可以说：

> No matter how small this gift is, since you thought about me, I feel really happy.

在 Part 3 中讲到对比，尤其是严重的问题，譬如机场建设是好事还是坏事？政府应该投钱给环保还是经济发展？

> No matter how many benefits there are in investing in economic development, it is undeniable that something in this world is once destroyed, irreversable, especially environment.

第三个让步表达是 even if（就算），让步状语是感受描述的黄金搭档。在 Part 1/2/3 中，**表达对某种东西的喜爱**。

> Even if I give up studying, I won't give up the passion for music. It's incomparable.

表达拒绝消极

> Even if people are disappointed about Chinese education, I still think we need to be optimistic about the future.

although 引导的是让步状语从句，but 引导的可不是让步状语从句，而是有转折意义的并列句，不是所有的转折都是让步。从字面意义上讲，让步就是"退一步讲"，表达"即使"、"尽管"的含义。

当然，正确的使用让步状语从句的精髓是——逻辑要好，许多同学经常在 Part 3 中犯这样的错误，在题目 Do you prefer eating at home or at restaurants? 中，有些同学会说"虽然现在很多人都喜欢在饭馆吃饭，因为种类多，不洗碗，但是我还是喜欢在家吃！"

这样讲我就听不明白了，不讲道理了对不对，你是想彰显个性吗？Part 3 考试呢需要考生具备一定的逻辑性，如果你喜欢在家吃饭，证明一下在家吃饭的好处，或者饭馆的坏处。而不是说了一大堆在外吃饭好，但是我就是不喜欢，这样你就误用了这个句型了。可千万别犯和这位同学一样的错误。

所以，让步和转折是两回事儿！千万记住！

01 改错：口语挑错

在 Part 2 帮助别人经历这道题中，看看下面的句子有错吗？

Although he looks really helpless, from my experience, he must be a fraud.

02 大闯关：口语闯关

试着用让步状语从句翻译下面的句子。

Why do some people like eating unhealthy food even if they know that they are unhealthy?

无论有多少人说这些食物不是很健康，年轻人都很难控制自己不被诱惑。

参考答案

01 让步状语从句在口语中错误率最高的就是 although 和 but 同时出现，英语表达习惯里，总是有主从句的区别，在上面这个例子中，每半句前面都有一个引导词（although，but，so），就造成了句子结构的混乱。另外让步状语表明的是自己的比较和推断，通常表达观点需要有逻辑性，而非任性。所以让步状语从句中很少出现 must 这种主观推断。就好比这几个例子，听了也会不舒服：

Although he looks handsome, he must be gay. 虽然他长得帅，但他一定是个同性恋。

Although she is rich, she must be a concubine. 虽然她有钱，但她一定是个小三。

02　No matter how many people say food is not healthy, young people can hardly control themselves from being tempted.

写作部分

让步状语从句总的来讲就是：虽然/尽管/即使/不论/无论……。

1 从句正常语序的让步状语从句

让步状语从句由以下词引导时，从句用正常语序：
虽然：although、though
即使：even if
无论是否：whether ... or not
例如：

> 2014 年 10 月 11 日　由于更多的使用手机和网络，人们正在丧失沟通能力吗？

> Although other conditions in social communication like instant messaging and social networks are perfect, people may still lack chances to interact with others directly.
> 虽然像即时通讯和社交网络这些社会交往领域的其它条件都很完美，人们仍会缺乏机会和他人直接互动。

这一句的主干是：

> Although other 相关领域的（形容词/名词词组） conditions are imperfect/perfect, sb（相关人群）may prevent/be trapped in 某种麻烦（名词/动名词词组）.
> 虽然相关领域的其他条件都很不完美/很完美，相关人群仍可能避免某种麻烦/陷入某种麻烦。

这一句的逻辑拿分点是强调，重点是强调这一段说明的分论点会导致的结果。比如"该鼓励孩子们规律性地看电视吗？"

这一段第一句的论点是：增强学习效果
↓
第二句论据是：能形成连续的学习过程
↓
这一句就要说：在这种情况下，哪怕电视节目的内容很晦涩，孩子们还是可以全面地接触到某一领域的知识。

这一句的逻辑难点是陷入的问题或者得到的好处必须要具体，一定不能变相地简单重复第一句的论点。

以下例句也应用了同一表达方式：

> 2014 年 10 月 2 日　除了奖学金政府提供外，大学其余资金该来自学费和私人机构吗？

> Even if the conditions in raising private capital are sound, universities may yet be in dire straits because of the non-profit nature.
> 哪怕在募集私人资金方面的条件都很健全，大学仍会因为非营利的本质而陷入极度的困境。

用表格来罗列同一语义的并列选项就是：

虽然相关领域的其他条件都很完美／不完美	相关人群	仍会陷入／避开	某种麻烦
否定立场：尽管其他条件都很完美 Although other 相关领域的 conditions are perfect, Even if other 相关领域的 conditions are sound, Though other 相关领域的 conditions are satisfied, Whether other 相关领域的 conditions are favorable or not,	名词	否定立场：仍会陷入 may still be trapped in may yet get into may nevertheless meet may still fall into	名词／动名词词组.
肯定立场：尽管其他条件都很不完美 Although other 相关领域的 conditions are imperfect, Even if other 相关领域的 conditions are incomplete, Though other 相关领域的 conditions are dissatisfied, Whether other 相关领域的 conditions are unfavorable or not,		肯定立场：仍可避免 may prevent may yet avoid the trouble in may still abstain from may nevertheless keep away from	

2 从句倒装语序的让步状语从句

下面的例句中句首的从句由以下词引导，从句用倒装语序：

尽管，哪怕：as、though

无论：no matter

> 2015 年 1 月 17 日　需要控制人们制造噪音还是相反？
>
> No matter how perfect environmental protection efforts are, people's activities and rest may nevertheless be broken by noise.
> 无论环保措施有多出色，人们的活动和休息仍会被噪音打断。

这一句的同义选项可以总结为下表：

虽然相关领域的其他条件都很完美／不完美，	相关人群	陷入／避开	某种麻烦
否定立场：尽管其他条件都很完美， excellent as 相关领域 conditions are, sound though the 相关领域 conditions are, no matter how perfect 相关领域 conditions are,	名词	否定立场：仍然陷入 may be trapped in may yet get into may nevertheless meet may still fall into	名词／动名词词组
肯定立场：尽管其他条件都很不完美， terrible as 相关领域 conditions are, unfavorable though 相关领域 conditions are, no matter how imperfect 相关领域 conditions are,		肯定立场：仍可避免 may prevent may yet avoid the trouble in may still abstain from may nevertheless keep away from	

练 习

01 改错：写作挑错

看看下面的句子有错吗？

2011 年 5 月 19 日　政府该为减少社会暴力而控制影视中暴力吗？

There would be no grand to limit any information transmitted by mass media if its contents follow the existing laws, although some people may try to muddle laws and business ethics.

没有任何理由限制媒体传播的信息，如果它的内容没有违反现行法律的话，虽然很多人也许想要混淆法律和商业道德的界限。

02 大闯关：写作闯关

翻译下面这句话，注意让步状语从句部分。

2013 年 6 月 8 日　鼓励消费的利弊

尽管购物狂的行为很引人注目，公众对于消费的喜好一般来讲还是积极的。

参考答案

01　当让步状语从句部分在说明一种假设的情况而不是事实时，通常用 though 不用 although。

There would be no grand to limit any information transmitted by mass media if its contents follow the existing laws, though some people may try to muddle laws and business ethics.

02　Although the behaviors of a compulsive spender are spectacular, the liking of consumption among the public is commonly believed to be positive.

7分见"鸭"在田 地点状语从句地图题必备

口语部分

地点状语从句和定语从句较难区分。

> I come from a place where you can see the beaches. where 引导定语从句，起解释说明作用。
>
> Let's go where we can see the beaches. where 引导地点状语从句。

长这么像却不一样，为什么呢？因为定语从句中 where 解释说明的是前面的名词 place，而地点状语从句是放在状语位置的，要么是动词后（像副词一样），要么是句首或句尾做一个地点，像 at the park 一样的地点。

再做一个对比吧：很多同学在国外会受到一些外国人恶意的诅咒：Go back where you come from！滚回你来的地方去！这个句子就是地点状语从句，因为 where 前面并没有任何名词。

搞清楚了吗？我们在基本信息题中曾经大量的运用 where 引导的定语从句，来限定修饰家乡、房间的各种布置。而这些都是定语从句：

> My hometown is a place where I was born and brought up.
>
> It's a place where I'm deeply attached to.
>
> Outside my window, it's a playground where you can see lots of kids playing around.

搞清楚这个概念以后，我们来说一下在雅思考试中怎么用这个句型：

> Where there is a will, there is a way. 有志者事竟成。

这句话可以用在 house or flat 的回答中，可以对考官说，我住在一个很小的房子里，但是和我的女朋友一起住，有她的地方就有家。

> Although the flat I'm living is not very spacious, I live there with my girlfriend. Where there is her, there is home.

在 leisure 题中，我们可以用地点状语从句表达：想去哪就去哪！

> When I have more free time, I can go where I want to go.

或者在周末题

> I like Saturday the most, because it gives me a chance to go where I want to go.

地点状语从句在中文的翻译基本就是三个模式：

1. 想去哪就去哪
2. 哪里有……哪里有……
3. 需要用到……的时候

比如在表达自己在哪个领域不太行，比如雅思考题"数学"或者"科学"，就可以说：I'm completely useless when math/logic is needed. 同样的道理，表达擅长某一领域，也可以这样说。比如"专业"，就可以说：I'm really gifted where design work is needed.

当然地点状语从句这个句子结构也可以放在 be 动词之后作补语，意思是 the place in which，或者 the point on which 的意思。

> That's just where you are wrong. 这就是你错的地方。
> You need to tell the children, after playing with the toys, to put them where they were. 你要和孩子们讲，玩完玩具记得放回去。
> I've put the photo where I could see it every day.
> 我把这个照片放在我每天都能看到的地方。

练 习

01 改错：口语挑错

看看下面的句子有错吗？

In the future, either I will go to where my father wants me or go to where my heart leads me.

02 大闯关：口语闯关

试着用地点状语从句翻译下面的句子。

正当我走神到了我和我小伙伴游泳的地方，一股恶臭冲进我的鼻子。

参考答案

01 这个句子很容易被地点状语从句的初学者弄错。where 作地点状语从句引导词，其功能相当于一个副词，前面是不能加 to 的，正确说法应该为：In the future, either I will go where my father wants me or go where my heart leads me.

02 As I was going traveling to where I used to swim with my playmates, a stinky smell suddenly was shoved into my nose.

写作部分

1 where 引导的地点状语从句

大家都知道"Where there is a will, there is a way. 有志者事竟成"，这句话确实非常有名。这里面前半句就是 where 引导的地点状语从句，表示"在……地方"的意思。

我们可以模仿这一句的结构在考试中造句，比如：

> 2016 年 1 月 9 日 Ａ卷 政府该为理科教育而不是社会科学投入更多吗？
>
> Where there is a defined wealth redistribution system developed by social science, there is more zeal for work and less social conflicts.
> 有了由社会科学设计的合理的财富再分配系统，就有更高涨的工作热情和更少的社会矛盾。

这一表达的难点不在于语法，而在逻辑，因为逻辑上这句话实际是"有了某一深层次的原因，就有与其相关的结果"，包含了两层逻辑解释，可以用于对于论点的阐述部分。

再来个例子大家体会一下分析的过程：

> 2015 年 3 月 14 日　能给小孩最好照顾的是育儿所还是家长？
>
> Where there are professional caregivers who master the knowledge of first aid, safety guiding and intelligence exploration, there are more guarantees for children's safety and intellectual development.
> 有了在急救、安全护理和智力开发方面具有专业的知识的专业保育员，对孩子们的安全和智力发展就有了更多的保障。

where 引导的地点状语从句还可以应用于图表作文中的线性图，用来强调某一时间点上的变化，比如：

> Approximately 45 percent of the world's population live where mosquitoes transmit malaria.
> 全球大约有45%的人口生活在蚊子传播疟疾的区域。

2　anywhere、everywhere 和 wherever 引导的地点状语从句

anywhere：无论何处
wherever：无论什么地方
everywhere：到处

这三个词都可以用来强调作用的普遍性。

句式结构我们还可以参照上面 where 引导的那句，只不过意思变成了"无论在哪/无论到哪……，……都是必然的"，比如：

2013年9月7日　核能是最好的能源吗？

> Wherever a nuclear power station is built, it is impossible to avoid the related menace to public security, because the corresponding technology support is too complex.
> 无论在哪里修建核电站，都无法完全避免对公众安全的威胁，因为相应的技术支持太复杂了。

再如：

2015年5月9日　该因为环境问题弃用科技还是科技会解决这一问题？

> Scientists will explore practical alternative energy that is environmentally friendly anywhere they can find it.
> 只要是实用的环保替代能源，无论在何方，科学家们都会将其开发出来。

再看 everywhere 的用法：

2015年1月29日　公众去未开发的地区游览的好处大于坏处吗？

> Everywhere tourists visit, they will bring domestic waste to there and taxes local ability to deal with waste.
> 游客到访任何地方，都会带去生活垃圾并将地方处理垃圾的能力推到极限。

练习

01 改错：写作挑错

看看下面的句子有错吗？

2014年9月4日 现代沟通和交通技术允许人们任意选择居所的好处大于坏处吗？

People prefer to live in where the air is fresher and the areas of gardens and parklands are larger.

人们更愿意生活在空气新鲜、公园绿地面积更大的地方。

02 大闯关：写作闯关

翻译下面的句子，注意地点状语从句的特殊表达。

2012年2月9日 同意跨国公司和全球化的增长对每个人都有利吗？

哪里有更开放的市场和更自由的竞争，哪里就有更活跃的经济活动和更多的社会财富。

参考答案

01　where 是修饰谓语 live 的地点状语从句，起到和副词一样的作用，那么 live 后面就不能接 in，因为 live in 后面要接宾语，而这一句中没有。

02　Where there are further open markets and more liberal competitions, there are more active financial activities and more social wealth.

方式状语从句给论述提供细节

口语部分

方式状语从句是个和比喻有关的句型，用中文来说就是表达"正如……""好像……""以……的方式""按照"这些意思。这是状语从句中，很多考生最不熟悉的一种从句。在雅思口语考试中它表达的意思是什么呢？

> I speak so as if I know it. 我说的好像我知道一样。

Part 2 中在描述自己最好的朋友时，我们就可以讲一个方式：没有人能用他懂我的那种方式懂我。

> Nobody understands me as he does. 没有人像他那样懂我。

说到自己受到爸妈影响的时候也可以说：

> I do things, make judgments, and speak the way my father does.
> 我做事情，做判断，说话都和我爸一样。

从这两句话中，大家大概可以感觉到，方式状语从句大体是表达我的行为方式，或者某人的行为方式和其他人一样或不同。而连接词就是 as 或者 the way。比如比较她和她妈妈：

> She is a good teacher, as her mother used to be.
> 她是个好老师，就像她妈妈过去那样。

美剧里警匪片经常出现一句话：Do as I say and sit down! 照我说的做，坐下！
在 Part 2 经历题中，我们经常会遇到等人、生气等问题。如果有人爽约，也可以说：

> He didn't show up as (he had) promised. 他没按约定出现。

as 有时候会和 so 连用，表示"和……一样"，这里也是一样。比如在 Part 3 中做男女对比：

> As women like bags and shopping, so men like sports and playing computer games.
> 就像女人喜欢包和买东西一样，男人喜欢运动和打游戏。

除了以上两种方式，as if 和 as though 作方式状语的连接词，表达"就好像"这个意思。比如在 Part 2 描述一个帮助别人的经历，就可以用到这种比喻：

> He looked at me as if I was his savior. 他看着我就好像我是他的救世主。

在 Part 1 中，表达喜欢某件事儿，也可以说：

> I think of music as if it's a part of my life. 我把音乐看作生命的一部分。

在 Part 2 中描述一个人的样子，比如在飞机上见到的一个人：

> She closed her eyes as though she was too tired.
> 她闭着眼睛好像特别累的样子。

还有在污染之地中描述难闻的气味，也可以说：

> It smelled as if someone left dead fish in the kitchen and forget to dump it for likely a month.
> 这味道闻着就好像有人把死鱼扔在厨房里，大概一个月没扔。

在借物经历中，描述一个人的内心戏或者表情：

> He looked as if he was very reluctant.
> 他看起来好像特别不情愿。

生气经历中，描述内心的情绪：

> I felt as though there is a volcano in my heart ready to erupt.
> 我感觉好像内心有个火山要喷发。

总而言之，方式状语从句多表达一种比喻，还表达按照某个人或者某种方式来做某事。要记得它的用法，只需记住它会出现的地方即可。

练 习

01 改错：口语挑错

看看下面的句子有错吗？

He stared at me as if to say something.

02 大闯关：口语闯关

试着用方式状语从句翻译下面的句子。

现如今的确有些人，看到垃圾桶了还把垃圾扔在地上，就好像和他们没关系一样。

参考答案

01 as if 引导方式状语从句时，后面可以直接跟 to do 或 doing，形容词或者介词短语。所以这句并没有错误。类似的说法还有：He rushed towards me as if in anger. 他冲向我好像很生气的样子。He stared me all the time as if never seeing a woman before. 他一直盯着我看，好像从没见过女人似的。

02 Nowadays, indeed there are people dumping the rubbish on the ground instead of the rubbish bin, even if they see a bin in reach, they treat it as if it's none of their business.

写作部分

方式状语从句用来交代主句的内容是以……的方式进行的，或者像……一样。

1 as、just as 引导的方式状语从句

表达的是都是"以……方式"或"就像……一样"的意思。

比如：

> 2013 年 7 月 27 日　保护古建筑的钱应用于建设新房屋和道路吗？
>
> Historical establishments serve local culture and traditions and bring a certain charm to neighborhood as they are the bridge connecting the past and the present.
>
> 历史建筑以连接过去和现在的桥梁的方式服务于地方文化和传统，并为社区带来独特魅力。

再如：

> 2012 年 4 月 21 日　同意计划未来不如专注当前吗？

If people have contingency plans through carefully planning just as they can foresee the proplems, the posibilities of failing would be minimized.

如果人们通过谨慎地制定计划来完善应急方案，就像他们能预见到问题所在一样，失败的可能性就将被最小化。

2 as if 和 as though 引导的方式状语从句

表示"就像……一样""如同……一样"的意思，因为是比拟，所以从句中多用虚拟语气，而在议论文写作中，这一虚拟一般是针对某些常规道理的分析论述，从句中的时态应该是一般过去时。

比如：

> 2014 年 2 月 15 日　成功靠努力和决心还是金钱外貌等其他因素？

To achieve great success, we must make full use of all the advantages we own as if a fighter made full use of all the weapons in their hand.

为了取得巨大的成功，我们必须充分利用我们拥有的所有优势，就像战士充分利用手边所有的武器一样。

上面这一句从修辞手法上讲，使用了比喻的修辞。一般来讲，论文等正式的学术写作中是要避免比喻的运用，在雅思这种议论文体中，比喻在有利于说理时可以运用，但数量不宜太多，一至两处足矣。

再看个例子：

> 2015 年 11 月 14 日 B 卷 自然资源高速消耗会导致什么问题？如何解决？

Humanity is over-reliant on fossil energy as though there is a bottomless reserve.

人类过度依赖化石能源，就像它是无穷无尽的一样。

3 in the same manner、in the same way 引导的方式状语从句

这两个词组表达的是"以同……一样的方式"的意思，连接的从句内容和主句是类比关

系，对主句涉及的方式进行类比说明，比如：

> 2015 年 7 月 4 日　要求年轻人为社区做义工的坏处会大于好处吗？

> We should encourage the next generation to be valuable social members by contributing more to the community in the same manner we encourage them to be exposed to society and gather experience by working part-time.
>
> 我们应该以同鼓励下一代通过兼职工作来接触社会并积累经验一样的方式来鼓励他们通过为社区做更多贡献而成为有价值的社会成员。

再如：

> 2014 年 10 月 6 日　学校教育的目的应偏重社会性多于个人性吗？

> Since all the taxpayers are the patrons, public education institutions must give absolute priority to social needs in the same way all the business operators pay the utmost attention to shareholders' interests.
>
> 由于所有纳税人都是出资者，公立教育机构必须给予社会需求以优先权，就如同所有的商务运营者都会优先考量股东利益一样。

在图表作文中，上诉的三类全部可以用来描述相似的数据变化趋势，比如：

> After 1988, the consumption of beef kept dropping in the rest of the time as the one of lamb did.
>
> 在 1988 年之后，牛肉的消耗量在余下的时间里以羊肉的消耗量呈现过的方式持续下降。

练习

01　改错：写作挑错

看看下面的句子有错吗？

2015 年 9 月 26 日　为什么一些国家废物回收量不足？如何鼓励回收？

In 1950s, the residents in developed countries started to sort garbage as they were told by the recycling handbooks from governments.

在 20 世纪 50 年代，发达国家的居民开始按照政府回收手册上的要求分类垃圾。

02 大闯关：写作闯关

试着翻译下面的句子，注意"不是……而是……"的翻译。

2016 年 4 月 2 日　多元文化社会给国家带来的好处多于坏处吗？

文化不是固定不变的，而是随着世界的变化而变化的，就和历史上的不同种族反复融合是一个道理。

参考答案

01　注意从句的时态，发生在主句之前，就要在主句的基础上往前提一个时态，这里主句开始分类垃圾是一般过去时，从句手册要求是在其之前发生的，应该用过去完成时。

In 1950s, the residents in developed countries started to sort garbage as they had been told by the recycling handbooks from governments.

02　Culture is not a definable thing, but rather changes as the world changes, in the same way different races integrated repeatedly in history.

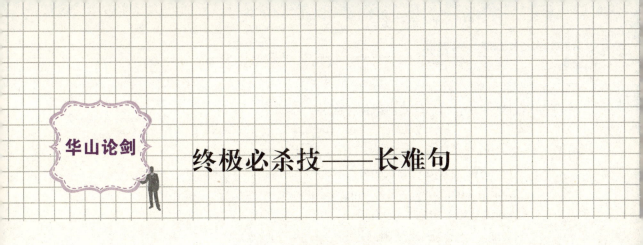

终极必杀技——长难句

口语部分

说起长难句,其实大部分时间,口语表达都是逆长难句而为的。但是在英剧美剧中,无论是《唐顿庄园》还是《生活大爆炸》,我们偶尔也会听到主人公秀口才似地说了一大段让我们感觉好佩服。所以作为追求多样性和丰富性的雅思口语考试,最地道的讲法是灵活地结合使用简单句和复杂句。要实现这一点,我们需要从两个角度来努力:

❶ 知道所有的句型用在哪里

❷ 避免错误的长句用法

在雅思口语当中,我们一直鼓励同学们苦练的是口语十大句型加分点:"状""定""主""宾""表""被""强""时""独""虚"。

语言的表达无非分为几个不同目的,遇到问题,回答时,先回应,再列举,后展开。在细节信息中,需要展示感受描述、场景描述、逻辑推导、举证、引述、对比、总结这样的不同技巧。在回应中,除了讲 Yes, I like it 或者 No, I don't like it. 还可以用虚拟语气或者反问来表达强烈的情绪:

> Honestly, if the pigs were to fly up, I would like museums.
> Who would say no to it?

在列举时,要有主次之分。很多同学都会简单处理这个句型,讲出 especially I like pop music and rock music. 其实这里的句型点有很多,比如:

> 完成时的使用:I've been interested in a lot of music types, by which I mean…
> 主语从句的使用:What I like the most is R & B, which is really expressive.
> 定语后置的使用:The music types I like include…
> 强调句型的使用:It's worth mentioning that I'm interested in …
> 被动语态的使用:Lots of square dancing can be seen in the park.

在场景描述当中，自然是要用到各种状语从句：

> As long as I have free time…
> Whenever I have spare time…
> Say if I'm not busy…/Say if the weather is not lousy…
> When I was in middle school…
> Usually, after school, when I am on the subway…

而题目需要举证的时候，就需要用到四项举证原则：

> 比较状语的使用：Nowadays, more and more people like to spend money on concerts.
> 被动语态的使用：It is often reported that…
> 宾语从句的使用：It occurs to me that…
> 定语从句的使用：The reason why I prefer to do this is because…

在表达感受的时候可以借助对话和内心戏灵活运用时态：

> 过去进行时：At that time, I was thinking, "God! How come it's so delicious."

表达总结时用表语从句：

> That's how it comes across. 我就是这么想的。
> That's why I like it. 这就是为什么我喜欢它。

在 Part 2 中我们也可以进行类似的内容结构划分，通过记住从句出现的位置来加以强化训练。通常 Part 2 都会有 4 个小问题，题目结构会相对来说比较固定。比如：

> Describe a person who moves to live with you
> You should say:
> Who this person is
> How you knew this person
> What you usually do together
> And explain why you like this person

我们把答题思路分为 4 个基本段：
第一段是介绍段，讲清名字、身份、评价、时间：

> 宾语从句的使用：I would say that
> 定语后置的使用：a person who moves to live with me that I knew about 4 years ago
> 被动语态的使用：is called Steven
> 定语从句的使用：who is a very amiable person

第二段是场景段，讲清人物形象描述（穿着、长相、性格、行为）：

> 条件状语从句的使用：If I remember well…
> 时间状语从句的使用：When I firstly met him…
> 过去进行时：He was wearing…
> 　　　　　　I was thinking…

第三段是细节段，讲清题目列举（总分结构、时间逻辑）：

> usually/sometimes
> 主语从句的使用：What I remember clearly is that…
> 被动语态的使用：I was told that…

第四段是逻辑段：

> 让步状语从句的使用：Although …, I still think…

当然，我们也需要注意一下这些常见的长难句易用错的地方。

易错点一：啰唆的重复

> He took her hand and (he) led her towards the house.
> When she recognized Morris she went pale, then (she) blushed.
> She swept (the floor) and polished the floor.
> I will not give up (my experiment) and will go on with my experiment.
> I am (your friend), and will still be your friends.

因为不会使用省略句，所以句子听起来特别啰唆，浪费时间。

易错点二：故意弄复杂的定语从句

> （错）I'd like to talk about a friend who is nice.
> （正）I'd like to talk about a nice friend.
> （错）The good leader that I admire who is a nice person who is my friend is Bob.
> （正）The good leader that I admire is Bob who is a nice friend to me.

在口语表达中，往往真的长难句是结合短句的成品，而非复杂的从句。举个例子：

> Do you like reading the newspaper?

> Well, living in this information age, honestly, newspapers which have been out of fashion for a while, is truly an antique already, as any current media, including mobile phone or TV can provide exactly what the newspaper can provide, and even comparatively more vivid content. For example, reality show, and interviews are the kind of things which we get information from. That's where newspapers are not able to be comparable with.

要想随意脱口而出长难句，还是需要各位读者认真从第一章细细读来，熟悉所有的句子成分和造句原理，假以时日，一定也可以脱口而出这样的句子。

练 习

01 改错：口语挑错

看看下面的句子有错吗？

Why do you think music can make people relaxed?

Well, to this question, I think we can understand relaxing in two different ways, physical relaxation and mental relaxation. For mental relaxation, music can release your pressure, empty your mind, especially some soft music like piano music. For physical relaxation, music can make you dance with the rhythm, stretch your body and relax yourself.

02 大闯关：口语闯关

试着把下面的语段用长难句翻译。

Why are fewer and fewer people likely to go to the cinema?

20年前，电影是主要的娱乐方式，提供极强的视觉感受，很多人看电影就是为了气氛，现在这些功能都被其他的东西代替了，像VR眼镜，家庭音乐，杜比音效之类的。互联网这么渗透我们的生活，人们也已经发现这种方便，哪也不去，就能在家享受同等规格、同等质量的服务，尤其是所有高度电子化的东西，像电影和歌。

参考答案

01 这是一个从学生课堂练习中摘出来的真实例子，很多同学为了讲两个层次，故意让句型层次分明，反而变得啰唆，且不口语化，传递信息的效率也极低。

Because some soft music like the piano is welcomed mostly for its function in releasing one's pressure and emptying one's mind. As for rock, which young people are crazy about in night clubs, helps to make people excited, then consequently stretch their arms and bodies to the rhythm. You can say music can make people relaxed both physically and mentally.

读读上面这个答案，是否要比之前的逻辑连接更紧密，更连贯，更有效传递信息。

02 Well, considering cinema, a major entertainment place 20 years ago, provided a great visual and audio effects with big 3D screen, most people went there for the great atmosphere which today has to some extent already been replaced by some alternatives, such as VR glasses, stereo home theatre systems, Dolby sound sets and so on. Being permeated by internet in modern life, people have found convenience of staying at home, and enjoying the same level and same quality service at home, especially everything in the electronic world, like films and songs.

写作部分

长难句其实就是包含多种句子成分和语法现象的复杂句。严格来讲，难句不一定长、长句不一定难。在各类出国考试（包括雅思）的写作部分当中，有个不成文的规矩，一句话的字数不应太多，一般25个左右就是上限了，这里面有两个原因：

一是考虑到阅读者的感受，太长、绕口、少间断、修饰关系层次过多的句子阅读和理解都很吃力，最典型的是法律文献，它们中为了表述严谨句子会非常长，读多了条款我们会有呕吐感，大家可以试试下面这个澳大利亚移民法的一条：

> This Division, the regulations made under it and any other provision of this Act as far as it relates to this Division or the regulations, apply to a partnership as if it were a person, but with the changes set out in this section and sections 140ZC and 140ZD.

二是我们会在尝试长句时犯下更多的错误或者落入俗套，错误我们下一节再讲，俗套就是我们喜欢使用多重定语从句互相限制，经验来讲，一句中代入两个以上的定语从句是不太符合中文和英文的语言习惯，在任何语言里都会拆分句子、避免限定成分过多。

我建议大家使用包含2-3种以前介绍过的语法现象的复杂句，就是每篇文章有目的地设计3-4句难句，以确保语法单项的分数。

那如何正确地写出复杂句呢？有下面几种方法：

1 组合简单句

只要上下文的简单句之间有逻辑联系（条件、限定、因果、并列等等），我们就可以利用前面的第五招到第三十四招中的方法将其组合起来，比如：

> 2013 年 2 月 23 日　为什么很多学生不愿学基础科学？会有什么影响？

> Graduates in basic science engaged in fundamental research.
> 基础科学专业的学生从事基础研究。
> Fundamental research is far away from the applied market.
> 基础研究远离应用市场。
> The positions in education institutions are ideal but limited.
> 基础科学毕业生难以找到理想的工作。
> It is hard for graduates in basic science to find other ideal jobs.
> 研究机构的职位是理想的但很有限。

我们把这四句结合成一句：

> Except limited positions in education institutions, it is hard for graduates in basic science to find ideal jobs, because they engage in fundamental research which is far away from the applied market.
> 除了在教育机构里的有限的职位外，基础科学专业的毕业生很难找到理想的工作，因为他们从事的是远离应用市场的基础研究。

组合简单句的时候，我们需要注意以下几点：

a. 避免重复用词

ideal、raduates in basic science、fundamental research 等在短句中重复，但在复杂句中只用了一次。

b. 必要时改句子为词组

The positions in education institutions are ideal but limited. 变成 limited positions in education institutions。

c. 添加连词和代词

复杂句加入了 except、they、which。

2 扩展简单句

我们还可以通过固定句子结构在简单句的基础上拓展出复杂句，举个例子：

简单句：　　　　　　主语　　　谓语 宾语.
　　　　　　　　　　↓

复杂句：条件状语/时间状语，主语，同位语，谓语 宾语 定语/定语从句.

比如：

> 2013年6月22日　国际实事该被列为中学课程还是纯粹是浪费时间？

简单句：
International news has become an important optional course.
　主语　　　　　　　谓语　　　　宾语
国际新闻已经成为一门重要的选修课。

复杂句：
In this globalization era, international news, the most effective way for
　　　时间状语　　　　　　　　　主语　　　　　　　同位语
children to establish more connection with realistic society, has become an
　　　　　　　　　　　　　　　　　　　　　　　　　　　　　　　　谓语
important optional course in compulsary education in most countries.
　宾语　　　　　　　　　定语
在这个全球化时代，国际新闻，一种对于孩子们建立和现实世界更多联系的最有效的方法，已经在大多数国家的基础教育里成为一门重要的选修课。

当然，这只是很多选择中的一个，大家可以自由发挥、自由组合。

练 习

01 改错：写作挑错

看看下面的句子，你能找出错误吗？

2012年9月12日　年轻人物质条件变好却不开心的原因和解决方法

The projects for youth psychological counseling via the effort of the public and the authorities are an opportunity to gather experience in youth mental health.

为年轻人做心理健康咨询的项目通过公众和当局的努力为在年轻人心理健康方面积累经验创造了机会。

02 大闯关：写作闯关

试着把下面几个单句组合成一个复杂句，注意对照这一节提过的三个原则。

2013 年 4 月 5 日　人们常换工作和住址是积极的还是消极的？

House prices perk up quickly and significantly in some areas.
某些地区房价上涨的速度快且明显。

Young people do not have too much income.
年轻人没有太多的收入。

Young people choose to change houses.
年轻人选择改变住址。

It is easy for young people to save living costs on rent.
年轻人可以轻松地节省在租金上的生活成本。

参考答案

01　在写复杂句时，一定要首先保证句子的基本结构是正确的、句子的主干成分（主谓宾或主系表）存在，特别是定语、状语过多时，上面的翻译缺谓语 create，应该是：

The projects for youth psychological counseling via the effort of the public and the authorities create an opportunity to gather experience in youth mental health.

02　When house prices perk up quickly and significantly in some areas, it is easy for young people without too much income to save living costs on rent by changing houses.
当某些地区房价上涨的速度快且明显时，没有太多收入的年轻人通过改变住址可以轻松地节省在租金上的生活成本。

减少常见错误
一定要把握细节

少了这些错误再提 1~2 分
（标点符号、格式、数的一致和名词的格的错误、中英文修饰成分的习惯性位置区别）

口语部分

在最后这一章，功成收式，我们来说一说口语考试中同学们的常见错误总结。

口语是一个要求即时反应的考试，所以大多数同学在应考时会采用不易犯错的短句并且重复使用。看似是个安全的策略，但却会失去语法得分，因为评分标准中鼓励考生使用复杂的语法结构。所以我们这里就列举一些，在授课过程中经常由学生犯的错误，以帮助有相同问题的同学快速纠错。

1 连读问题

时态问题在口语表达中主要涉及完成时态和过去时的使用。

第一个常见的小问题是连读。我们经常会说 I've been to many places that's the most interesting experience that I've ever had in my life. 有同学不适应连读这个技巧，总喜欢把 I've 拆开读成 I have，殊不知连读是 6 分以上发音的基本要求，如果不会连读而且这么明显地告诉考官，发音分显然只能低于 5.5 了。

那怎么练习这个连读的技巧呢？方法是：划线＋模仿。

我从模仿第一盘李阳疯狂英语磁带开始，就喜欢把文稿打印下来，把需要连读的地方全部划下来然后朗读。比如：

> I'm working-on-it.
> An-apple-a day keeps the doctor away.

可以先从短句开始训练，然后过渡到短文章。练习 20 篇基础语感就会培养出来了。

当然过去时的规避，我们在第一招就有提到，如何用一个动词代替所有动词，如果忘了，读者还可以再翻回去复习一遍。对于过去时的准确应用，我认为最好的方法就是记日记。用英文把每天发生的事儿记录下来，是对时态最好的修炼。

2 句子结构混乱

我上课时总说，主语从句是使用频率最高的从句。但也总有学生怎么学也学不会。在表

达"只要我有闲时间,我最喜欢做的事儿就是做饭。"很多同学会说:

> What I like the most the thing is to cook.
> I most like the thing is to cook.

这些错误都是句子成分学得不好造成的。许多初学者喜欢中文对英文逐字翻译,多数情况是翻译不对的。

主语从句和定语后置有相似之处:

我喜欢的事儿,英文表达为:The thing I like to do 或者 What I like to do。结尾是介词或者谓语动词,而不能出现第二个名词,否则位置冲突了。

解决办法:盯准一个模板句反复造句直至熟练。

3 介词的丢失与乱用

最常见的介词丢失莫过于 listen music,有许多考生有这个不良的表达习惯,听音乐不加 to。反而在邀请朋友来家里会说:invite my friend to home,以及去某地会说:the first time when I went to there。这些都是 to 的误用。

home 和 back 这两个词都可以直接放在动词后作副词,可以不作名词。回家就叫 go home,不用 go to home。同理,邀请朋友来家,也可以直接说 invite my friends home。here and there 更是副词,表示地点状语,也不作名词讲。既然口语表达里有 come here,去那当然是 go there。

解决办法:整理个错题本,把常见搭配问题好好复习复习,争取见到一个错误改正一个。

4 词性不分

许多同学对动词的 ing 形式比较敏感,譬如 cooking,swimming,可能背单词的时候就是见动名词比较多,所以在表达自己习惯时,也很容易讲错,比如:

> Do you like cooking?(题目中 like doing sth 是固定用法)
> Yes, I can cooking.(can 是情态动词,后应该跟动词原形)

对于词性不分的同学,错误率就比较高了,因为这是比较明显的错误。比如,说到老师,有同学说:

> He is very responsibility.（应该是形容词形式 responsible）
> You need to concentration on studying（动词正确形式应该是 concentrate）

解决办法：整理个错题本，把常见词性问题好好复习复习，争取见到一个错误改正一个。

5 男女不分

许多同学组句时，分不清 he 和 she，说的是同一个人，但是表达全过程男女混乱。几乎每一个学英语的中国人都会遇到这个问题。要想解决需要熟练即可。

6 乱搭配词汇和描述主体不清

许多同学以为只要记住单词的汉语意思，然后按照自己的意愿组合信息就可以参加考试了。殊不知这样的学习百害而无一利，用错的概率极高。

比如我的一个学生，在表达为什么觉得自己的这个室友是个好室友，他说：

> Because I don't like to do many things such as washing my clothes and washing the dishes that I had mentioned before, are all his job.

我就给这位同学点评说，说英语最怕绕圈。主句表达的意思必须是核心逻辑，这个句子看似复杂，但是最核心的句子是：I don't like to do many things. 他的室友之所以是好室友是因为他不喜欢做很多事。这是英语使用者首先会接收到的信息，这样就会造成逻辑理解困难。其实，这句话的核心观点是"我室友会做我不爱做的事"。那突出主题的词就是 helpful 或者 be willing to 或者 always kindly do。

而不是 are his job，job 表示"工作"，不表示"干活"。除非洗碗是他的工作，否则意思就偏离了。所以这个句子十分混乱，根本无法听懂，自然也不会给分，只会成为扣分项。正确的说法应该是：

> The reason why I like to live with him is because he is really helpful. He always kind to do all the housework, like washing clothes and dishes, which I don't like to do.

另外，such as 这个连接词后面不能跟句子，只能跟名词或动名词。这也是搭配失误所致。

改进建议：如果词汇搭配有明显问题的，建议不要强求逼自己讲复杂句。先把简单句练好，再循序渐进。多朗读，增加对长难句的理解。

7 语义正确语境错误

> Do you like going to the museum?
> No, I think the museum is boring. That's why I hate it.

很多同学想当然以为 like 的反义词就是 hate，但是翻译过来你会觉得很奇怪。"这就是为什么我恨博物馆。" 只是无感而已，不感兴趣，还谈不上恨吧。这个用词，很明显是过了。

关于常见错误在这一章就先列举这么多，如果大家有其他问题。欢迎添加公众微信号"晨说会道"（Liangchensun）向我反馈你在口语语法中遇到的问题。

01 改错：口语挑错

看看下面的句子有错吗？

What's your plan for the future?
Well, hopefully, if everything goes smoothly, I wish I could become an engineer.

02 大闯关：写作闯关

试着用 if 引导的虚拟语气翻译下面的句子。

2016 年 6 月 16 日　人们孤立生活不认识邻居的原因及解决方法

如果人们能够通过摆脱电子依赖的生活方式来在真实生活中参与更多的社交活动，问题至少会被部分地解决。

参考答案

01 题目中问 plan，表示的是清晰的计划，虚拟语气通常用来表达不太可能发生的事儿，遥不可及的奢望。那么这个句子中，答案倒不能算错，就是表达意思有歧义，考官会觉得，你到底想不想做 engineer 啊？

The unemployment rate would not be so high if higher education institutions had strengthened the bond between academic study and occupation training in the last education reform.

02 The problem will be solved, at least partly, if individuals could participate in more social events in real life via casting off cyberholic lifestyle.

写作部分

前面讲完了在文章中不同语法拿分点和逻辑结合以后的应用办法,在实战中,有了透彻的论证和多变的语法,但是分数还是不理想,最重要的原因就是错误数的问题、扣分太严重。

下面我按在实战中发现的比率从高到低来介绍一些常见的错误以及简单的解决方法:

1 单复数

包括:

主谓不一致,比如:Young people is too tired to handle their work.

单数可数名词不加冠词、数词或定冠词,比如:Student pays more attention to mobile phones than what teacher is teaching.

单复数形式与前面的修饰词不一致,比如:Many worker hate competition.

解决办法:

议论文中涉及名词一般是泛指,而可数名词都加复数可以指代同一类事物,那么除非有定语限定,否则我们可以把全部泛指一类事物的可数名词加复述、不加定冠词,这样就可以避开单复数和定冠词的纠结、不考虑谓语动词或系动词第三人称单数的问题,一次解决三个容易出错的地方。

同时注意,下列词后面接可数名词、而且必须是复数:a few、a number of、a variety of、few、many、numerous、some。下列词后面接不可数名词:a great deal of、a large amount of、a little、little、much。既可修饰可数名词(要求复数形式出现)也可修饰不可数名词:a great quantity of 、a lot of、lots of、plenty of。

2 定冠词的使用

大家经常搞不清什么时候加 the,什么时候不加,the 主要用于以下情况:

单数名词前表示一类人或事:The worker contributing more to work will win the employer's appreciation easily.

形容词、分词前表示一类人或事:The aged do not need to worry about living costs.

整体名词前:The working class has the right to enjoy more holidays.

特指:I am the doctor who cured him.

独有的:Without clear air and water, humans cannot live on Earth.

最高级:Education is the best way to prevent crime.

序数词:The consumption of chicken was the first one reaching 270 grams.

店铺:More people went to the cinema in 2000.

山川湖海专有名词以及一些国家名：the United States

解决办法：

记住上面罗列的情况，其余情况按单复数的解决办法中说明的：议论文大部分名词用于泛指，采用复数形式、不加 the。

3　句子结构

句子结构不全的问题主要出现在当句子的主语或状语是带长定语或定语从句的名词短语时，常见的错误是后面缺谓语动词、系动词或者其他基本句子成分，比如：

只有长主语和宾语，缺谓语：

> The expectation for getting a rational share in production and the best driving force is to explore workers' activeness and improve work efficiency.

只有长状语，缺主句：

> Personally, in view of the situation that they both ignored the significant differences in extends and qualities between different crimes.

解决办法：

确保句子主谓宾/主系表的基本结构存在，然后再注意句子的其他成分。

4　单词问题

词性错误

由于中文中同一词汇可以表示不同词性的含义，比如"教育"既是名词也是动词，而英文不同词性可能会有不同的单词，比如 educate 是动词教育、education 是名词教育，这就造成在使用中用错词性的现象，比如：

> Different personal feelings for happy（应该用名词 happiness）come from different psychology（应该使用形容词 psychological）conditions.

再比如：Lack（应该用 lack 的名词形式 lack of sth.，而不是其动词形式 lack sth）physical exercises will endanger children's health.

及物动词、不及物动词不分

同一动词可以是及物动词、不及物动词，或者二者都是但意义不一样。首先，不及物动词不能直接接宾语，其次，及物不及物含义不同时不能用错。比如

> Active consumption could raise people's living standards.

rise 作及物动词是"浮起、复活"的意思，不及物动词才是"增加、升高"的意思，这里应该用 raise。

格的错误

这个错误比较低级，但也很常见，就不举例了，把区别列成下表，大家记忆吧。

	你 & 你们	我	我们	她	他	他们	它们
主格	you	I	we	she	he	they	it
宾格	you	me	us	her	him	them	it
形容词所属格	your	my	our	her	his	their	its
名词所属格	yours	mine	ours	hers	his	theirs	its

解决办法：

记忆单词时注意词性、多重含义的适用情况、格的不同等。

除了上面这些之外，在每一节的讲解和练习部分，我们都附上了针对常见错误的改错练习，在此不再赘述，相应的出错点大家也必须注意。

练 习

01 改错：写作挑错

看看下面的句子，你能找出错误吗？

2015 年 10 月 31 日　对艺术创作的资助应该来源于政府还是其他渠道？

Governments should not play the role of market. Competition and commercialisation are the only way to boom any industry including the arts. That is because they can push the industry to meet the real needs of the public and achieve sustained development.

政府不应扮演市场的角色。竞争和商业化是使包括文化艺术在内的任何行业繁荣的唯一途径，因为它们可以推动行业去满足公众的真正需求并实现持续发展。

02 大闯关：写作闯关

试着翻译下面的句子，注意避免这一节介绍的所有常见错误。

2013 年 9 月 21 日　完美社会的要素是什么？如何使社会完美？

在一个更加平等的社会里，人们更愿意相信彼此、表达善意和同情、愿意切身参与到社会活动中去，因为收入和社会福利平等让每个个体感觉他们拥有同样的经济权利和政治权利。

参考答案

01 这句涉及格式问题：逗句号不分、句首字母不大写、逗号后首个字母反而大写。应为：

Governments should not play the role of market. Competition and commercialisation is the only way to boom any industry including arts, because they can push the industry to meet the real needs of the public and achieve sustained development.

02 In more equal societies, people are much more likely to trust each other, show goodwill and sympathy, and be deeply involved in the community, because equalities in income and social welfare make individuals feel they own equal economic and political rights.